British Animated Films, 1895–1985

Also by Denis Gifford

The Armchair Odeon
The Best of Eagle
British Cinema
The British Comic Catalogue 1874–1974
British Comics and Story-Paper Price Guide 1982
The British Film Catalogue 1895–1985
Chaplin
Cinema Britanico
Comics 101 Souvenir Book
The Complete Catalogue of British Comics
Discovering Comics
Eric and Ernie's TV Fun Book
Fifty Years of Radio Comedy
The Golden Age of Radio
The Great Cartoon Stars
Happy Days: 100 Years of Comics
The Illustrated Who's Who in British Films
The International Book of Comics
Karloff: The Man the Monster the Movies
Monsters of the Movies
The Morecambe and Wise Comic Book
Movie Monsters
A Pictorial History of Horror Movies
Quick on the Draw
Run Adolf Run: The World War Two Fun Book
Science Fiction Film
Stap Me: The British Newspaper Strip
Stewpot's Fun Book
Test Your N.Q.
The Two Ronnies Comic Book
Victorian Comics

British Animated Films, 1895–1985

A Filmography

by

Denis Gifford

McFarland & Company, Inc., Publishers
Jefferson, North Carolina, and London

Decorations: "Bonzo"
  by George Ernest Studdy

Library of Congress Cataloguing-in-Publication Data

Gifford, Denis.
  British animated films, 1895–1985.

  Includes index.
  1. Moving-picture cartoons — Great Britain —
Catalogs. I. Title.
PN1998.G53   1987   016.79143′75′0941   87-42507

ISBN 0-89950-241-5 (acid-free natural paper) ∞

Manufactured in the United States of America

McFarland & Company, Inc., Publishers
  Box 611, Jefferson, North Carolina 28640

for
BONZO
(not forgetting his master,
George Ernest Studdy)

Contents

Introduction

Ninety-one years ago readers of *The Referee,* an important weekly newspaper famous for its reviews of the latest theatrical occasions, turned to the report of the new show at the Alhambra Theatre in London's Leicester Square. The most exciting event of the decade — some would say of the century — had taken place there the previous Monday, March 25, 1896: the first performance in public of the Animatographe, England's answer to the new French invention, *le Cinématographe,* which had opened at the Alhambra's nearby rival, the Empire Theatre, a week or so previous. Here is a fragment of *The Referee's* review:

> The pictures for the most part represent variety artistes at their performances. There is a Lightning Caricaturist who draws the likeness of Bismarck before the audience. Better still is the reproduction of a young lady singing and dancing, and doesn't she know how to kick!

The Lightning Caricaturist may not have made quite the impact of the young lady with her high kick, but here, in the spring of 1896, we have the grandfather of all the thousands of film cartoonists who have since brightened the world's cinema screens with their lively lines. And this first cartoonist ever to be recorded on celluloid film by the brand-new, big-screen medium was British, a professional whose work appeared in many popular magazines towards the close of the nineteenth century. His pseudonym was Tom Merry; his real name was William Mecham.

Of course, none of the four short films that pioneer photographer Birt Acres made of Tom Merry was an animated cartoon. All four were simply moving photographic records of parts of his stage performance as a Lightning Cartoonist. But it was the beginning. Other artists followed, and soon an elementary form of animation began to appear as cartoonists found that they could not always complete their lightning sketches before the short (50-foot) lengths of film ran out in the cameras. So the photographers would film for a few frames, stop while the cartoonist filled in a few more lines, then crank the handle for a few frames more. The result when projected at normal speed (at the time, 16 frames a second) showed the cartoonist executing his drawings at a frantic rate. At last they were living up to their theatrical billing as Lightning Cartoonists!

The first cartoonist to take the technique a step further and make his drawings appear to move all by themselves was also an Englishman. His name was J. Stuart Blackton, and he drew cartoons for a New York newspaper. While visiting the moving picture pioneer Thomas Alva Edison for an illustrated interview, Blackton impressed Edison enough that the great inventor filmed the cartoonist at work for his peep-show device, the Kinetoscope. Inspired to become part of the exciting new entertainment medium, Blackton formed his own production company, Vitagraph. One of his first films, in 1900, was *The Enchanted Drawing*. Within its running time of one or two minutes, Blackton's drawings of funny faces changed their expressions by the use of editing techniques: the physical cutting and joining of the celluloid film.

Six years later Blackton attempted a second cartoon film, this time using the stop-frame process, then called "one turn–one picture," a technique that had been evolved for trick films requiring the movement, or animation, of actual objects. Blackton called his film *Humorous Phases of Funny Faces,* and copyrighted the four-minute short in Washington, D.C., on April 6, 1906.

One month later, the first British-made animated cartoon film was showing on theatre screens. Within those four brief weeks a conjurer called Walter R. Booth had obtained a print of Blackton's new production, studied it, discovered its techniques, and personally drawn, animated, and played the leading — only — role in a 200-foot, three-minute masterpiece entitled *The Hand of the Artist.* A year later the film was described as "having a phenomenal reception and sale, and still going strong." Booth made a second short called *Comedy Cartoons,* but this time animated artwork was but part of a parade of trick effects including superimposition and dissolves.

It was left to the French strip cartoonist Émile Cohl, born Courtet, to create the first 100 percent animated cartoon film, *Fantasmagorie,* in 1908. This little film, with its simple outline figures acting out a comedy plot in white on a black background, remains both comical and charming to this day. It also stands as the first lesson in "What Is an Animated Cartoon": It is something that can be achieved only by drawing, not something that uses drawing to imitate reality. This is a lesson many animators of the modern period have failed to learn.

The cartoon film gained a new lease on life when, in America, the Pathé Company adapted the newspaper comic strip *Mutt and Jeff* as an item for their weekly cinema newsreel. The same company's English operation decided to produce a weekly cartoon, too, but with no knowledge of the new animation techniques they fell back on the original concept of the Lightning Cartoonist. Max Martin, a cartoonist working for Pathé's weekly trade paper, had some stage experience and so was an obvious choice for the job. For nine months he turned out a weekly sequence of lightning cartoons for *Pathé Gazette*, all of them hand-drawn sketches speeded up by the stop-camera technique. They became the first regular series of British-made cartoon films.

The following year, Harry Furniss, the famous Irish-born cartoonist who had been writing and acting for Edison Films in New York, came home to set up his own small film studio beside the sea at Hastings, Sussex. He had barely begun production when, on August 4, 1914, England declared war on Germany. Furniss had given many an illustrated lecture in his time, a sort of superior Lightning Cartoonist act, so it was easy for him to convert his stage technique to films. He quickly produced an animated cartoon called *Peace and War Pencillings,* in which speeded-action sketches of one subject were suddenly stop-framed into another. As he later described his film for readers of *The Strand Magazine:*

> England's Strong Arm and Useful Left are actually the right and left arms of a man. England's Strong Arm is her Navy, so that in War we find the Right Arm metamorphosed into a Sailor, and the same process applied to the Left, turning it into a Soldier.

There was also some elementary animation: Kaiser Wilhelm's famous spiked moustache was compared with a barometer – it drooped down for "stormy"!

The Great War gave a great boost to British animation. As newspaper cartoons reached a new peak of patriotic popularity, it was natural to bring the same kind of cartooning to the cinema screen. Sidney Aldridge, a *Punch* contributor, produced his *War Cartoons,* a film featuring such topical comments as "Putting His Light Out," with Kaiser Bill as a dejected candle, very obviously "Made in Germany"!

George Ernest Studdy, later to make the first fully animated cartoon series in Britain, made his first tentative attempt at animation with his *Studdy's War Studies* for Gaumont, but it was left to a famous book illustrator of the period to become the real Founding Father of what soon came to be called the British School of Animation. Lancelot Speed, who had illustrated such classic works as Lord Lytton's *Last Days of Pompeii,* had been signed as the art director for Neptune Films, a new production company with studios at Elstree. Speed devised an animated logo showing King Neptune brandishing his trident, then went on to make the first of a long-running series of cartoon shorts, beginning with *Bully Boy No. 1.* On October 2, 1914, the trade paper *The Bioscope* called that film

> Considerably the wittiest and most ingenious topical skit that we have hitherto seen. It deals with the destruction of Rheims Cathedral by the Modern Atilla, and concludes with an amazingly realistic reproduction of the British Bulldog consuming the German Sausage.

In an interview for the same magazine, Speed made the first recorded comment on cartoon film production techniques:

> Audiences cannot realise the time devoted to the single move; the sixteenth part of a foot of film takes, at times, as long as twenty minutes to prepare. I am so far satisfied if I can manage to produce a *Bully Boy* in a fortnight, and this takes less than ten minutes to show on the screen.

In addition to the well-established techniques of speeded action and stop-frame, Speed introduced the cut-out: drawings of bodies and limbs made separately on thin card, then cut out and assembled into two-dimensional puppets which, with the aid of paper-clips fixed from behind as joints, could be moved fractionally against a separately drawn background. Other British cartoonists picked up this technique, including Dudley Buxton and Anson Dyer. Joining forces under the style of Kine Komedy Kartoons, these two kept British cartoon films on cinema screens at the rate of one new release every month through the darkening days of the Great War. And Dudley Buxton it was who first animated the sinking of the *Lusitania* in all its terrifying drama, three years before Winsor McCay tackled the same subject in the United States. Yet according to film history, McCay's version was the world's first dramatic cartoon film! Buxton's little epic was no flash in the pan, either. He later animated *The Raid on Zeebrugge*, which hit British screens only two months after the famous naval attack on the Belgian seaport. The review published in *Picturegoer* on April 23, 1918, is all we have left of this obviously remarkable film:

> The rush of the storming parties over the gangways while the night was alive with shells is an unforgettable incident, while the submarining of the Mole is another episode which will be followed with the keenest interest.

With the signing of the armistice in 1918 came a decline of public interest in British cartoon films. Anson Dyer joined Cecil M. Hepworth, foremost producer of romantic dramas, and at his studios in Walton-on-Thames made a short series of burlesques of Shakespeare plays: The hero of Dyer's *Hamlet* was an animated Charlie Chaplin! But cut-outs, however clever, could hardly match the now fully animated cartoons coming across from American studios.

The one thing American animators could not give English audiences was Britain's own native heroes. America's animated versions of such strip cartoon characters as *The Katzenjammer Kids* and *Krazy Kat* meant little to English audiences unfamiliar with the newspaper strip originals. This obvious opening was quickly filled by veteran Lancelot Speed, who animated 26 one-reel adventures of *Pip, Squeak and Wilfred*, the popular pets from the *Daily Mirror* children's strip by A.B. Payne. Then came G.E. Studdy, with lessons learned from his *War Studies*, with his own cartoon character,

G.E. Studdy's "Bonzo," the popular British pup who starred in 26 fully animated cartoons.

Bonzo. This chubby little puppy, much loved by readers of the glossy weekly *The Sketch,* turned up on postcards, cigarette cards, even molded glass ashtrays—so it was perhaps no wonder that he should turn up in animated cartoons, too. William A. Ward, later a prolific Disney strip artist for *Mickey Mouse Weekly,* was Studdy's chief animator and director for a year-long series of 26 Bonzo cartoons, the first British series to be made in the fully animated American style. Adrian Brunel, later to graduate to feature film directing, was one of Bonzo's scriptwriters.

In 1926 Pathé had trouble with Pat Sullivan, producer of the popular American series *Felix the Cat.* The famous film feline was dropped from Pathé's weekly cinemagazine, *Eve's Film Review,* and a British-made cartoon series was especially produced to fill the three-minute gap. Brian White, later to become famous for *The Nipper* strip in the *Daily Mail,* animated *Jerry the Troublesome Tyke* with Sid Griffiths. Griffiths would make a career in animation, working with Anson Dyer in the thirties through to Halas and Batchelor in the fifties.

Jerry the Tyke's adventures alternated with those of *Sammy and Sausage,* made by Joe Noble. Joe was the first British animator to mix cartoons with live action, in the style of Max Fleischer's popular *Out of the Inkwell* series. He was also the first animator to make a sound cartoon, rather than to put a soundtrack onto an existing silent cartoon. He produced 'Orace the 'Armonious 'Ound in 1928 and followed up with the first advertising cartoon in sound.

Another little-known British "first" is a full-length feature cartoon made by Anson Dyer in 1927. However, history may be forgiven for overlooking this, as the distributors cut it up into shorts, convinced that nobody would sit through 75 minutes of animation. As the film was a patriotic documentary entitled *The Story of the Flag,* they may well have been right!

It was Anson Dyer who kept the British flag flying in the field of animation through the thirties, too. This was the time when Walt Disney was the uncrowned king of the cartoons. No cinema worth its ninepence dared put on a program without a *Mickey Mouse* or a *Silly Symphony,* "all in Glorious Technicolor." But in 1936 Dyer dared to produce the first British color cartoon series. Starring *Old Sam,* these were all based on popular monologues spoken by the famous comedian Stanley Holloway, star of stage, screen, and now soundtrack!

Excellent as these cartoons were, they could not compete with Hollywood production-line cartoons. Neither could another series, *Come On Steve,* produced by Roland Davies from his own popular comic strip in the *Sunday Express.* Although amusing and inventive, the jerky animation and poorly recorded soundtracks were scorned at the time. Today the animation style is accepted technique for television series.

As another world war started in 1939, animation followed the path it had taken in 1914, but this time with government sponsorship. It was realized that animation could mix information with entertainment in a unique way, and so a new company combining the talents of a Hungarian animator and his British animator wife found itself busily employed making films for the Ministry of Information. John Halas and Joy Batchelor produced *Charley* cartoons to tell the British about the problems of farmers, health, schools and new towns on one hand, while on the other made commercial cartoons to tell the same British about the wonders of cornflakes and detergents! By the end of the war, Halas and Batchelor were the biggest and most experienced producers of animation in British film history. Yet they found it impossible to make cartoon films purely for cinema entertainment. Cash returns on a circuit booking failed to cover cost of production.

In 1947 this problem was realized by J. Arthur Rank, the wealthiest film producer in the United Kingdom. Determined to match Hollywood in every respect, he set up Gaumont British Animation to provide his Gaumont and Odeon cinema circuits with one new technicolor cartoon a month. To supervise he brought over David Hand from the Walt Disney Studios in Hollywood, and the GBA Studio was set up at Moor Hall, in Cookham, Buckinghamshire. The blend of British humor and American methods failed to gel, despite some visually attractive results. Ginger Nutt, squirrel star of the *Animaland* series, failed to win public affection, and the brave experiment was closed down during one of those recurrent cash crises that mark the history of British films.

Halas and Batchelor, with the field to themselves once again, made the first and only British stereoscopic cartoon, *The Owl and the Pussycat,* in 1953, and the following year produced the first proper full-length feature cartoon, *Animal Farm.* Adapted from George Orwell's symbolic fantasy of revolution in the farmyard, it had to be financed by the American producer of *The March of Time,* Louis de Rochemont. The film, perhaps also the first feature cartoon produced for adult entertainment, lost much of its impact by aping Disney styles and techniques.

Disney's grip on world animation was first broken by his own studio technicians, who revolted and formed United Productions of America in the forties. In England a similar revolt took place among the younger animators, who began to use the "limited animation" techniques pioneered by UPA as much from economic necessity as from artistic urgency. Bob Godfrey and his rebels set up Biographic Cartoons on the strength of their successful and hilarious amateur film *Watch the Birdie* (1954), and soon the new medium of independent television called for comedy animation in many of its 30-second commercials. Income from these cartoon commercials was used by both Godfrey and Richard Williams to finance personal cartoon productions for the cinema circuits. Following Williams' *The Little Island* (1958), the first British cartoon in cinemascope, George Dunning used his profits to produce the experimental *Flying Man* (1962), which told its brief tale in loosely splotched daubs of paint. Dunning later directed the extraordinary Beatles feature cartoon, *The Yellow Submarine* (1968), which, although American-financed and German-designed, used the four lads from Liverpool, and was sufficiently ahead of its time to still stand today as an inspiration for animators around the world. Finally British animated films, which had been winning awards at such specialized festivals as Annecy and Zagreb, won themselves a Hollywood Oscar for Bob Godfrey's eye- and ear-dazzling *Great* (1976); and it is exciting to add that as this manuscript was being completed for press, *Rupert and the Frog Song* (1984) won the British Film and Television Academy (BAFTA) Award as the best animated film of its year.

This book represents the first attempt to catalogue animated films made in Britain. It is as complete as humanly possible, the information being culled from many sources including, wherever possible, the credit titles of the films themselves. To give as full a picture of the genre, from its beginnings to the present day, I have included many types of film: the entertainment cartoon, the advertising cartoon, the instructional cartoon, and cartoons made for wartime propaganda, for experimental purposes, as "art films," and as student exercises. This latter area, a recent development as colleges and universities open their own animation departments, dominates the last years of this catalogue, for the reason that these are virtually the only animated films now shown on cinema screens, at festivals, and the like. British animation is now produced almost exclusively for television, either as commercials or for children's entertainment (Bob Godfrey's *Roobarb* series; Richard Williams' *A Christmas Carol*), and this catalogue is concerned only with films made for the cinema.

Extracts from reviews of the cartoons described in this volume are quoted wherever possible. The main sources of such reviews are the film trade papers *The Bioscope, The Cinema, The Kinematograph Weekly, Today's Cinema,* and *NSTA Reviews;* other trade and specialized papers: *Advertisers Weekly, Advertising World, Commercial Film, Documentary Newsletter, Monthly Film Bulletin, Film Sponsor, C.E.A. Film Report, Film User, Pathéscope Monthly;* catalogues: *British National Film Catalogue, Central Film Library, Pathéscope, Watsofilms;* and programs from the Cambridge Animation Festival, London Film Festival, Annecy Animation Festival, and Zagreb Animation Festival.

List of Abbreviations

Credits
A animation
C camera
D director
DES design
ED editor
M music
MD music director
P producer
S story
SC screenplay; script
SD sound
SUP supervisor
V voice
XP executive producer

Others
ABFD Associated British Film Distributors
AKA also known as (alternative title)
B&C British and Colonial Kinematograph Company
BFI British Film Institute
CEA Cinematograph Exhibitors Association
COI Central Office of Information
EFC Educational Film Centre
FBO Film Booking Offices
GB Gaumont British Picture Corporation
GFD General Film Distributors
GPO General Post Office
JWT J. Walter Thompson
MOI Ministry of Information
NSS National Screen Service
NSTA Newsreel and Specialised Theatres Association
ROSPA Royal Society for the Prevention of Accidents
TIDA Travel and Industrial Development Association
UA United Artists
YCC Yorkshire Cinematograph Company

How to Use This Book

Cartoons are listed under the year of their production, in chronological order of their release date (where known). Entries are presented according to the format shown below.

689[1] **The Wardrobe**[2] (180)[3]
   TV Cartoons[4] – Crispin[5]
   P:D:A: George Dunning, S: Stan Hayward[6]
   Eastmancolor[7]
   Short comedy cartoon. A man wearing old shoes climbs into a wardrobe. A second man wearing new shoes follows him. The first man then emerges wearing the new shoes.[8] "Whimsical, simply drawn against a white background, and punctuated by loud noises on the soundtrack." (*Monthly Film Bulletin* August 1970.)[9]

   1. entry number
   2. title
   3. footage
   4. production company
   5. distributor
   6. credits (see List of Abbreviations)
   7. color system
   8. description
   9. review quote

1895

1   **Tom Merry, Lightning Cartoonist: Kaiser Wilhelm** (40)
Birt Acres
P:D:C: Birt Acres
featuring Tom Merry
Not an animated cartoon, but the first film of a cartoonist in action
(see Introduction). Tom Merry, a popular magazine and stage cartoonist
of the period, performs one of his "Lightning Sketches" – of Kaiser Wilhelm
of Germany. Date uncertain, believed filmed in December 1895. Fragment
preserved in National Film Archive.

2   **Tom Merry, Lightning Cartoonist: Bismarck** (40)
Birt Acres
P:D:C: Birt Acres
featuring Tom Merry
Not an animated cartoon (but see Introduction). Tom Merry per-
forms one of his "Lightning Sketches." Date uncertain, believed filmed in
December 1895.

1896

3 Tom Merry, Lightning Cartoonist: Lord Salisbury (40)
Birt Acres
P:D:C: Birt Acres
featuring Tom Merry
Not an animated cartoon (but see Introduction). Tom Merry performs one of his "Lightning Sketches." Date uncertain, probably filmed December 1895, but exhibited March 1896.

4 Tom Merry, Lightning Cartoonist: William Gladstone (40)
Birt Acres
P:D:C: Birt Acres
featuring Tom Merry
Not an animated cartoon (but see Introduction). Tom Merry performs one of his "Lightning Sketches." Date uncertain, probably filmed December 1895, but exhibited March 1896.

1898

5   Little Stanley, Lightning Cartoonist (53)
Cinematograph Company
featuring Little Stanley
Not an animated cartoon. One-minute film of a young boy cartoonist drawing a "Lightning Sketch" in crayon. Released October 1898.

1899

6 Matches: An Appeal
Birt Acres (?)
D:S:A: Arthur Cooper
Animated matchsticks. A box of Bryant and May's matches opens and the matchsticks chalk up this appeal: "For one guinea Bryant and May will forward a case containing sufficient to supply a box of matches to each man in a batallion, with the name of the sender inside." The date of this film is controversial, as recent research sets it as produced in the Great War of 1914. This may, however, be a reissue as the setting of this film is identical with *Animated Matches* (1908). Print preserved in the National Film Archive.

1901

7 The Devil in the Studio (100)
R.W. Paul's Animatographe
D:S:A: Walter R. Booth
Trick film: live action/animation. "An artist is discovered in the studio preparing his palette for a masterpiece. As he squeezes a tube of vermillion it bursts into smoke and flame and he throws it to the floor aghast. Mephisto suddenly appears from the flaming colour and to the bewilderment of artist and model precipitates a large head of the former onto the black canvas. The painter is astonished to see the work done without effort and shakes his head dubiously at his own portrait filling the canvas, when Mephisto makes a second pass from model to easel, and vanishes. The canvas is once more blank, and as the artist stands between the two he perceives to his great amazement that the model is slowly fading from her platform and at the same time is gradually appearing on the canvas like a developing photograph. When the model is clearly defined the artist in a transport of delight at the production of a painting in a few seconds, rushes from the studio and quickly returns with the dealer, descanting to him as they come in on the merits of the masterpiece. Just as they turn to look at the picture, it immediately changes to a comical caricature making fun of them. The artist is about to apologise for the mishap when the dealer changes to our old friend Mephisto." (*Paul Catalogue* 1901.) Typical trick film of the period, inspired by the work of Georges Méliès in France. Released August 1901.

8 The Famous Illusion of De Kolta (120)
R.W. Paul's Animatographe
D:S:A: Walter R. Booth
Trick film: live action/animation. "A large frame stands in the centre of the picture, into which enters Pierrot in comical clowning mood. Picking up a piece of chalk he starts to make a sketch upon the board. Hardly has he commenced to do so when the drawing appears with marvellous rapidity, in fact, with a rapidity which would put any lightning cartoonist to the blush. The sketch represents an old toper with a whisky bottle. As Pierrot

5

stands to one side, the toper lifts the bottle to his lips, but the clown snatches it away and takes a drink himself. Finding, however, that it is not to his taste, he returns the bottle to its owner – on the nose. The figure at once vanishes and Pierrot starts a second sketch. This time a silkworm is drawn, resting upon a mulberry leaf. The clown flicks it with his finger, when it at once turns into a cocoon. This is lifted from the easel to a small table where it is seen to be round and solid. . . ." (*Paul Catalogue* 1901.) Released October 1901.

   9   Artistic Creation (85)
        Paul's Animatographe
        D:S:A: Walter R. Booth
        Live action/animation. "On the stage we see an elaborate easel and a table, the space under which is perfectly open. A Pierrot enters and rapidly sketches a lady's head, which comes to life on the canvas and speaks to him. He lifts it down and places it on the table, and proceeds to drawn an armless bust, which suddenly comes to life and is placed under the head. Two living arms are next produced in the same way, and attached to the bust, the skirt is added and the lady as a whole steps forward. The Pierrot gives her a seat and proceeds to draw a baby in long clothes, whom he takes down and comes rapidly towards the audience until the screaming infant fills the whole picture with the most ludicrous effect. This is considered the finest and smartest picture of the kind ever taken and a perfect photograph." (*Paul Catalogue* 1901.) Released October 1901. Obviously produced in tandem with the preceding film, *The Famous Illusion of De Kolta.*

   10   Dolly's Toys (80)
        R.W. Paul's Animatographe
        Live action/animated toys. A small girl falls asleep and dreams that her dolls come to life. The plot is so similar to many later films made by Arthur Cooper that it could be his first production. Cooper was working for Birt Acres at this time, and Paul released many of Acres' productions. Alternatively, it could be another of Walter R. Booth's regular trick films made at Paul's Animatographe Studio. Released December 1901.

1903

11 Political Favourites (150)
  Paul's Animatographe
  P: Robert W. Paul, D:S: Walter R. Booth
  Lightning cartoons, not animated but accelerated action. "It consists of a series of large cartoons, rapidly drawn, in view of the audience, by a skilful artist, the name of each leader appearing above his portrait. Included are Mr. Campbell-Bannerman, Mr. Balfour, Lord Rosenbery, the Duke of Devonshire, Sir William Harcourt, and the Right Honourable Joseph Chamberlain. The last holds two loaves of the same size bearing the words 'Protection' and 'Free Trade.'" (*Paul Film Catalogue* 1904.) Released January 1904; reissued January 1906 as *Free Trade and Protection Favourites.* The cartoonist is not known, and may be the writer/director Walter R. Booth himself, who is known to have been a capable cartoonist.

1904

12　The Enchanted Toymaker (190)
AKA: **The Old Toymaker's Dream**
Alpha Trading Company – Paul
P:D:S:A: Arthur Cooper

　　Animated toys/live action. "A busy toy maker is confronted by a good fairy who causes the toys to take to life. The Noah's Ark enlarges and the animals majestically enter. The man locks them in and sets a toy soldier on guard. The latter fires his gun to the shopman's bewilderment." (*Paul Film Catalogue* 1906.) The first animated film we can definitely attribute to Arthur Cooper, who had by this time left the employ of Birt Acres to establish his own small studio, the Alpha Trading Company, at St. Albans, Herts. Released June 1904.

1906

13 The Hand of the Artist (200)
   Urban Trading Company
   P: Charles Urban, D:S:A: Walter R. Booth
   The first British animated cartoon film, based on "Lightning Sketch"
routines with some live action. "Lifelike portrait sketches produced by the
Hand: a coster and his donah magically come to life, embrace, and dance
a cakewalk. Other surprising effects follow in rapid succession, the Hand
of the Artist repeatedly producing new wonders. After each subject plays
its part, the Hand crumples up the paper and dispenses it in the form of con-
fetti." (*Urban Film Catalogue* 1909.) Released April 1906.

14 The Fairy Godmother (140)
   AKA: **Noah's Ark**
   Alpha Trading Company — Cricks & Sharp
   P:D:S:A: Arthur Cooper
   Animated toys. Maidservant falls asleep and her young charge
watches a toy Noah's Ark whose animals come to life. Released December
1906. Print preserved in the National Film Archive under the title *Noah's
Ark*.

1907

15 Comedy Cartoons (280)
Urban Trading Company
P: Charles Urban, D:S:A: Walter R. Booth
Animated cartoon/live action: sequel to *The Hand of the Artist* (1906). "The Hand of the Artist draws outline faces upon a blackboard. The outlines fill and assume life, form and muscular movement. They eat, drink, smoke, express pleasure and satisfaction without leaving the blackboard, after which the images are removed by an ordinary duster, or disappear feature by feature." (*Urban Leaflet* April 1907.) Released April 1907.

16 The Sorcerer's Scissors (220)
Urban Trading Company
P: Charles Urban, D:S:A: Walter R. Booth
Animation with live action. "An ordinary pair of scissors appears in front of the title on the screen and cuts a woman's form from it. This comes to life in the shape of a pretty coster maiden. A paint brush appears, which gradually changes the coster girl's appearance to that of a French grisette, and the scissors reappearing clip a fresh garment which the girl dons and assumes the character of a Spanish dancer. . . ." (*Kinematograph Weekly* 5 March 1908.) Released October 1907; print preserved in the National Film Archive.

1908

17   Dreams of Toyland (350)
Alpha Trading Company – Walturdaw
P:D:S:A: Arthur Cooper
Animated toys. "Tommy is taken by his mother to the toyshop, where he is allowed to select a toy for himself. He chooses a mechanical motor bus, a very fine model of the real thing. Tommy and his mother are now seen leaving the shop, the youngster showing evident delight with his present. Next, bedtime arrives and Tommy is put in his cot. He falls to sleep and soon dreams of Toyland. His vision is depicted in the next picture, which shows a public thoroughfare inhabited by toy men and women, animals, carts, motors and all kinds of vehicles, all of which move about like marionette figures in a grotesque but amusing manner. It is a veritable miniature world with the most lively scenes imaginable. Every toy operates by its own accord in a remarkable manner. At last Tommy's new toy, the motor bus, comes upon the scene, crashes into other vehicles and there is an explosion. To sleeping Tommy it seems a reality and the moment the motor bus explodes he jumps in his sleep with such force as to throw himself out of bed upon the floor. This abrupt termination of his vision serves to awaken him, and he is now seen sitting half dazed on the bedroom floor, rubbing his eyes. Mother enters and puts him back into bed again. The subject has been produced at great cost, involving a great amount of apparatus to stage. It is thoroughly well worked out and forms the most fascinating spectacle it is possible to conceive for children. Order at once." (Walturdaw advertisement: *Bioscope* 27 February 1908.) Released February 1908; print preserved in the National Film Archive.

18   In the Land of Nod (365)
Alpha Trading Company – Walturdaw
P:D:S:A: Arthur Cooper
Animated toys. "This is a clever trick picture, the opening scenes showing children playing with their toys while their grandpa dozes in an armchair. Those which follow are his dream and what he has seen the children doing. The scene changes to the interior of a room in the doll's

11

house, which is one of the chief toys. The house catches fire and there is great excitement attending the turning out of the engine and escape. Several teddy bears keep the flames under control until the firemen arrive, and there are thrilling escapes with the aid of a long ladder. The effect is realistic for the sleeping man, and he wakes to find the children are playing a stream of water on his face from a toy engine." (*Bioscope* 5 January 1911.) Released April 1908; reissued by Cosmopolitan Films on 8 January 1911 as *Grandpa's Forty Winks*. Remade by Empire Films in 1912 as *Father's Forty Winks*.

19 Animated Matches (250)
Alpha Trading Company – Williamson
P:D:S:A: Arthur Cooper
Animated matchsticks. Matchsticks come to life and perform various gymnastic feats. Released April 1908. Print preserved in the National Film Archive.

20 The Lightning Postcard Artist (325)
Urban Trading Company
P: Charles Urban, D:S:A: Walter R. Booth
Animation/live action. "At the outset a plain card is presented upon which the hand of the artist rapidly outlines a cottage window. An animated toy policeman looks in and an equally wooden but loose-jointed butler hands him a bottle of wine . . . . The pencil's point is dull. A penknife then automatically sharpens the pencil, upon which it resumes work and draws a candle, candle stick, and matches which travel unaided across the table. A syphon, bottle, tumbler and smoking utensils next move into position. The candle bends over and sets on fire the matches. A puppet figure now rises from space and extinguishes the matches by means of the syphon . . . . There is presented a feeding bottle subject. Three of these infant necessities are drawn side by side upon the card. A baby's face then appears upon the flat surface of the outside bottles. The centre bottle obligingly bends alternatively to its companions on either side, from its own contents feeds the other two baby faces, and then mysteriously explodes. The film is a certain draw." (*Kinematograph Weekly* 6 August 1908.)

21 The Prehistoric Man (300)
Urban Trading Company
P: Charles Urban, D:S:A: Walter R. Booth, C: Harold Bastick
Animation/live action. "An artist in an idle moment has outlined on a sheet the figure of a conventional prehistoric ogre of forbidding aspect and threatening demeanour, armed with a prehistoric stone hammer. To the artist's own dismay the creature becomes possessed of life and movement and walks out of the wooden frame. Evidently looking upon the

draughtsman as the responsible author of his being, he attaches himself to
that unfortunate person and accompanies him wherever he goes. After in-
numerable calamities, a happy idea suggests itself to the artist who, returning to his studio, hastily draws a prehistoric animal, which also assumes life.
The man, entering the studio in search of his artist friend, is seized between
the fearsome jaws of the weird creature and swallowed whole. Only his
stone mallet remains, and this the artist uses as a weapon which cuts down
the inoffensive canvas upon which the creatures were drawn." (*Kinematograph Weekly* 17 September 1908.) Released September 1908. It is important to bear in mind that once the drawings "came to life" they changed into
real-life actors.

1909

22 The Sporting Mice (300)
Armstrong – Cricks & Martin
P:D:S:A: Charles Armstrong
Silhouettes. "A distinct and remarkable novelty consisting of the evolutions of performing mice and the contortions of a grotesque physiognomy, the whole being executed in living silhouette. A few of the many acts are juggling with a mouse on his elastic proboscis, a mouse walking on stilts, performing a record hoop trick, climbing a ladder held and swayed by another mouse, and performing various mystifying acrobatic turns." (*Bioscope* 27 May 1909.) Released May 1909. "Professor" Armstrong was the first animator to work in cut-out silhouettes. He produced many short films, including advertisements, at his studio, the Cumberland Works, in Kew. Only a handful are known by title.

23 Votes for Women: A Caricature (300)
Armstrong – Cricks & Martin
P:D:S:A: Charles Armstrong
Silhouettes. "One of this firm's noted series of silhouettes. A most grotesque film – a woman suffragette – Q.E.D. – all moonshine!" (*Bioscope* 17 June 1909.) Released June 1909.

24 Animated Cotton (340)
Urban Trading Company
P: Charles Urban, D:S:A: Walter R. Booth
Animated needle and cotton. "Intricate drawings, crochet work and darning are unaccountably executed in this film." (*Kine Monthly Record* June 1913.) Released September 1909; reissued 1913.

25 Sooty Sketches (395)
Urban Trading Company
P: Charles Urban, D:S:A: Walter R. Booth
Animation/live action: third of the *Hand of the Artist* films. "The artist is first seen holding a piece of cardboard over a lamp until it is well

14

covered with soot. This is then brought forward until it occupies the whole picture space, when a few deft touches with a brush reveal a silhouette figure of a negro minstrel, who juggles in expert fashion with his hat and banjo, and then fades away to make room for a garden scene. . . ." (*Kinematograph Weekly* 9 December 1909.) Released December 1909.

1910

26 The Clown and His Donkey (265)
Armstrong – Urban Trading Company
P:D:S:A: Charles Armstrong
Silhouettes. "A unique silhouette trick film in which a clown, a donkey, and an ape take part in some marvellous feats of jugglery, balancing, and acrobatic performances. The film is the result of great patience and ingenuity and was produced by Professor Armstrong." (*Bioscope* 28 April 1910.) Released March 1910. Print preserved in the National Film Archive.

27 Embroidery Extraordinary (225)
Hepworth Films
P:D: Cecil M. Hepworth
Animated needle and cotton. "A good trick film in which some wonderful designs make themselves, ending with a 'good-bye.'" (*Bioscope* 6 October 1910.) Released 6 October 1910.

28 The Toymaker's Dream (420)
Alpha Trading Company – Tyler Films
P:D:S:A: Arthur Cooper
Animated toys. Old toymaker falls asleep on the job and dreams that his toys come to life. Two toy airplanes crash into each other. "A very clever trick film and a good advertisement for the *Daily Mail*." (*Bioscope* 27 October 1910.) Released 30 October 1910. Remade as *The Old Toymaker's Dream* (1913).

1911

29 Animated Putty (375)
Kineto Films
D:S:A: Walter R. Booth
A lump of putty shapes itself into an eagle's head, a bunch of roses, a windmill, a girl in a hat, a devil, and a boy. "A very clever trick picture with many wonderful effects." (*Bioscope* 26 January 1911.) Released 2 February 1911; reissued 1913. Print preserved in the National Film Archive.

30 Ta-Ta! Come Again (70)
Armstrong—New Agency
P:D:S:A: Charles Armstrong
Silhouettes. "Good-night" from the cinema manager is spelled out in letters juggled by an elephant and a jackdaw. "A good short-length trick silhouette film." (*Bioscope* 23 February 1911.) Released February 1911.

31 Mr. Asquith and the Clown
Armstrong
P:D:S:A: Charles Armstrong
Silhouette. Politician has trouble with a clown.

32 The Best Cigarette Is a Jones
Armstrong
P:D:S:A: Charles Armstrong
Silhouette. Advertisement for Jones Cigarettes.

33 The Little Artists (325)
Cricks & Martin
P: G.H. Cricks, D: J.H. Martin
Animated needle and cotton. "Two children are shown, one holding a teddy bear, while the other girl sketches on a blackboard, and then the latter is replaced by a frame of canvas to which a thread is attracted, which by its own volition forms a star, and in closer view is then seen to take various other shapes—a child's photograph, a lighthouse, Humpty

17

Dumpty before his fall, the Man in the Moon, a picture of a rabbit, and portraits of King George V and his consort, the thread finally tracing the legend,
'Au Revoir' with which the film concludes." (*Bioscope* 15 June 1911.) Released 22 June 1911.

34   Road Hogs in Toyland (330)
Empire Films – Butcher
P: Frank Butcher, D:S:A: Arthur Cooper.
Animated toys. "A story enacted entirely with mechanical toys. A picture that will please the youngsters. All their pet characters introduced."
(Advertisement *Bioscope* 30 November 1911.) "All the youngsters' pet toys
in animation, it will make them scream with delight, and will bewilder their
parents." (Advertisement *Bioscope* 7 December 1911.) "A smart little film
which should prove very popular." (*Bioscope* 23 November 1911.) Released
16 December 1911.

35   A Merry Christmas to All Our Friends (90)
Crystal Films – Cosmopolitan
D:A: Stuart Kinder
Animated letters form the title phrase as a greeting from the cinema
manager to his patrons. Released December 1911.

1912

36 **Animated Toys** (365)
Urban Trading Company
P: Charles Urban, D:S:A: Walter R. Booth
Animated toys. "Certain geometric squares and circles appear on the screen and from these are evolved, in a marvellous manner, all kinds of toys and domestic utensils. The whole of the processes are produced with remarkable rapidity and marvellous ingenuity." (*Bioscope* 14 March 1912.) Released 20 March 1912.

37 **Paper Cuttings** (325)
Kineto Films
D:S:A: Walter R. Booth
Animated cut-outs. "An amusing and novel trick subject in which a pair of scissors, apparently without direction, by any human agency, cut lengths of paper into strange and unexpected shapes. The film concludes with a reference to the coal strike, which will be sufficiently fresh in the public recollection to make the picture interesting." (*Bioscope* 25 April 1912.) Released 2 May 1912.

38 **A Modern Mystery** (290)
Urban Trading Company
P: Charles Urban, D:S:A: Walter R. Booth
Animated clay. "This is an interesting and clever trick film showing the art of clay modelling to perfection; followed by a conjurer who, by the touch of his wand, produces all sorts of wonderful things." (*Kine Monthly Film Record* May 1912.) Released 8 May 1912.

39 **Wooden Athletes** (330)
Empire Films—M.P. Sales
P: Frank Butcher, D:S:A: Arthur Cooper
Animated toys. "A unique trick film. It consists of a troupe of acrobats and equilibrists made up of ordinary wooden dolls, and their performances are wonderful. The outside of a travelling showman's booth is first shown,

and the 'band' consisting of the big drum and pipes is braying out to a gaping crowd. The boss showman is strutting up and down the front of the booth. When all the dolls have crowded in the interior is shown, and the performance goes on. There is weight-lifting extraordinary, jumping through hoops, walking and dancing on the tightrope, and a number of other circus eccentricities. After each turn the oddities come to the front and bow to the audience." (*Bioscope* 9 May 1912.) Released 15 May 1912. Print preserved in the National Film Archive.

40 Father's Forty Winks (330)
Empire Films—M.P. Sales
P: Frank Butcher, D:S:A: Arthur Cooper
Animated toys. "Paterfamilias, weary of replying to his boys' questions regarding their toys, falls asleep and dreams that the toys have come to life, and the picture illustrates his dream. A street scene is shown, and all the usual characters are represented by mechanical figures. A large house catches fire, the police ring up for the fire brigade, which arrives drawn by mechanical dogs. The house is blazing away, and some thrilling rescues are effected by teddy bears, etc. The dream ends by paterfamilias being rudely awakened by the squirting of water from a toy engine, in the hands of one of his boys." (*Kine Monthly Record* June 1912.) Released 23 June 1912; remake of *In the Land of Nod* (1908).

41 Sports in Moggyland (340)
Diamond Films—Cosmopolitan
Animated toys. "The patience displayed by the trainer of the lower animal kingdom sinks into insignificance compared with what must be requisite in order to bring a company of Dutch dolls to such a pitch of perfection as is evinced by the participators in *Sports in Moggyland*. For it is quite impossible after seeing them to believe that these puppets are not endowed with an intelligence which enables them fully to appreciate and enjoy the antics they engage in. They drill with the precision and enthusiasm of Boy Scouts. They leap hurdles, negotiate the Giant's Stride, and engage in desperate tournaments which would be almost too sensational in point of danger were it not for the comforting reflection that nothing really matters much as in the constantly recurring threat of total dismemberment. They show a marvellous aptitude for getting themselves joined together again." (*Bioscope* 5 September 1912.) Released September 1912.

42 The Cats' Cup Final (360)
Empire Films—M.P. Sales
P: Frank Butcher, D:S:A: Arthur Cooper
Animated toys. "An ingenious trick film." (*Kine Monthly Film Record* November 1912.) Toy cats play a football match. Released 3 November 1912.

43   Old Mother Hubbard (410)
Empire Films – M.P. Sales
P: Frank Butcher, D:S:A: Arthur Cooper
Animated toys. Traditional nursery rhyme of Mother Hubbard, her dog and her cupboard. Released 24 November 1912. Not reviewed.

44   In Gollywog Land (590)
Natural Colour Kinematograph Company
P: Charles Urban, D: F. Martin Thornton, A: Edgar Rogers, Walter R. Booth
Kinemacolor
Animated puppets/live action; first animated film in color. "The golly-wog manages to dodge the apples but when the dough covers the basin, six little wogs break through. Then the gollywog gives a conjuring act with flowers, and later goes for a ride in his auto-boot, runs into a rival motorist, and has to amputate his leg. First aid with a vengeance!" (*Bioscope* 16 November 1916.) Released November 1912. Retitled *Gollywog's Motor Accident* for U.S. release; reissued in 1916 in monochrome by Kineto Films.

45   Cinderella (997)
Empire Films – M.P. Sales
P: Frank Butcher, D:S:A: Arthur Cooper
Animated toys. "This film represents the well-known story of Cinderella, the various parts being taken by nursery dolls." (*Kine Monthly Film Record* December 1912.)

46   Ten Little Nigger Boys (380)
Empire Films – M.P. Sales
P: Frank Butcher, D:S:A: Arthur Cooper
Animated toys. "An up-to-date version of the old nursery rhyme enacted entirely by mechanical toys. A too plentiful diner, a police trap, a monstrous fish, an accident while dropping sticks, a hive of bees, a shell, a tree, a lion, and a gun, successively account for the nigger boys, the survivor shrivelling up in the sun. The tricks are performed with unusual cleverness." (*Bioscope* 23 January 1913.) Released December 1912.

47   Santa Claus (2000)
Natural Colour Kinematograph Company
P: Charles Urban, D: F. Martin Thornton, R.H. Callum, A: Walter R. Booth, Edgar Rogers, S: Alfred De Manby, Leedham Bantock, Harold Simpson
Kinemacolor
featuring Leedham Bantock (Santa Claus), Margaret Favronova (Tingaling)

Live action/animated toy sequences. Elsie goes to sleep on Christmas Eve and dreams that Father Christmas arrives down the chimney and transforms her into Tingaling, a fairy. They travel by reindeer sledge to his home at the North Pole where busy little gnomes are making toys for the Christmas delivery. She helps him in his deliveries to rich and poor children, and Santa enlists the aid of Father Neptune to help a sea captain return to his family. First shown December 1912 at the Scala Theatre; released December 1913.

48   **Modelling Extraordinary** (1000)
     Natural Colour Kinematograph Company
     P: Charles Urban, D:S:A: Walter R. Booth
     Kinemacolor
     Animated clay modeling. "A very clever little trick picture presenting a series of humorous animated clay models. The various effects are exceedingly neatly executed and are of a somewhat original character." (*Bioscope* 26 November 1914.) Released December 1912; reissued 21 December 1914 in monochrome by Kineto Films.

1913

49 The Nightmare of the Gladeye Twins (770)
Kineto Films
D:S:A: Edgar Rogers
Animated dolls/live action. "Pretty little Elsie, tired out after playing with her giant dolls, falls asleep and dreams that they all come to life, and her especial pets, 'the twins,' indulge in wonderful exploits. Remarkably clever is the photographic illusion. The twins steal a pearl necklace and bury it in the garden. They find the milk can at the front door, drink it, fill up the can with ink, and the policeman drinks this (a sorry libel on the force). This is amusing and clever enough to find a place in every Christmas holiday programme." (*Bioscope* 9 November 1916.) Released 15 June 1913; reissued November 1916 as *Elsie's Nightmare.*

50 The Old Toymaker's Dream (325)
Empire Films – M.P. Sales
P: Frank Butcher, D:S:A: Arthur Cooper
Animated toys. "The old toymaker falls asleep and dreams that his toys come to life. He sees many funny scenes in the streets of Toy Town, and a big aeroplane race across country, round St. Paul's, and on to a cannibal island." (*Kine Monthly Film Record* June 1913.) Released 16 June 1913.

51 Pathé Cartoons (series)
Pathé Frères Cinema
D:S:A: Max J. Martin
The first animated cartoon series, live action with some animation. Max Martin's hand sketches topical cartoons in accelerated action. Advertised in *Pathé's Cinema Journal* 22 November 1913: "What's this? Well, it's Number One of Pathé Cartoons. Something that will catch on immediately. We foresee for this special film a great rush; and, Mr. Exhibitor, if you want something really humorous, just secure at once No. 1 Pathé Cartoons, a Satirical Review of Topical Events – ready now! Price 55 shillings first week, 30 shillings second week, 15 shillings third week."

1913

24 Nov	No. 1
1 Dec	No. 2
8 Dec	No. 3
15 Dec	No. 4
22 Dec	No. 5
29 Dec	No. 6

1914

5 Jan	No. 7
12 Jan	No. 8
19 Jan	No. 9
26 Jan	No. 10
2 Feb	No. 11
9 Feb	No. 12
16 Feb	No. 13
23 Feb	No. 14
2 Mar	No. 15
9 Mar	No. 16
16 Mar	No. 17
23 Mar	No. 18
30 Mar	No. 19
6 Apr	No. 20
13 Apr	No. 21
20 Apr	No. 22
27 Apr	No. 23
4 May	No. 24
11 May	No. 25
18 May	No. 26
25 May	No. 27
1 Jun	No. 28
8 Jun	No. 29
15 Jun	No. 30
22 Jun	No. 31
29 Jun	No. 32
6 Jul	No. 33
13 Jul	No. 34
20 Jul	No. 35
27 Jul	No. 36
3 Aug	No. 37

52   Love and War in Toyland (3000)
Natural Colour Kinematograph Company
P: Charles Urban, D: F. Martin Thornton, A: Edgar Rogers
Kinemacolor
Animated toys. "This is claimed to be the most wonderful trick film ever produced, and we can quite believe that the producers are fully justified in their assertion. When we admire the patience exhibited by the trainers of animals possessing the intelligence of elephants and dogs, what must we think of that which enables some hundreds of toys to give an

animated and life-like three act drama of love, battle and revenge? When it is estimated that the production required some 200,000 changes of position in photographing, and that it occupied nearly 4,000 hours of hard work, it will be seen that the result has not been easily carried out. The pitched battle between the leaden troops of the Lovelanders and the Nogoods, and the fearsome onslaught by every wild beast ever conceived by the designers of Gamages, take rank with the greatest of battle films, while the aeroplane duel which takes place many inches above the earth, is amazing in its manipulation and daring. The colouring of the film embraces all the tints of the spectrum, and is a continual delight to the eye." (*Bioscope* 18 December 1913.) Released December 1913.

53   Larks in Toyland (496)
Empire Films — Davisons
P: Frank Butcher, D:S:A: Arthur Cooper

Animated toys. "A cleverly contrived comic with real dolls as the artistes and toys galore to appeal to the kiddies." (*Bioscope* 11 December 1913.) Released 25 December 1913.

1914

54 Isn't It Wonderful? (465)
Armstrong – Andersons
P:D:S:A: Charles Armstrong
Silhouettes. "Trick silhouette film in which the antics of members of the Playtown Circus are very entertaining." (*Bioscope* 19 February 1914.) Released February 1914.

55 The Little Picture Producer (950)
Natural Colour Kinematograph Company
P: Charles Urban, D: F. Martin Thornton, A: Edgar Rogers
Kinemacolor
Live action/animated toys. Three children use their animated toys to produce a western film. Listed in *Bioscope* 26 March 1914, but not reviewed.

56 The Tangram (370)
Kineto Films
D:S:A: Walter R. Booth
Animated pieces of a traditional Chinese puzzle form themselves into King Henry VIII, Lloyd George, and act out a Chinese love drama. "An amusing film in which the rectilineal pieces of an ancient Chinese puzzle are arranged into various comic caricatures from the much married Henry to the mightily maligned George." (*Bioscope* 2 April 1914.) Released 13 April 1914.

57 Kine Kartoons (500)
Barker Motion Photography
P: Will Barker, D:S:A: F. Gandolphi, C: Leslie Eveleigh
Cut-out animation. "The first few numbers deal in a humorous manner with such subjects as 'How a Budget Is Made' (showing Lloyd George drawing his inspiration from an animated mangel wurzel), 'The Dress Germ' (offering an ingenious bacteriological explanation of the various phenomena in modern dress), 'How I Killed My First Jaguar by

26

Colonel Teddy' (depicting the manner in which the ex–President of the United States makes a successful kill), and 'Broncho Billy Loops the Loop' (illustrating some surprising aeronautical feats by a cowboy). The cartoons are very well drawn, and they are set in motion by means of exceedingly clever trick effects. The extent of their animation is, in fact, one of their most notable and unique features." (*Bioscope* 21 May 1914.) Released May 1914.

58   Anima Drawings (561)
Cartoonlets – M.P. Sales
"A magic pencil draws comic figures before our eyes, when they are at once imbued with life, performing many ludicrous antics." (*Kine Monthly Film Record* July 1914.) Released June 1914.

59   An Adventure in Impland (425)
Hepworth Films
P: Cecil M. Hepworth
"Comic drawings by a rapid fire cartoonist, the two imps and their glad-eye consorts having a merry time." (*Bioscope* 9 July 1914.) "We feel certain that everybody will be both interested and amused at the innocent adventures of Limpy and Lumpy. A striking little novelty." (*Kine Monthly Film Record* July 1914.) Released 23 July 1914.

60   A Little Lady Cartoonist (470)
Kineto Films
D:S:A: Walter R. Booth
Live action/animation. "A child is seen drawing caricatures of well-known people. After drawing these and by the aid of a few taps on the anvil, she is seen on the canvas impersonating the caricatures of life." (*Kine Monthly Film Record* July 1914.) Released July 1914.

61   Peace and War Pencillings by Harry Furniss (430)
Furniss Films
P:D:S:A: Harry Furniss
Live action/animation. Cartoonist draws lightning topical sketches at accelerated speed. "For instance there is an innocent suggestion of John Bull at peace comfortably reading a paper by the light of a candle, the candle being placed in a high candlestick. The second stage of this involves the changing of the scene to Trafalgar Square, the flame being turned into Nelson, the candlestick into Nelson's Column, and a slight suggestion added of the lions at the base and of the National Gallery in the background. Then – War. On the newspaper the word is rapidly written, the dome of the National Gallery becomes the Kaiser, the position of John Bull's head is shifted within a few strokes, the lions spring from their pedestals, the fountains represent cannonading, and, well, that is War."

(Harry Furniss: "The Magic Hand": *Strand Magazine* December 1914.) Premiered early August at the London Coliseum. Print preserved in the National Film Archive.

62 War Cartoons by Dudley Tempest (180)
Bamforth Producing Company – Y.C.C.
D:S:A: Dudley Tempest
Live action/animation. Cartoonist draws lightning topical sketches at accelerated speed. Filmed at their Holmfirth (Yorkshire) Studios by Bamforth, who produced both films and postcards. Dudley Tempest was a staff postcard artist. Released 28 August 1914.

63 Magic Squares (498)
British & Colonial – Davisons
D:S:A: Louis Nikola
Animated cut-outs. "Quite a novelty in trick films, the squares of paper assuming various forms and enacting a comedy, then depicting various popular sports and amusements. Produced by a famous illusionist." (*Bioscope* 3 September 1914.) Released 14 September 1914.

64 Cine War Cartoons No. 1 (500)
R. Prieur
Live action/animation. "A screamingly funny film that will fill your theatre." (*Bioscope* 10 September 1914.) No further details traced.

65 War Cartoons (276)
Furniss Films – H.A. Browne
P:D:S:A: Harry Furniss
Live action/animation. Second edition of topical cartoons drawn in accelerated action by a famous cartoonist of the period. Released September 1914.

66 War Cartoons by Sidney Aldridge (456)
Aldridge – Warner's Features
P:D:S:A: Sidney Aldridge
Live action/animation. "This issue is very opportunely timed and well displays in a new direction the clever work of a famous contributor to *Punch*. So good, in fact, are the various cartoons that the task of comparison is one of extreme difficulty. Perhaps the best of a most entertaining series are 'Putting His Light Out,' with the Kaiser as a dejected candle very obviously Made In Germany; the Dachshund incident, with its comical sequel, and 'The Unmailed British Fist,' which enables the final laugh. All are, needless to say, well drawn, and witty enough to appeal wherever shown." (*Bioscope* 17 September 1914.) Released September 1914.

67   The Voice of the Empire (1100)
B.B. Films—Fenning Film Service
The longest cartoon to date, a full 1,000-foot reel running some 15 minutes. "A descriptive cartoon shows Kitchener's appeal for volunteers, and how Britain responds by giving him a first instalment of 500,000 men. Cartoons show how London, Scotland, Ireland, and Wales responded, also how the Colonies—Canada, New Zealand, Newfoundland, India, etc.—answer the call. King George V visiting HMS New Zealand. Types of Australian Army. The West Indian Regiment at Kingston, Jamaica. Scottish Regiments. Empire Day celebrations. And finishing up with an original cartoon, 'The Rousing of the British Lion.' (*Bioscope* 8 October 1914.) Released October 1914.

68   The Humpty Dumpty Circus (448)
Humpty Dumpty Films—R. Prieur
Animated toys. Wooden dolls come to life and perform circus stunts. Released October 1914.

69   The Kaiser's Nightmare (500)
Charing Cross Film Company
D: F. Baragwanath, S: J.S. Norton
Nonanimated cartoons. "As the title suggests, this little film is a semi-humorous review of the present European situation, presented for the most part in satirical manner from the Kaiser's point of view. The travesty poem by Mr. J.S. Norton, upon which it is based, and quotations from which appear on the screen, is published in the form of a penny booklet, and the caricatures, cartoons and other drawings shown in the film are the work of Mr. F. Baragwanath. It is, perhaps, rather a pity that the latter should all be 'still drawings' as opposed to the 'animated cartoons,' since, under the circumstances, they gain nothing from their cinematographic presentation, and might have been produced with equal effect as lantern slides." (*Bioscope* 1 October 1914.) Released October 1914.

70   Bully Boy No. 1 (435)
Neptune Films
D:S:A: Lancelot Speed, C: Claude McDonnell
Live action/animation. The first film in a series in which the notable cartoonist and illustrator draws topical cartoons at accelerated speed, and they then animate. "Considerably the wittiest and most ingenious topical skit that we have hitherto seen. It deals with the destruction of Rheims Cathedral by the modern Attila, and concludes with an amazingly realistic reproduction of the British Bulldog consuming the German Sausage. The living line drawings in which these subjects are dealt with are executed with remarkable ability by Mr. Lancelot Speed. Although keen and

stinging, the humour of the pictures never degenerates into mere vulgarity." (*Bioscope* 8 October 1914.) Previewed at the Shaftesbury Avenue Pavilion 2 October 1918. Print preserved in the National Film Archive.

71   Wireless from the War Series
London Exclusives
Live action/animation. Series of short films made in the "Lightning Cartoonist" technique showing the artist's hand rapidly sketching topical comments. None received a review in the trade press, but No. 5 is preserved in the National Film Archive. It contains three items: Uncle Sam saying "Nothing doing" to a German woman; a Russian soldier asking for 8,000,000 tickets to Berlin at the Frontier Booking Office; German soldiers stranded by the Belgians who have flooded Termonde.

8 Oct	**No. 1** (250)
15 Oct	**No. 2** (250)
22 Oct	**No. 3** (250)
29 Oct	**No. 4** (250)
5 Nov	**No. 5** (250)

72   Winchelsea and Its Environs (430)
Furniss Films — Davison
P:D:S:A: Harry Furniss
Live action/animation. Combination of photographic views of and accelerated sketches of a seaside town. "Novel and highly interesting combination of illustrated art and scenic photography. As various scenes are represented, the rich historical associations of the neighborhood are drawn and illustrated by the artist. A species of lightning sketching tour and enjoyable throughout." (*Bioscope* 22 October 1914.) Released October 1914.

73   The Kineto War Map Series
Kineto Films
P: Charles Urban, D:S:A: F. Percy Smith
Series of animated maps depicting the progress of the war. "This little film introduces an idea so strikingly excellent and effective that one wonders it has not been made use of before, and like other great ideas it is exceedingly simple. It is a war map in animation showing with graphic precision the exact course of the war." (*Kine Monthly Film Record* October 1914.)

1914	
22 Oct	**No. 1** (500)
3 Dec	**No. 2** (305)

1915

4 Feb	**No. 3** (515)
11 Mar	**No. 4** (500)
15 Apr	**No. 5** (380)
1 Jul	**No. 6** (405)
30 Aug	**No. 7** (620)
11 Oct	**No. 8** (480)
29 Nov	**No. 9** (435)

1916

27 Jan	**No. 10** (550)
23 Mar	**No. 11** (500)
27 Apr	**No. 12** (650)
18 May	**No. 13** (600)
10 Aug	**No. 14** (580)
7 Sep	**No. 15** (470)

74   French's Contemptible Little Army (375)
Neptune Films (Bully Boy Series No. 2)
D:S:A: Lancelot Speed, C: Claude McDonnell
Live action/animation. Empire soldiers combine to cook the Prussian Goose. "Mr. Speed is an exceedingly clever draughtsman who has been able to appreciate to the full the unique possibilities offered by the moving picture camera in conjunction with work of this sort. Possessed thus of every advantage he is taking this new form of comic pictorial art several steps further forward than it has yet been developed." (*Bioscope* 29 October 1914.) Released 24 October 1914.

75   British War Sketches (498)
Bamforth Producing Company – Y.C.C.
D:S:A: Dudley Tempest
Live action/animation: cartoonist sketches topical comments. "Smartly drawn in a popular vein, these pictures are quite a good example of their kind. Mr. Dudley Tempest, the artist, has achieved some capital results, especially in the portions entitled 'His Master's Voice' and 'It's a Long Way to Tipperary.'" (*Bioscope* 29 October 1914.) Released October 1914.

76   Christmas War Sketches (590)
Bamforth Producing Company – Y.C.C.
D:S:A: Dudley Tempest
Live action/animation. "In a further series of topical cartoons, Mr. Dudley Tempest gives evidence of his pleasing and decisive style. Splendidly drawn and most aptly titled throughout, probably the best being 'A Christmas Salute' and 'Footing the Bill,' both referring to a certain self-deified individual." (*Bioscope* 12 November 1914.) Released 2 November 1914.

77   **Fourth Harry Furniss Cartoon** (240)
      Furniss Films – Davison
      P:D:S:A: Harry Furniss
      Live action/animation. Cartoonist draws topical comments. No synopsis or review traced. Released 2 November 1914.

78   **Sleepless** (400)
      Neptune Films (Bully Boy Series No. 3)
      D:S:A: Lancelot Speed, C: Claude McDonnell
      Live action/animation. Artist draws topical comments including a doctor's sleeping draft which fails to cure the Kaiser's insomnia. Released 5 November 1914. Print preserved in the National Film Archive.

79   **War Skits by Sidney Aldridge** (325)
      Aldridge – New Agency
      P:D:S:A: Sidney Aldridge
      Animated cartoons. "An unusually clever series of humorous trick drawings as befitting the times, of a popular nature. The ingenious contributor to *Punch* hits off the new Napoleon, otherwise 'Bill,' in fine style, and ends the film with a fine drawing of 'K of K' (i.e. Kitchener of Khartoum)." (*Bioscope* 12 November 1914.) Released 17 December 1914.

80   **Sports in Toyland** (310)
      Excel Films – R. Prieur
      D:S:A: Stuart Kinder
      Animated dolls. "A fairly well executed trick picture showing wooden dolls at various sports. The film finishes with a 'Good Night' device and is therefore suitable for the end of a programme." (*Bioscope* 12 November 1914.) Released 21 December 1914.

81   **Proverbs and War Topics** (511)
      AKA: **War Cartoons Series 1**
      Tressograph – Davison
      P: Henry Tress, D:S:A: Dudley Buxton
      Live action/animation. The first cartoon film by the popular postcard and magazine cartoonist, Dudley Buxton, destined to become a major force in British animation. "Your audience will always show their delight for clever cartoons. We have something absolutely new, attractive and original by the eminent lightning cartoonist, Dudley Buxton." (advertisement November 1914.) "The first of a series of cartoons by Mr. Dudley Buxton. Without being particularly original he is clever and amusing." (*Bioscope* 12 November 1914.) Released 19 November 1914.

82 War Cartoons Series 2 (421)

Tressograph — Davison
P: Henry Tress, D:S:A: Dudley Buxton
Live action/animation. Topical sketches in accelerated action.
Released 26 November 1914. Not reviewed.

83 The Doll's Circus (500)

Goblin Films — R. Prieur
Animated toys. Dolls give a circus performance. Listed in *Bioscope*
26 November 1914; released 7 December 1914. Not reviewed.

84 Merry War Jottings (478)

Bamforth Producing Company — Y.C.C.
D:S:A: Dudley Tempest
Live action/animation. Artist draws several topical cartoons including "The Peace He Wanted," "Try Again Billy," and "The Joy Wheel."
"Another smart series of cartoons in which that conspicuously clever
draughtsman Mr. Dudley Tempest makes merry at the expense of a
muchly-moustached monarch. The quaint manner in which the artist
'blacks in' certain important details arouses one's interest to a very marked
degree, just as he dashes away to another and probably much more important part of the subject. The completed results in every case bespeak a complete mastery and a wonderful eye to exact proportion, while the addition
of a witty title gives the necessary topical touch." (*Bioscope* 10 December
1914.) Released 30 November 1914.

85 War Cartoons Series 3 (408)

Tressograph — Davison
P: Henry Tress, D:S:A: Dudley Buxton
Live action/animation. Cartoonist draws topical comments at ac-
celerated rate. Not reviewed; released 3 December 1914.

86 Transformations (470)

Kineto Films
P: Charles Urban, D:S:A: F. Percy Smith (?)
"A series of very ingenious and effective animated topical cartoons.
Pictures of various well-known persons and objects are deftly transformed
by the draughtsman into other pictures of correlative spirit. Novel in con-
ception and cleverly executed, the film should be exceedingly popular."
(*Bioscope* 3 December 1914.)

87 Sea Dreams (360)

Neptune Films (Bully Boy Series No. 4)
D:S:A: Lancelot Speed, C: Claude McDonnell
Live action/animation. Cartoonist executes high-speed drawings

which come to life. The British Navy destroys Kaiser Wilhelm's dream of a German Empire. "This one is a real scream, the dreamer, of course, being the German Emperor. There is no better cartoonistic work on the screen anywhere than that put into this series by Mr. Speed." (*Pictures & Picture-goer* 7 January 1915.) Released 10 December 1914.

88   A Box of Matches (396)
Humpty Dumpty Films — R. Prieur
Animated matches come out of their matchbox and perform stunts. "A very clever and somewhat original trick film introducing a series of pro-digious feats admirably performed by a box of matchsticks. Really very in-genious and quite skilfully done." (*Bioscope* 17 December 1914.)

89   Studdy's War Studies No. 1 (450)
Gaumont
D:S:A: George E. Studdy
Lightning cartoons. The first attempt at animation by George E. Studdy, a popular press cartoonist who had worked in comic strips ("Pro-fessor Helpemon" in *The Big Budget* 1904), and would later create the popular dog "Bonzo" and bring him to the screen in full animation. "The series is of a topical character, and a number of humorous aspects of the Great War are presented on the screen. The rapid building-up of the sketch, which speedily takes definite shape before our eyes, is distinctly fascinating." (*Kine Monthly Film Record* January 1915.) Released 28 December 1914.

1915

90 Studdy's War Studies No. 2 (450)
Gaumont
D:S:A: George E. Studdy
Lightning cartoons. "Perhaps the favourite of the series will be the evolution of the German sausage into the perfected Super-Hun, an admirable portrait of the Kaiser, in which, with subtle sarcasm, he is depicted with his sword carried on the wrong side. The other subjects treated include an allusion to the Scarborough Raid, the Kaiser choosing a new suit and complaining that the Spring fashions offer nothing but 'checks,' and a very amusing study of the man in the street struggling with the pronunciation of Russian names." (*Bioscope* 28 January 1915.) Released 15 January 1915.

91 A Chip Off the Old Block; or, The Half-a-Crown Prince (360)
Neptune Films (Bully Boy Series No. 5)
D:S:A: Lancelot Speed, C: Claude McDonnell
Lightning cartoons. "The fifth of this series of clever animal sketches by Mr. Lancelot Speed is, if possible, more amusing than its predecessors. *Bully Boy Cartoons* are so successful that one sees them in almost any picture show that one visits, and very frequently they form a turn at some of the best music halls." (*Pictures & Picturegoer* 6 February 1915.) Advertised in *Bioscope* dated 7 January 1915; released 18 January 1915.

92 The Adventures of Willie Woodbine and Lightning Larry (710)
Aldridge – New Agency
P:D:S:A: Sidney Aldridge
Animated cartoon (?): "The first of a series by Sidney Aldridge by a combination of trick scenic effects and knockabout business." (*Bioscope* 21 January 1915.) Subtitled *A Joy-Ride to the Cannibal Islands,* no further episodes in this projected series were produced. "Lightning Larry and Willie Woodbine are presented with a magic wand and magnet. Larry espies a balloon, gets it down by the aid of the magnet, and they start on their joy ride. The balloon arrives over the village of Slopton-on-Mud. Here

35

they lower the magnet and one by one the houses become attached to it, and are stowed inside the car. They then arrive at the Keil Canal, bombs are thrown down, and Admiral Jellicoe is caused a deal of bother. The balloon then arrives over the Cannibal Islands, where King Howdedo gives them permission to settle. They then depart and after an adventure with two dusky flappers, plant the model village of Slopton-on-Mud."

93   His Birthday Present (77)
Pathé
Newsreel cartoon included in Pathé News released 27 January 1915. Kaiser Wilhelm's moustache falls off when he is menaced by the British lion. Preserved in the National Film Archive.

94   Humpty Dumpty R. A. (525)
Humpty Dumpty Films – R. Prieur
Animated doll/lightning cartoons. "An animated doll executed lightning cartoons of men famous at the present moment, including Admiral Jellicoe, General French, Winston Churchill, Sir Edward Grey, and Lord Kitchener. The sketches might have been executed just a little nearer to the camera, but they are cleverly done, and are excellent likenesses, whilst the general idea of the film is very well carried out." (Bioscope 28 January 1915.)

95   Studdy's War Studies No. 3 (450)
Gaumont
D:S:A: George E. Studdy
Lightning cartoon. Not reviewed. Released 25 February 1915.

96   Armstrong's Trick War Incidents (360)
Armstrong – G. Serra
P:D:S:A: Charles Armstrong
Silhouettes. "This is a trick film bearing upon the war, in which some animated silhouettes go through some interesting manoeuvres. Sergeant Cox performs with his bulldog and his donkey, and is very expert at bringing down enemy airships. It is a novel entertainment, and the little figures are very amusing." (Bioscope 8 April 1915.)

97   John Bull's Animated Sketchbook No. 1 (450)
Cartoon Film Company
P: J.A. Clozenberg, D:S:A: Dudley Buxton
Animated cartoon. The first production of the first British company set up purely to produce animated cartoons. "The first of a series of film cartoons by this popular artist were shown at a recent trade review and elicited laughter and praise from a class of people notoriously difficult to arouse to any display of emotion, to wit, the trade press. The various popular and

unpopular personages were admirably represented, each giving point to a really good joke, and considerable ingenuity was displayed in pictures which showed bomb-dropping by 'Zepp,' submarine exploits, and a reproduction of the destruction of the 'Blucher.' The effect of shellfire and a running sea added considerable realism to the latter." (*Bioscope* 15 April 1915.) Released 10 April 1915.

98   The Jolly Roger (338)
Neptune Films (Bully Boy Series No. 6)
D:S:A: Lancelot Speed, C: Claude McDonnell
"The sixth and in all probability about the most amusing of this famous series by Lancelot Speed. Topical and typical of this clever artist's style." (*Bioscope* 1 April 1915.) Released 17 April 1915.

99   His Winning Ways (65)
Gaumont (Studdy's War Studies No. 4)
D:S:A: George E. Studdy
Lightning cartoon, included in *Gaumont News* No. 427, released 26 April 1915. The cartoonist's hand draws a German U-Boat named "The U-Limit," and gives it the Kaiser Bill moustache. Exclaiming, "Gad, I'm great at knocking down girls!" he punches Miss Trawler, Miss Collier, Miss Falaba and Miss Neutral. Print preserved in the National Film Archive.

100   John Bull's Animated Sketchbook No. 2 (500)
Cartoon Film Company – Ruffell's Exclusives
P: J.A. Clozenberg, D:S:A: Dudley Buxton
Animated cartoon. Released April 1915. Not reviewed.

101   Turkish Delight
Neptune Films (Bully Boy Series No. 7)
D:S:A: Lancelot Speed, C: Claude McDonnell
Released 5 May 1915. Not reviewed.

102   The Adventures of Big and Little Willie (355)
Mario-Toons – Yorkshire Cine Company
S: William K. Haselden
Animated puppets. Based on the topical cartoons currently appearing in the *Daily Mirror,* as drawn by W.K. Haselden. "The novelty of this film consists in the use of marionettes which portray the quaint ideas of W.K. Haselden, the *Daily Mirror* cartoonist. An ingenious trick issue fairly well carried out, with some amusing topical bits." (*Bioscope* 6 May 1915.) Big and Little Willie were Haselden's versions of Kaiser Wilhelm and the Crown Prince.

103 Topical Sketch No. 1 (316)
By Say Films – Davison
P:D:S:A: "Say"
Lightning cartoons. "The first of a novel series by a gifted artist, whose invisible pencil mysteriously evolves some magnificent linework, the effects being in almost every case, white upon a black background. A cheering variety and several novel features that will appeal to the exhibitor are seen in an entirely satisfactory issue." (*Bioscope* 20 May 1915.) The white lines appearing on a black background was the style originally used by Émile Cohl, and was probably achieved in the same way: by drawing in black on white and projecting the negative. Released 5 July 1915.

104 John Bull's Animated Sketchbook No. 3 (500)
Cartoon Film Company
P: J.A. Clozenberg, P:S:A: Dudley Buxton
Released May 1915. Not reviewed.

105 Topical Sketch No. 2 (299)
By Say Films – Davison
P:D:S:A: "Say"
Lightning cartoons. "More clever cartoons drawn in masterly style by Say, and emphasised in value by his witty allusions to various everyday topics." (*Bioscope* 3 June 1915.) Items: "War Babies"; "Belgium Pie"; "The New Game of Scooter"; "Portrait of the Late R.W. Poulton-Palmer"; released 12 July 1915.

106 Topical Sketch No. 3 (315)
By Say Films – Davison
P:D:S:A: "Say"
Lightning cartoons. "In all probability the best so far of this series. Say's witty answer to Mr. Filbert, the gentleman who wants excitement, is especially good, and very apposite to the times. 'The Order of the Garter' is also cleverly achieved. A novelty in topicals and well worth the viewing." (*Bioscope* 10 June 1915.) Items: "Percy the Filbert Wants a Change"; "The Order of the Garter"; "The Order of the Boot"; "Puzzle – Find the Sergeant Major." Released 19 July 1915.

107 Topical Sketch No. 4 (210)
By Say Films – Davison
P:D:S:A: "Say"
Lightning cartoons. "Another brief but entirely successful addition to this series of cartoons." (*Bioscope* 17 June 1915.) Released 29 July 1915.

108   John Bull's Animated Sketchbook No. 4 (435)
Cartoon Film Company
P: J.A. Clozenberg, D:S:A: Dudley Buxton
"It shows Kaiser Bill in difficulties with his halo, which, after various diverting contortions, eventually chokes him. The *Lusitania* disaster is then grimly and decisively portrayed, the moral of it pointed with a picture of Von Tirpitz plus the famous whiskers, in an Iron Cross frame, which, by some clever touches, is turned into the Jolly Roger adorned with skull and crossbones. The next item shows the Kaiser and his enterprising son motoring at full speed for Calais, but receiving a nasty setback from the British Lion." (*The Cinema* 24 June 1915.) Released 21 June 1915. This cartoon also includes animated caricatures of Harry Tate and Charlie Chaplin. Preserved in the National Film Archive.

109   John Bull's Animated Sketchbook No. 5 (435)
Cartoon Film Company
P: J.A. Clozenberg, D:S:A: Dudley Buxton
"No. 5 of the series will touch, we understand, upon John Bull's recipe for making soldiers; the entry of Italy into the war, and a comic sketch entitled 'All's Fair in Love and War.' We confidently recommend these highly interesting and ingenious cartoons, of which not the least notable feature is the manner in which the titles troop onto the screen in a jumble of letters and arrange themselves in proper order." (*The Cinema* 24 June 1915.) Released July 1915.

110   Bully Boy No. 8 (332)
Neptune Films
D:S:A: Lancelot Speed, C: Claude McDonnell
Trade show announced for 21 May 1915 but postponed to 25 June 1915. Reviews not traced.

111   John Bull's Animated Sketchbook No. 6 (500)
Cartoon Film Company
P: J.A. Clozenberg, D:S:A: Dudley Buxton
Released 6 August 1915. No reviews traced.

112   Dicky Dee's Cartoons No. 1 (541)
British & Colonial – Davison
P: J.B. McDowell, D:S:A: Anson Dyer
Lightning cartoons. The first production by Ernest Anson Dyer, an ecclesiastic stained glass artist who would become the leading animator in pre–World War Two British cartoons. "A very up-to-the-minute and original series of humorous and topical sketches executed in black and white by an artist possessing exceptional skill and facility." (*Kine Monthly*

Film Record October 1915.) "Excellently drawn and fairly interesting series of topical cartoons." (*Bioscope* 2 September 1915.) Released 18 October 1915.

113 All for the Love of a Lady (563)
Cartoon Film Company
"John Bull's Animated Sketchbook" No. 7
P: J.A. Clozenberg, D:S:A: Dudley Buxton
Released September 1915; reviews not traced.

114 Dicky Dee's Cartoons No. 2 (578)
British & Colonial – Davison
P: J.B. McDowell, D:S:A: Anson Dyer
Lightning cartoons. "These clever animated cartoons, being of British origin, and mainly of a topical character, should be particularly useful. They are clearly executed and very amusing. No. 2 includes 'The Peace Monger' (the Kaiser), 'The Zeppelin Raid,' and 'A Puzzle Portrait.' (*Bioscope* 7 October 1915.) "Dicky Dee's magic pen changes Charlie Chaplin into the Right Honourable Lloyd George." (*Kine Monthly Film Record* December 1915.) Released 25 November 1915.

115 Dicky Dee's Cartoons No. 3 (352)
British & Colonial – Davison
P: J.B. McDowell, D:S:A: Anson Dyer
Lightning cartoons. "Two subjects, one Christmassy the other patriotic, are dealt with in the latest edition of these popular cartoons." (*Bioscope* 25 November 1915.) "Good as previous numbers of this clever and novel series have been, this one surpasses them. It consists of two subjects, 'The Dream Man,' a humorous portrayal of an altogether seasonable topic, and a particularly clever 'quick-change' sketch in a fine patriotic vein." (*Kine Monthly Film Record* January 1916.) Released 13 December 1915. Print preserved in the National Film Archive.

116 John Bull's Animated Sketchbook No. 8 (700)
Cartoon Film Company
P: J.A. Clozenberg, D:S:A: Anson Dyer
Released 25 November 1915. Anson Dyer's first cartoon for this series. Not reviewed.

117 John Bull's Animated Sketchbook No. 9 (750)
Cartoon Film Company
P: J.A. Clozenberg, D:S:A: Dudley Buxton
Released 23 December 1915. Not reviewed.

118   A Pencil and Alick P.F. Ritchie (436)
   Favourite Films
   D:S:A: Alick Ritchie
   Lightning cartoons. Cartoonist's drawings come to life: Turkey falls into the soup; Zeppelin drops bomb which bounces off John Bull's chest. Print preserved in National Film Archive. Released 3 January 1916 as *Alick Ritchie's Frightful Sketches* (No. 1). "Topical, screamingly humorous, and clever. There are three of them and each one distinctly touches the public taste upon some topical theme of thought." (*Kine Monthly Film Record* March 1916.)

1916

119   Alick Ritchie's Frightful Sketches (336)
Favourite Films
D:S:A: Alick Ritchie
Lightning cartoons. "Clever and original comic trick cartoons on topical subjects, including excellent caricatures of leading Hun personalities." (*Bioscope* 17 February 1916.) Released 30 March 1916.

120   Before the Beak (577)
Cartoon Film Company
"John Bull's Animated Sketchbook" No. 10
P: J.A. Clozenberg, D:S:A: Anson Dyer
Released February 1916; not reviewed.

121   John Bull's Animated Sketchbook No. 11 (607)
Cartoon Film Company
P: J.A. Clozenberg, D:S:A: Dudley Buxton
Released 9 March 1916; not reviewed.

122   The Early Bird (566)
Cartoon Film Company
"John Bull's Animated Sketchbook" No. 12
P: J.A. Clozenberg, D:S:A: Anson Dyer
"There is an abundance of real bustling fun in a rich succession of scenes, introducing all kinds of funny characters, and it possesses the flavour of the old Harlequinade minus clown and pantaloon. We have the comic policeman, the loafing worker or shirker, the down-at-heel broken-down swell, a glimpse of a frustrated love affair, and many other ingredients that make up a really novel and amusing little entertainment, which reflects every credit upon Anson Dyer, the clever artiste." (*Kine Monthly Film Record* April 1916.) Released 10 April 1916.

123   John Bull's Animated Sketchbook No. 13 (718)
Cartoon Film Company
P: J.A. Clozenberg, D:S:A: Dudley Buxton
Released April 1916; not reviewed.

124   John Bull's Animated Sketchbook No. 14 (683)
Cartoon Film Company
P: J.A. Clozenberg, D:S:A: Anson Dyer
Released May 1916; not reviewed.

125   John Bull's Animated Sketchbook No. 15 (500)
Cartoon Film Company
P: J.A. Clozenberg, D:S:A: Dudley Buxton
Released 1 June 1916; not reviewed.

126   John Bull's Animated Sketchbook No. 16 (690)
Cartoon Film Company
P: J.A. Clozenberg, D:S:A: Anson Dyer
Released 22 June 1916; not reviewed.

127   Gossip (600)
Cartoon Film Company
"John Bull's Animated Sketchbook" No. 17
P: J.A. Clozenberg, D:S:A: Dudley Buxton
"Excellent animated cartoon burlesquing the female habit of gossip, the domestic slave who voices his patriotism of love and freedom, and Jellicoe and the Kaiser as rival shop-keepers." (*Bioscope* 20 July 1916.) Released 4 September 1916.

128   Alick Ritchie's Frightful Sketches (486)
Favourite Films – B&C
D:S:A: Alick Ritchie
Lightning cartoons. "A hand steals across the screen, grasps a pencil, and quickly writes the words 'Murderer of Babies.' A few deft strokes and the German Emperor is seen in all the majesty of his frightfulness. A brave little British boy faces him. After a few comical skirmishes the Lord High Kaiser is blown to nothingness. Another picture shows the North Sea of German notion. A neutral is sailing, much to the annoyance of a big German warship, who asks 'Vere is the British?' The German then throws a few mines overboard to make more frightfulness possible. A very big fish, scenting a tasty meal, swallows the mines, and the Kaiser too. The German sailor, seeing the swollen proportions of the fish, takes the same for a British submarine and rams it with a disastrous effect to one of the Kaiser's vaunted navy, which is seen all smoke, steam and splinters." (*Kine Monthly Film Record* August 1916.) Released 31 August 1916.

129   The Battle of Jutland
Kine Komedy Kartoons
"Britannia's Budget" No. 1
P: Frank Zeitlin, D:S:A: Ernest H. Mills
First cartoon film of a new production company, drawn and animated by a well-known press cartoonist of the period, and following the Lancelot Speed technique of combining Lightning Cartoons with cut-out animation. Dramatic cartoon depicting the recent Naval battle. Not reviewed; released 7 September 1916.

130   John Bull's Animated Sketchbook No. 18 (600)
Cartoon Film Company
P: J.A. Clozenberg, D:S:A: Anson Dyer
Not reviewed; released September 1916.

131   John Bull's Animated Sketchbook No. 19 (600)
Cartoon Film Company
P: J.A. Clozenberg, D:S:A: Dudley Buxton
Not reviewed; released September 1916.

132   Supremacy (600)
Kine Komedy Kartoons
"Britannia's Budget" No. 2
P: Frank Zeitlin, D:S:A: Ernest H. Mills
Not reviewed; released 29 September 1916.

133   John Bull's Animated Sketchbook No. 20 (570)
Cartoon Film Company – Ashley
P: J.A. Clozenberg, D:S:A: Anson Dyer
Not reviewed; released 19 October 1916.

134   Magic Embroidery (294)
H. & B. Films
Animated needle and cotton. "An ingenious trick picture in which a magic thread is seen to assume embroidery designs of every description." (*Kine Monthly Film Record* October 1916.) Released 4 December 1916.

135   What London Saw (550)
Kine Komedy Kartoons
"Britannia's Budget" No. 3
P: Frank Zeitlin, D:S:A: Ernest H. Mills
Animated drawings and models. "It professes to be a moving picture of the Zeppelin raid that took place on September 3rd when Lieutenant Robinson brought down the airship at Cuffley. We see the searchlights

picking up the raider, the airman's attack upon it, and the final blaze and fall to the ground, terminating with a splendid portrait of the smiling airman after receiving the Victoria Cross. Included in the subjects are many of the clever animated sketches, notably the netting of submarines and scenes in London before and after the first appearance of the Zepps." (*Kine Monthly Film Record* November 1916.)

136   John Bull's Animated Sketchbook No. 21 (600)
   Cartoon Film Company
   P: J.A. Clozenberg, D:S:A: Dudley Buxton
   Not reviewed; released November 1916.

137   John Bull's Animated Sketchbook No. 22 (600)
   Cartoon Film Company
   P: J.A. Clozenberg, D:S:A: Anson Dyer
   Not reviewed; released 18 December 1916.

138   Waterman's Ideal Ink
   Kineto Kino–Ads
   D:A: Walter R. Booth (?)
   Animated advertisement. "Waterman's Ideal Ink is packed in a wooden outer case shaped very much like an explosive shell. In the Kino-Ads film this box appears side by side with a Waterman's Pen. By a process more mysterious to the public than to the cinematographer, the box acquires hands and arms and becomes a moveable imp. The imp stalks across the screen and seizes the pen. It writes a message. Another sheet descends and another message is inscribed. The imp faces the audience, lifts its cap, and moves two little goggle eyes from side to side." (*Bioscope* 14 December 1916.) One of many animated advertisements made by Kineto Films during this period.

1917

139 The Romance of David Lloyd-George (750)
Kine Komedy Kartoons – Broadwest
P: Frank Zeitlin, D:S:A: Ernest H. Mills
Advertised as "founded on sittings specially given to the artist by the Prime Minister." "In an altogether novel and interesting way the artist portrays incidents in the life of the Premier with the utmost fidelity – his younger days in his native Welsh village, his first contact with the House, on which occasion he was lucky enough to hear Gladstone speak; his dramatic escape from Birmingham Town Hall when he was mobbed whilst making a speech during the Boer War; his Insurance Act, the Old Age Pension, and many other incidents." (*Bioscope* 4 January 1917.)

140 The Devil's Little Joke (750)
Kine Komedy Kartoons – Broadwest
P: Frank Zeitlin, D:S:A: Dudley Buxton
"The important feature of this film is that it has reference to what is at present the most discussed topic of the day – Peace. The subject is cleverly and very ably handled by Mr. Dudley Buxton, and shows what the Kaiser would like to do, and also what will really happen." (*Bioscope* 11 January 1917.) Released 19 February 1917.

141 Tank Pranks (575)
Speed Cartoons – Jury
P: William Jury, D:S:A: Lancelot Speed
First of a new series of topical cartoons by Lancelot Speed, produced for exclusive distribution by Jury's Imperial Pictures. "Tommy and Jack are seen hobnobbing together when something strikes their notice, which one believes to be a rhinoceros and the other a motor lorry. Each is right to a certain extent, for the tank is imagined by the artist in an amazing combination of both, with a suggestion of the chameleon and a suspicion of the lobster. The tanks depart on their mission with the good wishes of Britannia, and all surmises as to how they were smuggled into France with so much secrecy are put to an end by the revelation that they found their own way

across the channel in a manner which has hitherto been considered only possible to an intelligent submarine. Having safely landed and found their way to the front, we see further evidence of their adaptability, when they come to the Rhine, which they cross in a manner peculiarly their own. Nothing stops their irresistible progress until they encounter the Supreme War Lord himself, compel him to accept their hospitality, and eventually land him where all surely hope he may soon find himself." (*Bioscope* 8 February 1917.)

142   The Entente Cordiale (710)
Kine Komedy Kartoons—Broadwest
P: Frank Zeitlin, D:S:A: Ernest H. Mills
Not reviewed. Advertised 22 February 1917; released 26 March 1917.

143   By the Sad Sea Waves (600)
Kine Komedy Kartoons—General
P: Frank Zeitlin, D:S:A: Dudley Buxton
Not reviewed. Released April 1917.

144   The U Tube (700)
Speed Cartoons—Jury
P: William Jury, D:S:A: Lancelot Speed
    "We are not sure whether it was Count Zeppelin or Von Tirpitz who gave the Kaiser the idea of boring a tube from Berlin to Birmingham, but we are quite sure that Mr. Speed has done good service in exposing the plot. This is surely the most highly imaginative cartoon we have seen and the drawing and animation, apart from the conception, are wonderfully amusing." (*Bioscope* 10 May 1917.) Print preserved in the Imperial War Museum.

145   Bairnsfather Cartoons (series)
Cartoon Film Company—FBO
P: J.A. Clozenberg, D:A: Jack Dodsworth, DES: Bruce Bairnsfather
    Lightning cartoons. The humorous drawings of Captain Bruce Bairnsfather, the soldier cartoonist whose sketches of life in the trenches were first published in *The Bystander,* recreated for the screen. A series of twelve numbered cartoons released from 31 May 1917 to 13 November 1917. Each 1,000 foot reel contained eight cartoons. "Captain Bruce Bairnsfather draws these reproduced cartoons before our eyes—at least, we suppose he does (you see only his hand)—and the pictures and their legends, which have amused thousands in the pages of our contemporary and in bound volume form, will serve to amuse and cheer millions of picturegoers. Rightly, the first cartoon is the immortal 'If you know of a better 'ole, go to it!'" (*Bioscope* 31 May 1917.) "These productions in cartoons are, we

understand, in greater demand even than Chaplin Comedies. They are certainly most popular, and decidedly so. It would, however, be an advantage to picturegoers if the artist for the screen would draw his life figures bigger and bolder. In a big theatre the faces of Bill, Walrus, and other heroes of the battlefield, are barely seen amidst the wealth of graphic detail." (*Bioscope* 28 June 1917.) Series did not have individual titles, but No. 2, released 15 June, contained: "That Hat"; "Coiffure in the Trenches"; "Another Maxim"; "Trouville-sur-Somme"; "Situation Shortly Vacant"; "The Nest"; "Keeping His Hand In."

146   How to Run a Cinema (835)
Kine Komedy Kartoons
P: Frank Zeitlin, D:S:A: Dudley Buxton
Burlesque on contemporary films. Released 21 June 1917.

147   The Romance of President Wilson (922)
Kine Komedy Kartoons
P: Frank Zeitlin, D:S:A: Ernest H. Mills
Pictorial biography of the American President; released 29 June 1917.

148   Food for Reflection (700)
Kine Komedy Kartoons
P: Frank Zeitlin, D:S:A: Anson Dyer
Not reviewed; released 29 June 1917.

149   The Kaiser's Record (835)
Kine Komedy Kartoons — Jury
P: Frank Zeitlin, D:S:A: Anson Dyer
    "The gramophone records that do not please the Royal Hun are John Bull's song, 'We Don't Want to Fight,' 'The Kiel Row' (the canal), and Von Tirpitz 'Asleep in the Deep.' These and others are cleverly and amusingly drawn for the screen, and with a musical director who can play up to the artist, are sure of a hearty welcome." (*Bioscope* 12 July 1917.) Released 30 July 1917.

150   Raemakers' Cartoons (series)
Cartoon Film Company
P: J.A. Clozenberg, D:A: Jack Dodsworth, DES: Louis Raemakers
    Lightning cartoons. The serious war cartoons of the Dutch artist Louis Raemakers, reprinted in a British magazine, recreated for the screen. A series of twelve numbered cartoons released from 10 July 1917. "The first series includes 'Murder on the High Seas'; 'The Zeppelin Triumph' (a figure of a pretty child asking her widowed father, 'But mother had done nothing wrong, had she, Daddy?'); 'The Crucifixion of Belgium'; and 'The German

Tango' are perhaps the best known of the set. The last named is a wonderful conception: the skeleton figure of Death dancing with a crowned female, 'From East to West and West to East I Dance with Thee.'" (*Bioscope* 19 July 1917.)

151   Russia the Resolute (868)
Kine Komedy Kartoons – Jury
P: Frank Zeitlin, D:S:A: Ernest Mills
"Although this clever cartoon was produced before the recent deplorable debacle in the Russian armies, it is very clever and interesting, if only for the skilful portraits of the ex-Tsar, the Grand Duke Nicholas, General Brusiloff, and the Dictator Kerensky. Especially clever is the picture of the Tsar with Rasputin and the Kaiser whispering devilish advice in his ears." (*Bioscope* 2 August 1917.) Released 10 September 1917.

152   The Plot That Failed (654)
Kine Komedy Kartoons
P: Frank Zeitlin, D:S:A: Dudley Buxton
"The funniest allotment gardeners in furious rivalry, each hampering the other's efforts to produce prize vegetables. Then a bomb dropped from a Zeppelin destroys both plots, and the land is now to let. Real humour and clever animation of the figures of the suburban gardeners." (*Bioscope* 2 August 1917.)

153   The Golfing Cat (340)
Gaumont
P: H.D. Wood, D: George Pearson, S:A: Louis Wain
"A quaint example of the work of the famous artist, Louis Wain, whose cats are known the whole world over." (*Bioscope* 16 August 1917.) Louis Wain drew cartoons featuring comic cats in many children's books and adult magazines. He called his animated cat "Pussyfoot."

154   The Hunter and the Dog
Gaumont
P: H.D. Wood, D: George Pearson, S:A: Louis Wain
The second cat cartoon by the magazine artist Louis Wain. Print preserved in the National Film Archive, but no trace of a review or release date suggests it was probably included as an item in the *Gaumont Magazine* film series.

155   Humours of a Library (425)
Kineto Films
P: Charles Urban, D:S:A: Leonard Summers
"Well-drawn but over-small illustrations of the types that frequent public libraries, such as Agriculture; Philosophy; The Turf; Spiritualism;

Romance (Eastern); Fiction (Sentimental); Plain Fact; Arts and Crafts; Finance; The Porter, Stout and (H)ale; Literature for Dogs." (*Bioscope* 16 August 1917.)

156 Humours of Football (410)
    Kineto Films
    P: Charles Urban, D:S:A: Leonard Summers
    Sequence of gags illustrating football terms: A Half Back; a Full Back; a Scottish High-land; a Slight Touchdown; a Little Highland Gathering; Another Little Gathering; Excitement Running High; a Runaway; a Half Time Draw; After the Fray; Victory; Beloved by All, the Referee; Far From the Madding Crowd. "The photographic quality is excellent." (*Bioscope* 13 September 1917.) Released 18 October 1917.

157 Humours of Advertising (375)
    Kineto Films
    P: Charles Urban, D:S:A: Leonard Summers
    Sequence of gags. "Leonard Summers is the artist who by means of sandwichmen illustrates advertisements. The drawing is rather elementary and the idea of the contrast between the sandwichman himself and the advertisement on his board does not lend itself effectively to the humour of antithesis." (*Bioscope* 18 October 1917.) A Man's Shadow; Where to Get a Good Dinner; The Best Boots in London; Try Our Noted Hats; Keep Dry; The Glad Eye; a Windy Day; a Pair of Spectacles; The Liars; Sleeping Beauty. Released 22 November 1917.

158 Peter's Picture Poems
    Kine Komedy Kartoons – Broadwest
    P: Frank Zeitlin, D:S:A: Anson Dyer
    Artist illustrates verses by the poet Peter, including one in which the Kaiser tries to turn Russia into Prussia, but the United States objects. Print preserved in the National Film Archive. Released November 1917.

159 The History of a German Recruit (1000)
    Birmingham Film Producing Company
    P: C.T. Mitchell, D:S:A: Tom Webster
    Satire on the methods of treating new recruits in the German Army. The first provincially produced cartoon, drawn by a Birmingham newspaper cartoonist who would later become the most famous sports cartoonist in Britain, Tom Webster. Premiered at the New Street Picture House, Birmingham, on 21 November 1917.

160   A Patriotic Message (350)
Kincartoons – War Aims Committee
P:D:S:A: E.P. Kinsella, Horace Morgan
Propaganda film. "The cartoon is designed by Mr. Kinsella, so well known for his clever work in the illustrated weekly magazines, and shows how the working class family is robbed of its daily bread by the under-sea methods by which the enemy is carrying on its warfare. The appeal is a forcible one." (*Bioscope* 6 December 1917.) Sponsored by the Ministry of Food.

161   Admiral Beatty and the Nelson Touch (727)
Kine Komedy Kartoons – Walturdaw
P: Frank Zeitlin, D:S:A: Ernest H. Mills
"Ernest H. Mills, whose topicality and inspired drawings have placed him in the front rank of cartoonists, presents a series of sketches of the Victory and Admiral Lord Nelson, the nation's hero of bygone days, and the modern battle flagship of Admiral Beatty; hearts of oak and gunners of old, men of iron and the fighting sailors of today." (*Bioscope* 6 December 1917.) Released 31 December 1917.

162   Old King Coal (834)
Kine Komedy Kartoons – Broadwest
P: Frank Zeitlin, D:S:A: Anson Dyer
"Anson Dyer gets a lot of fun out of animated cardboard figures. His cat is a conception and insists on laughs, and the old cat (the housewife) certainly makes the cat laugh; and when James, her husband, is smothered in the coal cellar, everybody laughs. This is quite a good comic cartoon with clever punning subtitles." (*Bioscope* 6 December 1917.) Released 14 January 1918.

163   Agitated Adverts (592)
Kine Komedy Kartoons – Walturdaw
P: Frank Zeitlin, D:S:A: Anson Dyer
The cartoonist depicts the people who insert various types of advertisement in a newspaper. Print preserved in the National Film Archive. Released 20 December 1917.

164   Ever Been Had? (640)
Kine Komedy Kartoons – Broadwest
P: Frank Zeitlin, D:S:A: Dudley Buxton
The Man in the Moon descends to Earth to interview the last survivor of a global holocaust: he turns out to be a film extra! Released 31 December 1917.

1918

165 More Agitated Adverts (670)
Kine Komedy Kartoons – Walturdaw
P: Frank Zeitlin, D:S:A: Anson Dyer
Sequel to the successful *Agitated Adverts* (1917). Released 22 February 1918. Not reviewed.

166 The Story of the Camel and the Straw (350)
Kincartoons – War Aims Committee
P:D:S:A: E.P. Kinsella, Horace Morgan
Propaganda film. The parable of the last straw which broke the camel's back, as adapted for a War Savings Committee appeal. Released as a segment of *Pathé's Animated Gazette* newsreel for 25 February 1918.

167 Stand by the Men Who Have Stood by You
Kincartoons – War Aims Committee
P:D:S:A: E.P. Kinsella, Horace Morgan
Propaganda cartoon with live-action sequences. After a reenactment of the execution of Nurse Edith Cavell, John Bull fires British soldiers across the channel to kill Germans. Britannia implores the audience to buy War Bonds. Print preserved in the Imperial War Museum.

168 Charlie at the Front (1000)
Birmingham Film Producing Company
P: C.T. Mitchell, D:S:A: Tom Webster
Tom Webster's second animated cartoon. "I must admit that it is quite the cleverest and most humorous thing Mr. Webster has yet drawn. The Mule, Tank, and Trench incidents, the titbits of the film, are far better seen than described." (*Kinematograph Weekly* 7 March 1918.)

169 Tommy Atkins (800)
Speed Cartoons – Jury
P:D:S:A: Lancelot Speed
"It is the story of the clerk who enlisted and Mr. Levinski (Mr. Smith & Co) wouldn't make him an allowance. He drills, fights in the

trenches, is taken prisoner, escapes, and comes back an officer who kicks Levinski and his Russian partner out of the office, and the police tell them to enlist or deport themselves." (*Bioscope* 14 March 1918.)

170 John Bull Cartoons (series)
Pathé
D:S:A: Leslie Holland
Series of 52 short cartoon items, redrawing the topical cartoons from the weekly magazine *John Bull,* and included in the magazine film series *Pathé's Weekly Pictorial,* released from 4 April 1918 to 1 May 1919. "One of the most interesting items is the sketching of the weekly *John Bull* cartoon." (*Kinematograph Weekly* 2 May 1918.)

171 The Office Boy's Dictionary
Kine Komedy Kartoons
P: Frank Zeitlin, D:S:A: Dudley Buxton
Not reviewed; released April 1918.

172 The British Through German Eyes
Kine Komedy Kartoons
P: Frank Zeitlin, D:S:A: Anson Dyer
Not reviewed; released April 1918.

173 A Plane Tale (186)
Anson Dyer–MOI
D:S:A: Anson Dyer
Propaganda film for the Ministry of Information. A print is preserved in the National Film Archive, but no details of release date can be traced.

174 Old Father William
Speed Cartoons–War Savings Committee
D:S:A: Lancelot Speed
Propaganda cartoon based on Lewis Carroll's poem. A young man asks Old Father William why he is so happy, and he replies that in his youth he bought War Savings Certificates. Print preserved in the Imperial War Museum.

175 Twice Nightly
Kine Komedy Kartoons–Walturdaw
P: Frank Zeitlin, D:S:A: Victor Hicks
Cartoon burlesque of a typical Music Hall program. Not reviewed; released June 1918.

176   Britain's Effort (1000)
Speed Cartoons—Jury
P:D:S:A: Lancelot Speed
"In this we see by striking comparisons the proportions of Britain's vast contributions to the war. For instance, to illustrate the output of munitions, Mr. Speed first shows the pyramids, 480 feet in height; by the side of these a small mound of munitions grows, increasing rapidly until it completely overshadows the huge Egyptian monuments." (*Kinematograph Weekly* 27 June 1918.) Print preserved in the Imperial War Museum.

177   The Raid on Zeebrugge (670)
Kine Komedy Kartoons—FBO
P: Frank Zeitlin, D:S:A: Dudley Buxton
Dramatic documentary cartoon of the British Naval attack on the Belgian port on 3 April 1918. "Particularly effective is the view of the Mole, later to be the scene of the last grand stand of those splendid old cruisers Vindictive, Iphigenia, Intrepid and their other comrades. The rush of the storming parties over the gangways while the night was alive with shells and death seemed the only certainty, is one unforgettable incident, while the submarining of the Mole is another episode which will be followed with the keenest interest." (*Pictures and Picturegoer* 20 July 1918.) Released 22 July 1918.

178   Charlie Joins the Navy (1000)
Birmingham Film Producing Company
P: C.T. Mitchell, D:S:A: Tom Webster
"Series number two of the famous Tom Webster Charlie Chaplin Cartoons were also shown, depicting the one and only Charlie Chaplin in a variety of roles." (*Kinematograph Weekly* 11 July 1918.)

179   Allotments (500)
Kineto
"Adventures of Slim and Pim" No. 1
P: Charles Urban, D:S:A: Leslie Dawson
"Amazing new series of the most fantastic mirth-provokers imaginable. Every one an example of perfect mechanical production, timed to a second and go like a clock. They'll keep your audiences roaring and your box office receipts up." (Kineto Films advertisement 25 July 1918.) "Slim and Pim are growers of produce. Slim is very successful, but Pim cannot get his vegetables to grow. He discovers a wonderful fertilizer and upon applying it has the most remarkable results from which many amusing incidents arise, and various complications from a dream nearly produce a tragedy." (*Bioscope* 15 August 1918.) Released 12 September 1918.

180   Blood and Iron (650)
Kine Komedy Kartoons
P: Frank Zeitlin, D:S:A: Dudley Buxton
War cartoon; not reviewed. Released 28 August 1918.

181   Pim Falls in Love (500)
Kineto
"Adventures of Slim and Pim" No. 2
P: Charles Urban, D:S:A: Leslie Dawson
"Showing their rivalry for the fair lady and their frantic efforts to cut one another out in her affections. Going to the desperate lengths of rigging out a monkey in a suit exactly like Pim's, it is not to be wondered at that the girl collapses at the sight of the animal all dressed up and nowhere to go, as Slim gets the fair one into a cab with a veritable nightmare of a horse who lets both friends down." (*Bioscope* 29 August 1918.) Released 28 September 1918.

182   A Child's Dream of Peace (700)
Kine Komedy Kartoons – Walturdaw
P: Frank Zeitlin, D:S:A: Anson Dyer
"This is a very attractive Christmas playlet in which figures a Santa Claus present given to a child in bed. The little one dreams a dream of Nazareth, the new-born child, the pilgrimage of the wise men past the pyramids of Egypt, the Star of Bethlehem. It is dignified in treatment and artistic in conception, really not a cartoon in the strict sense of the word." (*Kinematograph Weekly* 10 October 1918.) Animation with live action sequences.

183   A Nautical Adventure (525)
Kineto
"Adventures of Slim and Pim" No. 3
P: Charles Urban, D:S:A: Leslie Dawson
"Slim and Pim exchange a goat for a submarine in which they have some great adventures. The submarine careens madly along and dashes halfway through a whale, whirls, and thus fixed, Slim and Pim go through the window and find themselves in the interior of the whale. They reach its mouth, which they mistake for a shelter. They marry two mermaids, but finding that their better halves are half human and half fish, they order them into the sea." (*Kine Monthly Film Record* October 1918.) Released 17 October 1918.

184   Foch the Man (850)
Kine Komedy Kartoons – Ashley
P: Frank Zeitlin, D:S:A: Anson Dyer
"Starting with a pen picture of the soldier's birthplace, set amid the

snow-capped mountains of the Pyrenees, the illustration goes on to give incidents which have helped to make the name of Foch a household word. His habits and sayings are typified briefly and his methods shown." (*Kinematograph Weekly* 24 October 1918.) Animated biography of the French Field-Marshal.

185   Called Up (550)
Kineto
"Adventures of Slim and Pim" No. 4
P: Charles Urban, D:S:A: Leslie Dawson
"Not being considered quite the right shape for the trenches, they are made into camp cooks. They make sausages out of anything they can find. The steam attracts Old Bill, who advises our friends to take them to the boys, but they lose their way. Yet the delicious smell travels on to where the Kaiser and Willie are vowing to enter Paris forthwith. They need no encouragement when they smell the steam of their national food coming through the window. The Kaiser and Willie immediately fall to and start to devour the tasty repast, when they are 'laid out,' one being stuffed into a large saucepan, and the other in the oven. Our heroes then draw the stove back to camp and make known their capture. They are each passed a VC which the King presents to them." (*Kinematograph Weekly* 10 October 1918.) Released 10 November 1918.

186   In the King's Navee (550)
Kineto
"Adventures of Slim and Pim" No. 5
P: Charles Urban, D:S:A: Leslie Dawson
"They join the Navy, but although they muddle through, they get a certain amount of work done. It is nothing to them to stop flying shells and hurl them back at the enemy, or direct the shells' course. At one time our friends are in a perfect hail of shells, and use umbrellas to protect themselves, for they insist on finishing a game of tiddley-winks in spite of parts of the ship being blown to pieces all round them. A final explosion on board blows them sky high, but they fall into a seaplane. Starting it off they think that their troubles are over, but in its course it cannons an enemy observation gasbag. This is sent spinning, Slim and Pim finding themselves clinging to it. The seaplane falls into the sea, likewise the two Germans who were in the balloon. Slim and Pim sail through space. A star comes up and the gasbag bursts. Our heroes fall down! down!! down!!! through the roof of a house, where they find themselves in chairs at a table with the tea all ready." (*Kinematograph Weekly* 28 November 1918.) Released 28 November 1918.

1919

187 A Genii and a Genius (650)
Kine Komedy Kartoons – Phillips
P: Frank Zeitlin, D:S:A: Victor Hicks

"Charlie Chaplin is picturised visiting the realms of fantasy, and his journey through Mars and the Milky Way are worth going a long way to see." (Phillips Films advertisement: March 1919.) "Take the case of Spick and Span with the Moon en route to Mars from Piccadilly. It took three days' work to complete the drawings for one section of this episode, and this after I had got my ideas cut and dried on paper; and after this an equally long period was spent in photographing the result." (Victor Hicks: *Picture Plays* 20 December 1919.)

188 Well I'll Be Blowed! (500)
Kine Komedy Kartoons – Phillips: "Cheerio Chums" No. 1
P: Frank Zeitlin, D:S:A: Dudley Buxton

"Series of three cartoons depicting the adventures of ex-service men and their adventures in commerce." (Phillips Films advertisement: 20 March 1919.) "Jerry receives the balance of his mother's pension, a trifle of £1000, and together with Nobbler goes into business as a kinema proprietor. Their big opening feature is *East Lynne*. The audience, however, will not be drawn, and to one man the great programme is shown, a programme in which everything goes wrong, and the greater portion of the feature gets dropped in the mud, fourteen reels of it." (*Kinematograph Weekly* 13 March 1919.) Released 8 May 1919.

189 Uncle Remus No. 1 (500)
Kine Komedy Kartoons – Phillips
P: Frank Zeitlin, D:A: Anson Dyer, S: Joel Chandler Harris

"Three cartoons telling in motion the whimsical stories of Brer Fox and Brer Rabbit, as told by Uncle Remus." (Phillips Films advertisement: 20 March 1919.) Released 15 May 1919.

190   **Zig-Zags at the Zoo No. 1** (500)
      Kine Komedy Kartoons – Phillips
      P: Frank Zeitlin, D:A: Ernest H. Mills, S:DES: J.A. Shepherd
      First in a series of three cartoons adapted from the drawings by J.A.
Shepherd appearing monthly in *The Strand Magazine*. Released 22 May
1919.

191   **Poy Cartoon No. 1** (500)
      Kine Komedy Kartoons – Phillips
      P: Frank Zeitlin, S:DES: Percy Fearon
      "Three cartoons reproducing his actual work in *The Evening News*,
by the famous caricaturist, Poy." (Phillips Films advertisement: 20 March
1919.) Released 29 May 1919. Poy was the pen-name of the newspaper cartoonist Percy Fearon.

192   **Britain's Honour** (1000)
      Speed Cartoons – Jury
      P:D:S:A: Lancelot Speed
      "In addition to the heroes who have fought, worked and died in the
cause of humanity, we are shown the victims of child labour, bad housing,
disease, and other evils, the dragon that preys on humanity and that can
only be vanquished by justice, truth, and right, aided by science rightly applied." (*Bioscope* 29 May 1919.)

193   **Hot Stuff** (500)
      Kine Komedy Kartoons – Phillips: "Cheerio Chums" No. 2
      P: Frank Zeitlin, D:S:A: Dudley Buxton
      Not reviewed. Released 5 June 1919.

194   **Zig-Zags at the Zoo No. 2** (500)
      Kine Komedy Kartoons – Phillips
      P: Frank Zeitlin, D:A: Ernest H. Mills, S:DES: J.A. Shepherd
      Not reviewed. Released 12 June 1919.

195   **Uncle Remus No. 2** (500)
      Kine Komedy Kartoons – Phillips
      P: Frank Zeitlin, D:A: Anson Dyer, S: Joel Chandler Harris
      Not reviewed. Released 19 June 1919.

196   **Poy Cartoon No. 2** (500)
      Kine Komedy Kartoons – Phillips
      P: Frank Zeitlin, S:DES: Percy Fearon
      Not reviewed. Released 26 June 1919.

197   Cheerio Chums No. 3 (500)
Kine Komedy Kartoons – Phillips
P: Frank Zeitlin, D:S:A: Dudley Buxton
Title unknown. Not reviewed. Released 3 July 1919.

198   The Tiger, Clemenceau
Kine Komedy Kartoons – Ashley
P: Frank Zeitlin, D:S:A: Ernest H. Mills
Biographical cartoon. "One of the greatest personalities of modern times. The life of a statesman who has helped to make the new map of Europe." (Ashley Films advertisement: *Bioscope* 3 July 1919.)

199   Zig-Zags at the Zoo No. 3 (500)
Kine Komedy Kartoons – Phillips
P: Frank Zeitlin, D:A: Ernest H. Mills, S:DES: J.A. Shepherd
Not reviewed. Released 10 July 1919.

200   Uncle Remus No. 3 (500)
Kine Komedy Kartoons – Phillips
P: Frank Zeitlin, D:A: Anson Dyer, S: Joel Chandler Harris
Not reviewed. Released 17 July 1919.

201   Poy Cartoon No. 3 (500)
Kine Komedy Kartoons – Phillips
P: Frank Zeitlin, S:DES: Percy Fearon
Not reviewed. Released 24 July 1919.

202   The Merchant of Venice (800)
Hepworth Picture Plays
P: Cecil M. Hepworth, D:S:A: Anson Dyer, S: William Shakespeare
Burlesque of the Shakespeare play. "The artist takes some of the bard's characters and twists them to meet his own wicked purposes. Antonio is an ice cream merchant; Bassanio a navvy; Portia a housemaid ('featuring Miss C. de Mopp'); and Shylock a Hebraic gentleman ('featuring Mr. Warder Street'). Bassanio loves Portia but hurts one hand; harder still for the ice cream merchant in a snow storm. So they go to the Pathé corner of Wardour Street and there Antonio borrows from Shylock, pledging himself to the loss of a pound of flesh should he fail to pay the money. Of course he can't, in due course he finds himself in the County Court, but Portia comes to the rescue and Shylock, having been discovered to have used all his meat tickets, is non-suited. So the tragedy ends happily." (*Kine Monthly Film Record* September 1919.)

203   Romeo and Juliet (850)
Hepworth Picture Plays
P: Cecil M. Hepworth, D:S:A: Anson Dyer, S: William Shakespeare
Burlesque of the Shakespeare play. "A novel and intriguing feature
of the cartoon is the introduction of Charlie Chaplin and Miss Mary
Pickford as Romeo and Juliet. With quite extraordinary skill Mr. Dyer has
caught the mannerisms of these two film favourites, reproducing in an
amazingly lifelike way the famous Chaplin walk and the Pickford smile. An
amusing typical touch is the introduction of Mr. Pussyfoot as a means of
bringing the story to a happy ending." (*Bioscope* 23 October 1919.)

204   'Amlet (600)
Hepworth Picture Plays
P: Cecil M. Hepworth, D:S:A: Anson Dyer, S: William Shakespeare
Burlesque of the Shakespeare play. "A vision of Charlie Chaplin as
the moody Dane, supported by Mr. (Horatio) Bottomley as Horatio. Mr.
Dyer shows Hamlet reconstructing his wicked uncle's crime (which consists in this case of profiteering in butter) by means of the cinematograph.
Invited to the Elsinore Picture Palace by his stepson, the guilty King is confronted with a daring film record of his deed, while Hamlet, disguised as
a theatre attendant, studies his blanched features with the aid of an electric
torch." (*Bioscope* 11 December 1919.)

205   Ophelia (850)
Hepworth Picture Plays
P: Cecil M. Hepworth, D:S:A: Anson Dyer, S: William Shakespeare
Burlesque. "Mr. Dyer exhibits a remarkable mastery of the intricate
technique of the cinema cartoon, besides possessing an infinite fund of
humour and imagination." (*Bioscope* 1919.)

1920

206 In the Spring a Young Man's Fancy (500)
Kine Komedy Kartoons – General: "Bucky's Burlesques" No. 1
P: Frank Zeitlin, D:S:A: Dudley Buxton
"A young man is infatuated with the song 'Come and Squeeze Me.'
His efforts on the piano, in which he finds a feline specimen with its young,
is ludicrous. His discovery of a pair of lovers, his hasty flight, in the erratic
manner of cartoon comedy, is all delightfully funny." (*The Cinema* 24 June
1920.)

207 Clutching Eyebrows (500)
Kine Komedy Kartoons – General: "Bucky's Burlesques" No. 2
P: Frank Zeitlin, D:S:A: Dudley Buxton
"Adventures of an over-zealous detective who holds up everything
with his revolver, even the railway signals." (*Kinematograph Weekly* 22 July
1920.)

208 Othello (850)
Hepworth Picture Plays
P: Cecil M. Hepworth, D:S:A: Anson Dyer, S: William Shakespeare
Burlesque of the Shakespeare play. "The Moor of Venice becomes a
seaside Nigger Minstrel whilst Desdemona (known as Mona for short) is the
lovely daughter of the local bathing machine proprietor. After many
humorous adventures in which the main parts of the famous tragedy are
ingeniously if irreverently introduced, Othello smothers Desdemona with
burnt cork and kisses." (*Bioscope* 29 July 1920.)

209 The Daring Deeds of Duckless Darebanks (500)
Kine Komedy Kartoons – International
P: Frank Zeitlin, D:S:A: J.L. Anderson
The American animator J.L. Anderson was brought over to England
to introduce the American technique of cel animation to British cartoon
makers. "The plot can be told in three words – Doug rescues the girl, but
the real fun which is to be found in the drawings could not be indicated

in many. The film is quite good as a caricature of the ever-smiling Fairbanks, but it depicts more stunts than he would dare, now that he has Mary (Pickford) to consider." (*The Cinema* 12 August 1920.)

210   Running a Cinema (456)
Kine Komedy Kartoons – Anchor: "Memoirs of Miffy" No. 1
P: Frank Zeitlin, D:S:A: Dudley Buxton
The first in a short-lived series, "The Memoirs of Miffy," in which Dudley Buxton used the American cel method of animation, as introduced to the Kine Komedy Kartoons company by J.A. Anderson. Although the series did not last long in the cinema, Buxton continued the character in a syndicated comic strip which appeared in several provincial newspapers for some years. A print of the film is preserved in the National Film Archive.

211   The Taming of the Shrew
Hepworth Picture Plays
P: Cecil M. Hepworth, D:S:A: Anson Dyer, S: William Shakespeare
Burlesque of the Shakespeare play. This film was announced in *The Cinema* dated 3 June 1920, but no review or release date has been traced. Possibly not completed.

212   A Fishy Business (500)
Kine Komedy Kartoons – Anchor: "Memoirs of Miffy" No. 2
P: Frank Zeitlin, D:S:A: Dudley Buxton
"Miffy on this occasion is concerned to avenge an insult to his wife by a burly fishmonger, who received him so vigorously that he has recourse to a physical culture expert for instruction in methods of offence. A blow from the professor sends him into the land of dreams, and he has amazing conflicts with the wild animal inhabitants of a desert isle before plunging into the sea, to awake to find that his instructor is reviving him with a pail of water." (*Kinematograph Weekly* 25 November 1920.)

213   The Smoke from Gran-Pa's Pipe (500)
Kine Komedy Kartoons – General
P: Frank Zeitlin, D:S:A: J.L. Anderson
Grandfather recalls his boyhood adventures: fishing, boxing, and a visit to a circus. Print preserved in the National Film Archive.

1921

214 The Wonderful Adventures of Pip, Squeak and Wilfred (series)
Astra Films
D:A: Lancelot Speed, S: Bertram Lamb, DES: Austin Payne
Series of 26 one-reel (1,000 foot) episodes featuring the comic strip characters created by A.B. Payne (artist) and B.J. Lamb (writer) in *The Daily Mirror*. Weekly release from 17 February 1921 to 11 August 1921. "There seems to be about as much footage devoted to subtitles as to pictures in the first episode. From the artistic and technical point of view, it would be an advantage to cut all of them out. The pictures themselves are undoubtedly well done, and the solidity of the drawing and the care in detail provide a change from the old kind of cartoon. While there is no definite plot, the action is sufficiently consecutive and generally brisk." (*Kinematograph Weekly* 20 January 1921.) Episode 6, *Over the Edge of the World,* is preserved in the National Film Archive.

215 Bobby the Scout No. 1 (600)
Hepworth Picture Plays
P: Cecil M. Hepworth, D:S:A: Anson Dyer
"The scout is so anxious to put in his one good deed a day that, after he has advised a donkey not to eat thistles in case he pricks his mouth, and acted as a human cushion for a bony lady on a rustic seat, he proceeds to heaven in search of further subjects, and finally reconciles Jupiter and Juno, who are an ill-matched couple in Cloudland. The dog is responsible for many laughs, particularly when he retrieves a thunderbolt which Jupiter hurls to Earth as part of his daily duties." (*Kinematograph Weekly* 16 June 1921.)

216 Bobby the Scout No. 2 (700)
Hepworth Picture Plays
P: Cecil M. Hepworth, D:S:A: Anson Dyer
"In a cavern of Olympus, Bobby meets a centaur whom he dissuades from sampling the whiskey dropped by a balloonist. Meanwhile, his faithful hound is swallowed by a horrible serpent, which Bobby promptly

cuts in two. Mr. Dyer displays even more than his usual fertility of imagination in devising humorous incidents, and many of his effects are as ingenious as they are funny." (*Bioscope* 13 October 1921.)

217   Bobby the Scout No. 3 (600)
Hepworth Picture Plays
P: Cecil M. Hepworth, D:S:A: Anson Dyer
"Bobby plays upon his harp, whereupon trees and rocks go into transports of delight, and even a lion, who would dearly like to eat Bobby, is reduced to tears. Bobby's dog plays his part as usual, and helps to contribute to the fun." (*Kinematograph Weekly* 10 November 1921.)

218   Crock and Dizzy (series)
B & J Productions – M.P. Sales
P: Broda and Jenkins, D:S: Tom Titt, A: W.D. Ford, Joe Noble
Series of 12 half-reel (500 foot) cartoons featuring the characters Crock and Dizzy. No trace of titles, reviews, or release dates (1921–1922).

1922

219   The Noah Family (series)
Gaumont
S: J.F. Horrabin
Animated models (?). Adapted from the daily cartoon strip for children in *The Daily News,* featuring wooden toys who live in Mr. Noah's Ark. Included as an item in the cinemagazine series *Around the Town:* "Japheth's Fishing Adventure" Part 1 in No. 114; Part 2 in No. 115. Preserved in the National Film Archive.

220   Little Red Riding Hood (850)
Hepworth Picture Plays: "Kiddiegraph" No. 1
P: Cecil M. Hepworth, D:S:A: Anson Dyer
Marion Dyer: The Child
Live action with animation, featuring the cartoonist's daughter, Marion Dyer, as the little girl to whom the story is told. "Tells the well-known tale in a manner that will appeal to old and young." (*Kinematograph Weekly* 7 December 1922.) Print preserved in the National Film Archive.

221   The Three Little Pigs (850)
Hepworth Picture Plays: "Kiddiegraph" No. 2
P: Cecil M. Hepworth, D:S:A: Anson Dyer
Anson Dyer: The Artist, Marion Dyer: The Child
Live action with animation. The cartoonist, Anson Dyer, tells the story to his own daughter, Marion. "An artist is shown telling his children of the three pigs' adventures by means of drawings." (*Kinematograph Weekly* 7 December 1922.) Print preserved in the National Film Archive.

222   Tishy (1000)
Webster Cartoons – Napoleon Films
P:D:S: Tom Webster, A: W.D. Ford, Joe Noble, C: Tom Aitken
By 1920 Tom Webster had become the leading sports cartoonist of the *Daily Mail.* His interest in animation continued, and he financed and produced several successful cartoon films. "The subject of the film is the

now famous racehorse, Tishy, who is shown plaiting her legs in readiness for the start, and then advising the jockey to get off and take a taxi. Although the rest of the field has long since passed the winning post, Tishy continues her shambling way, while the crowd waits patiently for her arrival. Night falls, and the moon climbs high into the sky, before she completes the course and drops, a shapeless mass of twisted limbs, at the post. Thanks to Mr. Webster's brilliant draughtsmanship and inimitable captions, the film is even finer than the original cartoons." (*Bioscope* 1 February 1923.) The film was given a royal premiere at the London Hippodrome on Tuesday 12 December 1922.

1923

223 Adlets Advertising Budget (series)
Adlets
Advertising shorts including a number of animated cartoon items in each. Details unknown save for one issue preserved in the National Film Archive which includes: "Clark's Creamed Barley"; "Eno's Fruit Salt"; "Gibbs' Dentifrice"; "Hennessey's Brandy"; "The LMS Railway"; "Sandeman's Port."

224 Jimmy Wilde
Webster Cartoons – Napoleon Films
P:D:S: Tom Webster, A: W.D. Ford, Joe Noble, C: Tom Aitken
Cartoon featuring the famous boxer. No trace of reviews or release date.

225 Inman in Billiards
Webster Cartoons – Napoleon
P:D:S: Tom Webster, A: W.D. Ford, Joe Noble, C: Tom Aitken
Cartoon featuring the famous billiard player. No trace of reviews or release date.

1924

226 Pongo Arrives (250)
Pathé: "Pongo the Pup" No. 1
D:S: Dudley Buxton, A: Dudley Buxton, Joe Noble
First of a series of seven short cartoons included in the weekly magazine film, *Pathé Pictorial*, from October 1924. The series was initiated to replace the popular American cartoons of Felix the Cat. "This new All British cartoon series will soon rival the popularity of the famous Felix the Cat, and in all probability the slogan, 'Pongo keeps on running' will become as much a household word as the pedestrianism of Felix. The first cartoon shows the arrival of Pongo by aeroplane, his reception by the crowd, his arrival at the Pathé studio, and his joy at finding himself a film star." (*Kinematograph Weekly* 9 October 1924.)

227 Pongo Gets a Meal (250)
Pathé: "Pongo the Pup" No. 2
D:S: Dudley Buxton, A: Dudley Buxton, Joe Noble
"Pongo the Pup has his second adventure but, clever though the cartoons are, they will undoubtedly suffer through their close likeness to the immortal Felix." (*Kinematograph Weekly* 16 October 1924.)

228 Bonzo (687)
New Era: "Bonzo" No. 1
P: Gordon Craig, D: William Ward, S:DES: George E. Studdy, A: William Ward, Percy Vigas, H. McCready, M. Matheson, M. York, P.G. Tobin, S.G. Castell, Marjorie Drawbell, Charles de Mornay, Kevin Moran, Brian White
First in a series of 26 cartoons featuring "Bonzo," the cartoon puppy created by George Ernest Studdy in *The Sketch*, a popular magazine. Premiered at the Marble Arch Pavilion, London, on Tuesday 14 October 1924. "A cartoon subject which will rival Felix the Cat and provide excellent items for all programmes. Bonzo is by no means a slavish copy of his predecessors. He is, in fact, a very doggy dog, whom it is a delight to watch. The producer, W.A. Ward, has collaborated admirably with the artist, and

we look forward to seeing more of their work. The first example is most amusing and shows Bonzo's acrobatic efforts to capture some sausages out of his reach on a shelf, incidentally allowing for a scrap with a kitten. The conception is extremely simple, but also it is typically doggy, and there is no need for explanations to point the working of a dog's mind." (*Kinematograph Weekly* 23 October 1924.) Print preserved in the National Film Archive. Released 26 January 1925.

229   Pongo's Day Out (250)
Pathé: "Pongo the Pup" No. 3
D:S: Dudley Buxton, A: Dudley Buxton, Joe Noble
Item in *Pathé Pictorial.*

230   Pongo Cleans Up the Goat Family (250)
Pathé: "Pongo the Pup" No. 4
D:S: Dudley Buxton, A: Dudley Buxton, Joe Noble
Item in *Pathé Pictorial* No. 345. Released 10 November 1924.

231   Pongo Catches the Crossword (250)
Pathé: "Pongo the Pup" No. 5
D:S: Dudley Buxton, A: Dudley Buxton, Joe Noble
Item in *Pathé Pictorial* No. 360. Released 23 February 1925.

232   Pongo's Super Gazette (250)
Pathé: "Pongo the Pup" No. 6
D:S: Dudley Buxton, A: Dudley Buxton, Joe Noble
Item in *Pathé Pictorial.*

233   Pongo's Rodeo (250)
Pathé: "Pongo the Pup" No. 7
D:S: Dudley Buxton, A: Dudley Buxton, Joe Noble
Item in *Pathé Pictorial.*

1925

234 Bonzo No. 2 (500)
New Era
(credits as for **Bonzo** [entry 228])
Second in series; title unknown. "Bonzo is depicted making a pie of weird ingredients which include whisky, a dead mouse, a cheese, and other comestibles. Having made it, he puts it in the oven and is eventually blown through the wall when the pie explodes." (*Kinematograph Weekly* 5 February 1925.) Released 23 February 1925.

235 Bonzo No. 3 (500)
New Era
(credits as for **Bonzo** [entry 228])
Third in series; title unknown. "Studdy has made Bonzo steal a goose, get chased by a policeman, put in the dock, and finally escape with his spoil, which looks like compounding a felony! Topicality is introduced when Bonzo climbs a pipe-stack in brilliant cat burglar style." (*Kinematograph Weekly* 12 March 1925.) Released 9 March 1925.

236 Bonzo No. 4 (500)
New Era
(credits as for **Bonzo** [entry 228])
Fourth in series; title unknown; not reviewed. Released 23 March 1925.

237 Bonzo No. 5 (521)
New Era
(credits as for **Bonzo** [entry 228])
Fifth in series; title unknown. Bonzo dreams he is chased by cats and turned into sausages. Released 6 April 1925.

238 Chee-kee the Vamp (500)
New Era: "Bonzo" No. 6
(credits as for **Bonzo** [entry 228])
Sixth in series. Bonzo has trouble with Chee-kee, his Pekinese sweetheart. Print preserved in the National Film Archive. Released 20 April 1925.

239   Bonzo No. 7 (459)
New Era
(credits as for **Bonzo** [entry 228])
Seventh in series; title unknown; not reviewed. Released 4 May 1925.

240   Playing the Dickens in an Old Curiosity Shop (459)
New Era: "Bonzo" No. 8
(credits as for **Bonzo** [entry 228])
Eighth in series. Bonzo, working in an antique shop, has trouble with
the clocks. Print preserved in the National Film Archive. Released 18 May
1925.

241   Bonzo No. 9 (500)
New Era
(credits as for **Bonzo** [entry 228])
Ninth in series; title unknown; not reviewed. Released 1 June 1925.

242   Bonzolino or Bonzo Broadcasted (465)
New Era: "Bonzo" No. 10
(credits as for **Bonzo** [entry 228])
Tenth in series. When Bonzo is rejected by his Pekinese sweetheart,
he transmits himself to Hollywood by radio waves and becomes the film
star "Bon Chaney." Released 15 June 1925.

243   Bonzo No. 11 (500)
New Era
(credits as for **Bonzo** [entry 228])
Eleventh in series; title unknown; not reviewed. Released 29 June
1925.

244   Bonzo No. 12 (500)
New Era
(credits as for **Bonzo** [entry 228])
Twelfth in series; title unknown; not reviewed. Released 13 July 1925.

245   Jerry the Troublesome Tyke
U.I.C. Productions – Pathé
P:D:S:A: Sid Griffiths, C: A.A. Bilby
First in a series of short cartoon items included in the magazine film
series *Pathé Pictorial*. Not all titles and episodes can be traced. "A new
series of cartoons of British origin describing the adventures of Jerry, a
puppy. Jerry's character appears to be influenced partly by the antics of
Felix the Cat, and partly by his fellow, Bonzo, but he will no doubt acquire
a personality of his own." (*Bioscope* 23 July 1925.) "The items shown

introduce him and then deposit him in some adventures under the sea, which are very cleverly done. Unlike Felix, the series superimposes at times the cartoons on actual locations in a very effective manner." (*Kinematograph Weekly* 23 July 1925.) Included in *Pathé Pictorial* No. 382; released 27 July 1925.

246   Detective Bonzo and the Black Hand Gang (506)
New Era: "Bonzo" No. 13
(credits as for **Bonzo** [entry 228])
S: Adrian Brunel
Thirteenth in series. Bonzo foils the Black Hand Gang in their plot to kidnap a jockey. Print preserved in the National Film Archive. Released 27 July 1925.

247   Bonzo No. 14 (500)
New Era
(credits as for **Bonzo** [entry 228])
Fourteenth in series; not reviewed; title unknown. Released 10 August 1925.

248   Honesty Is the Best Policy
U.I.C. – Pathé: "Jerry" series No. 2
P:D:S:A: Sid Griffiths, C: A.A. Bilby
Second in series; not reviewed. Included in *Pathé Pictorial* No. 385; released 17 August 1925.

249   Polar Bonzo (500)
New Era: "Bonzo" No. 15
(credits as for **Bonzo** [entry 228])
Fifteenth in series. Bonzo's adventures at the North Pole. Print preserved in the National Film Archive. Released 24 August 1925.

250   Bonzo No. 16
New Era
(credits as for **Bonzo** [entry 228])
Sixteenth in series; not reviewed; title unknown. Released 7 September 1925.

251   Treasure Island Travel
U.I.C. – Pathé: "Jerry" No. 3
P:D:S:A: Sid Griffiths, C: A.A. Bilby
Third in series; not reviewed. Included in *Pathé Pictorial* No. 390; released 21 September 1925.

252 Jerry Tracks Treasure
U.I.C. – Pathé: "Jerry" No. 4
P:D:S:A: Sid Griffiths, C: A.A. Bilby
Fourth in series; not reviewed. Included in *Pathé Pictorial* No. 392; released 5 October 1925.

253 The Topical Bonzette (463)
New Era: "Bonzo" No. 17
(credits as for **Bonzo** [entry 228])
S: Adrian Brunel
Seventeenth in series. Burlesque on the *Topical Gazette* type of newsreel: a new horse trough in Piccadilly Circus; Jack Bonzobbs the cricketer; Professor Bonzo the fancy diver; Joe Bonzo the boxer in training. Print preserved in the National Film Archive. Released 21 September 1925.

254 Sandy MacBonzo or Bonzo Goes to Scotland (500)
New Era: "Bonzo" No. 18
(credits as for **Bonzo** [entry 228])
Eighteenth in series. Bonzo visits Scotland. Print preserved in National Film Archive. Released 5 October 1925.

255 Booster Bonzo or Bonzo in Gay Paree (500)
New Era: "Bonzo" No. 19 (?)
(credits as for **Bonzo** [entry 228])
Bonzo visits Paris. Print preserved in National Film Archive. Released 19 October 1925.

256 There's Many a Slip
U.I.C. – Pathé: "Jerry" No. 5
P:D:S:A: Sid Griffiths, C: A.A. Bilby
"The cartoons suggest that the artist is becoming much more at home with his medium. We would suggest, however, that the imposition of drawings on camera shots should be abandoned. The one example in this issue is not very effective." (*Kinematograph Weekly* 22 October 1925.) Included in *Pathé Pictorial* No. 394; released 19 October 1925.

257 Bonzo the Traveller (500)
New Era: "Bonzo" No. 20 (?)
(credits as for **Bonzo** [entry 228])
Released 2 November 1925; reissued on 9.5 mm, 1935. "Here is Bonzo's first picture (on 9.5 mm) which depicts him in Gay Paris, and later, having tired himself out swimming the channel, in a cinema and dreaming that he finds the actual North Pole. Then he wakes up!" (*Pathéscope Monthly* April 1935.)

258 Jerry's Test Trial
U.I.C. – Pathé: "Jerry" No. 6
P:D:S:A: Sid Griffiths, C: A.A. Bilby
Not reviewed. Included in *Pathé Pictorial* No. 396; released 2 November 1925.

259 Tally Ho Bonzo (500)
New Era: "Bonzo" No. 21 (?)
(credits as for **Bonzo** [entry 228])
Released 16 November 1925; reissued on 9.5 mm, 1935. "Bonzo covets some aniseed balls, steals a bagful, and gets his deserts in the form of one of the sweets in a tin can securely tied to his tail. Pack of hounds! Bonzo does not see why he should let them capture Master Reynard (the fox). With the aid of the aniseed ball he lays a false scent and succeeds in hoodwinking all but one of the pursuing pack." (*Pathéscope Monthly* June 1935.)

260 The Expedition
U.I.C. – Pathé: "Jerry" No. 7
P:D:S:A: Sid Griffiths, C: A.A. Bilby
"These cartoons are still remarkable for the skill with which they are drawn, but suffer somewhat from a paucity of ideas." (*Kinematograph Weekly* 19 November 1925.) Included in *Pathé Pictorial* No. 398; released 16 November 1925.

261 Bonzoby (500)
New Era: "Bonzo" No. 22 (?)
(credits as for **Bonzo** [entry 228])
Bonzo replaces Dog Toby in a street Punch and Judy show. Released 30 November 1925.

262 Joy Provided
U.I.C. – Pathé: "Jerry" No. 8
P:D:S:A: Sid Griffiths, C: A.A. Bilby
"The new instalments of Jerry the cartoon dog have a pleasant atmosphere of Christmas, and display more ideas than have been noticed in previous episodes. The drawing of these cartoons is now admirable; improvement is desirable only in the scripts." (*Kinematograph Weekly* 17 December 1925.) Included in *Pathé Pictorial* No. 401; released 7 December 1925.

263 Bonzo No. 23 (500)
New Era
(credits as for **Bonzo** [entry 228])
23rd in series; not reviewed; title unknown. Released 14 December 1925.

264 **Never Say Die**
U.I.C. – Pathé: "Jerry" No. 9
P:D:S:A: Sid Griffiths, C: A.A. Bilby
Included in *Pathé Pictorial* No. 403; released 21 December 1925.

265 **Bonzo No. 24** (500)
New Era
(credits as for **Bonzo** [entry 228])
24th in series; not reviewed; title unknown. Released 28 December 1925.

266 **The Bedtime Stories of Archie the Ant (series)**
Smith
P:D:S:A: Frank Percy Smith
1: Bertie's Cave (635)
2: The Pit and the Plum (423)
3: The Tale of a Tendril (602)
Series of three half-reel films using animated puppets produced by Frank Percival Smith, the natural history film pioneer. Not released commercially to cinemas. Preserved in the National Film Archive. 1: Bertie Beetle's store of food is saved from enemies by a friendly spider. 2: Three beetles bury a plum and repel marauders. 3: Bertie Beetle tries to pluck a tendril for Flutterby, his girlfriend, but is captured by Bogie Bug.

1926

267 Wild Oats (500)
Ideal Films: "Alfred and Steve" No. 1
P:S: Tom Webster, A: Dick Friel, Joe Noble
First in a series of cartoons featuring Alfred the racehorse and Steve his trainer, created by the sports cartoonist of the *Daily Mail*, Tom Webster, and animated by the expert American animator Richard Friel. "Tom Webster's pencil is as full of cleverness on the screen as in print, but the essential humour is not so apparent. There are too many subtitles, and the incidents are not funny in themselves." The story is "Alfred's reprehensible behaviour in going to a horse's nightclub on the eve of a race." (*Kinematograph Weekly* 21 January 1926.)

268 Won by a Nose (500)
Ideal Films: "Alfred and Steve" No. 2
P:S: Tom Webster, A: Dick Friel, Joe Noble
Second in the series. "Shows how Alfred wins a race harnessed in a hansom cab." (*Kinematograph Weekly* 21 January 1926.)

269 The Deputy
U.I.C. – Pathé: "Jerry"
P:D:S:A: Sid Griffiths, C: A.A. Bilby
"Jerry as a vaudeville act, deputising for a famous pianist. He introduces an act a la Grock which, however, ends in disaster." (*Kinematograph Weekly* 21 January 1926.) Included in *Pathé Pictorial* No. 408; released 25 January 1926.

270 Weather or Not
U.I.C. – Pathé: "Jerry"
P:D:S:A: Sid Griffiths, C: A.A. Bilby
"Jerry is introduced speeding for dear life with a tin can tied to his tail. He escapes and boards a liner. A storm crops up (giving a chance for good 'combination photography') and Jerry leaves the boat. He calls on the Clerk of the Weather, finds him sleepy, and alters the weather to 'calm,'

then returns to receive his reward." (*Kinematograph Weekly* 21 January 1926.) Included in *Pathé Pictorial* No. 410; released 1 February 1926.

271   Weight and Sea
   U.I.C. – Pathé: "Jerry"
   P:D:S:A: Sid Griffiths, C: A.A. Bilby
   Included in *Pathé Pictorial* No. 412; released 15 February 1926.

272   Ten Little Jerry Boys
   U.I.C. – Pathé: "Jerry"
   P:D:S:A: Sid Griffiths, C: A.A. Bilby
   Burlesque of the nursery rhyme "Ten Little Nigger Boys" featuring ten Jerry the Tykes. Included in *Pathé Pictorial* No. 414; released 1 March 1926.

273   One Exciting Nightmare
   U.I.C. – Pathé: "Jerry"
   P:D:S:A: Sid Griffiths, C: A.A. Bilby
   Jerry the Tyke has an alarming nightmare. Included in *Pathé Pictorial* No. 416; released 15 March 1926.

274   All Cod
   U.I.C. – Pathé: "Jerry"
   P:D:S:A: Sid Griffiths, C: A.A. Bilby
   Jerry the Tyke's adventure with a fish. Included in *Pathé Pictorial* No. 418; released 29 March 1926.

275   Down and Out (1000)
   Ideal Films: "Alfred and Steve" No. 3
   P:S: Tom Webster, A: Dick Friel, Joe Noble
   Third in series. "Tom Webster's cartoon jockey and steed are here seen in an attempt to win a race disguised as a zebra, whose faked stripes are washed away by the rain. Some ingenious gags and quaint movements make it funny enough to go down anywhere." (*Kinematograph Weekly* 1 April 1926.)

276   Both Biters Bit
   U.I.C. – Pathé: "Jerry"
   P:D:S:A: Sid Griffiths, C: A.A. Bilby
   Included in *Pathé Pictorial* No. 420; released 12 April 1926.

277   When Jerry Papered the Parlour
   U.I.C. – Pathé: "Jerry"
   P:D:S:A: Sid Griffiths, C: A.A. Bilby
   Jerry the Tyke tries to decorate his room. Included in *Pathé Pictorial* No. 422; released 26 April 1926.

278   There's a Long Long Trail a-Winding (600)
Pathé
D:A: Brian White
Cartoon version of the popular song. "Clever sketches and good timing ensure that any audience will be both interested and quickly moved to sing." (*Kinematograph Weekly* 20 May 1926.)

279   Wireless Whirl
U.I.C. – Pathé: "Jerry"
P:D:S:A: Sid Griffiths, C: A.A. Bilby
"Jerry the Troublesome Tyke in a delightful wireless travesty." *Kinematograph Weekly* 1 July 1926.) Included in *Pathé Pictorial,* released June 1926.

280   Jerry Sacks a Saxophone
U.I.C. – Pathé: "Jerry"
P:D:S:A: Sid Griffiths, C: A.A. Bilby
Included in *Pathé Pictorial.*

281   C.O.D.
U.I.C. – Pathé: "Jerry"
P:D:S:A: Sid Griffiths, C: A.A. Bilby
Included in *Pathé Pictorial.*

282   He Gets Fixed
U.I.C. – Pathé: "Jerry"
P:D:S:A: Sid Griffiths, C: A.A. Bilby
Included in *Pathé Pictorial.*

283   Grown Up
U.I.C. – Pathé: "Jerry"
P:D:S:A: Sid Griffiths, C: A.A. Bilby
Included in *Pathé Pictorial.*

284   Old King Cole
Ideal Films: "Sing Song Series" No. 1
D:A: Norman Cobb
Cartoon version of the popular song, designed to encourage the cinema audience to join in and sing with the "Bouncing Ball." "They comprise familiar British melodies that people love to sing together. They are British throughout, the songs, the funny drawings and effects, photography, orchestration, printing, etc. A full orchestral score by Horace Shepherd, Mus. Bac. is given free with each of the series." (Advertisement 24 June 1926.) Released June 1926.

285 **The Bonnie Banks of Loch Lomond**
Ideal Films: "Sing Song Series" No. 2
D:A: Norman Cobb
"Bouncing Ball" song cartoon; released June 1926.

286 **Rule Britannia**
Ideal Films: "Sing Song Series" No. 3
D:A: Norman Cobb
"Bouncing Ball" song cartoon; released June 1926.

287 **Clementine**
Ideal Films: "Sing Song Series" No. 4
D:A: Norman Cobb
"Bouncing Ball" song cartoon; released July 1926.

288 **John Peel**
Ideal Films: "Sing Song Series" No. 5
D:A: Norman Cobb
"Bouncing Ball" song cartoon; released July 1926.

289 **There Is a Tavern in the Town**
Ideal Films: "Sing Song Series" No. 6
D:A: Norman Cobb
"Bouncing Ball" song cartoon; released July 1926.

290 **Comin' Thro' the Rye**
Ideal Films: "Sing Song Series" No. 7
D:A: Norman Cobb
"Bouncing Ball" song cartoon; released July 1926.

291 **Hearts of Oak**
Ideal Films: "Sing Song Series" No. 8
D:A: Norman Cobb
"Bouncing Ball" song cartoon; released July 1926.

292 **Sally in Our Alley**
Ideal Films: "Sing Song Series" No. 9
D:A: Norman Cobb
"Bouncing Ball" song cartoon; released July 1926.

293 **We Nearly Lose Him**
U.I.C. – Pathé: "Jerry"
P:D:S:A: Sid Griffiths, C: A.A. Bilby
Included in *Pathé Pictorial* No. 432; released 12 July 1926.

294 Burlington Bertie
Ideal Films: "Sing Song Series" No. 10
D:A: Norman Cobb
"Bouncing Ball" song cartoon; released 19 August 1926.

295 Stop Your Ticklin' Jock
Ideal Films: "Sing Song Series" No. 11
D:A: Norman Cobb
"Bouncing Ball" song cartoon; released 19 August 1926.

296 The Midnight Son
Ideal Films: "Sing Song Series" No. 12
D:A: Norman Cobb
"Bouncing Ball" song cartoon; released 19 August 1926. "Vesta Til-
ley's famous number enjoyed a vogue on two continents, and its inclusion
in the Sing Song Series will set many people singing or humming it again.
The Ideal trade mark is used in place of a ball to guide the singing, and the
cartoon accompanying the words is cleverly timed and amusing."
(Kinematograph Weekly 23 September 1926.)

297 He Breaks Out
U.I.C. – Pathé: "Jerry"
P:D:S:A: Sid Griffiths, C: A.A. Bilby
Included in Pathé Pictorial No. 434; released 26 July 1926.

298 A Splash and a Dash
U.I.C. – Pathé: "Jerry"
P:D:S:A: Sid Griffiths, C: A.A. Bilby
Included in Pathé Pictorial No. 436; released 9 August 1926.

299 The Language of Cricket No. 1
Unity Films
D:A: Hiscocks, S: G.B. Savi
"The first opens with illustrations of what cricket might be like in
different lands." (Kinematograph Weekly 26 August 1926.)

300 The Language of Cricket No. 2
Unity Films
D:A: Hiscocks, S: G.B. Savi
"The second shows a deputy for Strudwick taking eight wickets for
nought, and is followed by a series of jokes entitled 'Filmericks.'"
(Kinematograph Weekly 28 August 1926.)

301 A Flash Affair
U.I.C. – Pathé: "Jerry"
D:S:A: Sid Griffiths, C: A.A. Bilby
"Jerry the Tyke in the funniest footage we have seen lately, as a photographer. This British cartoon creation can now rank in quality with its Max Fleischer godfather." (*Kinematograph Weekly* 9 September 1926.) Included in *Pathé Pictorial* No. 440; released 6 September 1926.

302 Football
U.I.C. – Pathé: "Jerry"
P:D:S:A: Sid Griffiths, C: A.A. Bilby
Included in *Pathé Pictorial* No. 444; released 4 October 1926.

303 Dismal Desmond (series)
Gaumont
D:S:A: Joe Noble, C: Freddie Young
Series of untitled episodes included in the weekly magazine film series *Gaumont Mirror,* commencing with No. 1, premiered at the New Gallery Kinema, London, 18 November 1926, before royalty. "Dismal Desmond the Doleful Dalmatian is the most popular mascot figure since Felix. His lugubrious countenance is seen in every toy shop and has been extensively advertised in the press. As a cartoon character he will create another furore that means lots of money at the paybox. Dismal Desmond, a picture of pathos and profit." (Gaumont Company advertisement, *Kinematograph Weekly* 4 November 1926.)

304 Land of Hope and Glory (600)
Pathé
D:A: Brian White
Cartoon version of the song by Edward Elgar. "The jumping dot on the words has underneath it constantly changing and varied typical British scenes of a patriotic and artistic kind." (*Kinematograph Weekly* 18 November 1926.)

305 Going West
U.I.C. – Pathé: "Jerry"
P:D:S:A: Sid Griffiths, C: A.A. Bilby
"The Troublesome Tyke in a funny cowboy escapade." (*Kinematograph Weekly* 16 December 1926.) Included in *Pathé Pictorial;* released December 1926.

306 The Happy Iron
Colman
Advertising cartoon film for Colman's Mustard.

307 Stopping the Rot
Colman
Advertising cartoon for Colman's Mustard.

1927

308　His Birthday
U.I.C. – Pathé: "Jerry"
P:D:S:A: Sid Griffiths, C: A.A. Bilby
Included in *Pathé Pictorial* No. 462; released 7 February 1927.

309　In and Out of Wembley
U.I.C. – Pathé: "Jerry"
P:D:S:A: Sid Griffiths, C: A.A. Bilby
Jerry the Tyke visits the Wembley Exhibition. Included in *Pathé Pictorial*.

310　A Bird in the Hand
U.I.C. – Pathé: "Jerry"
P:D:S:A: Sid Griffiths, C: A.A. Bilby
Included in *Pathé Pictorial*.

311　Too Canny for Cannibals
U.I.C. – Pathé: "Jerry"
P:D:S:A: Sid Griffiths, C: A.A. Bilby
Included in *Pathé Pictorial*.

312　Jerry's Done It Again
U.I.C. – Pathé: "Jerry"
P:D:S:A: Sid Griffiths, C: A.A. Bilby
Included in *Pathé Pictorial*.

313　A Sticky Business
U.I.C. – Pathé: "Jerry"
P:D:S:A: Sid Griffiths, C: A.A. Bilby
Included in *Pathé Pictorial*.

314　Am I Wasting My Time on You (500)
Luscombe British – Pioneer
"Bouncing Ball" song cartoon; released March 1927.

315   Bye Bye Blackbird (500)
Luscombe British – Pioneer
"Bouncing Ball" song cartoon; released March 1927.

316   The Frothblowers' Anthem (500)
Luscombe British – Pioneer
"Bouncing Ball" song cartoon of "The More We Are Together"; re-
leased March 1927.

317   It Made Me Happy When You Made Me Cry (500)
Luscombe British – Pioneer
Cartoon of the song by Walter Davidson. A small man skips from
word to word of the chorus, performing an appropriate mime with each
word. Print preserved in the National Film Archive. Released March 1927.

318   Let Me Call You Sweetheart (500)
Luscombe British – Pioneer
"Bouncing Ball" song cartoon; released March 1927.

319   Perhaps You'll Think of Me: I Love You (500)
Luscombe British – Pioneer
"Bouncing Ball" song cartoon; released March 1927. Print preserved
in the National Film Archive.

320   Shepherd of the Hills (500)
Luscombe British – Pioneer
"Bouncing Ball" song cartoon; released March 1927.

321   Tonight You Belong to Me (500)
Luscombe British – Pioneer
"Bouncing Ball" song cartoon; released March 1927. Print preserved
in the National Film Archive.

322   The Story of the Flag (series)
Nettlefold Films – Butcher
P: Archibald Nettlefold, D:S:A: Anson Dyer
1: The Union Jack (636), **2: The Naval Ensigns** (735), **3: The Royal
Standard** (573), **4:** (593), **5:** (632), **6:** (563)
Originally conceived as a feature-length animated film, but broken down
into six episodes and released as half-reel shorts. "Opening with much information of the antiquarian order, light is thrown on the remarkable
alterations which have taken place in the Royal Standard of England,
largely owing to dynastic changes, notably in the accession of James I,
William III, and George I." (*Bioscope* 1 December 1927.) The series,

although silent, was reissued in 1935 for educational purposes, and the first three episodes were reviewed in the *Monthly Film Bulletin* for February 1935. One: "Includes a note on Oliver Cromwell's introduction of the Irish Harp, and a useful observation on degrading the flag." Two: "Adds some pictures of the Kew flagstaff and the Douglas firs in British Columbia." Three: "Illustrates the Fleur-de-Lys quarters introduced by Edward I and traces their gradual elimination."

1928

323 Putting the Wind Up Winnie
Pathé: "Sammy and Sausage" No. 1
D:S:A: Joe Noble, C: Mr. Fisher
First in a series of cartoons featuring Sammy, a boy, and Sausage, his dog. Included in *Eve's Film Review* (a weekly magazine film series) No. 363; released 24 May 1928.

324 Television
Pathé: "Sammy and Sausage" No. 2
D:S:A: Joe Noble, C: Mr. Fisher
Included in *Eve's Film Review* No. 364; released 30 May 1928.

325 The Pipe of Peace
Pathé: "Sammy and Sausage" No. 3
D:S:A: Joe Noble, C: Mr. Fisher
Included in *Eve's Film Review* No. 366; released 13 June 1928.

326 Shadows
Pathé: "Sammy and Sausage" No. 4
D:S:A: Joe Noble, C: Mr. Fisher
Included in *Eve's Film Review* No. 367; released 20 June 1928.

327 Inside Information
Pathé: "Sammy and Sausage" No. 5
D:S:A: Joe Noble, C: Mr. Fisher
Included in *Eve's Film Review* No. 368; released 27 June 1928.

328 Fowl Play
Pathé: "Sammy and Sausage" No. 6
D:S:A: Joe Noble, C: Mr. Fisher
Included in *Eve's Film Review* No. 370; released 11 July 1928.

329 Crossing the Line
Pathé: "Sammy and Sausage" No. 7
D:S:A: Joe Noble
Included in *Eve's Film Review* No. 372; released 25 July 1928.

330 **The Good Old Days**
Pathé: "Sammy and Sausage" No. 8
D:S:A: Joe Noble
Included in *Eve's Film Review* No. 373; released 2 August 1928.

331 **Onion Is Strength**
Pathé: "Sammy and Sausage" No. 9
D:S:A: Joe Noble
Included in *Eve's Film Review* No. 375; released 15 August 1928.

332 **The Lie-Do Cup**
Pathé: "Sammy and Sausage" No. 10
D:S:A: Joe Noble
Included in *Eve's Film Review* No. 377; released 29 August 1928.

333 **A Big Draw**
Pathé: "Sammy and Sausage"
D:S:A: Joe Noble
Included in *Eve's Film Review* No. 380; released 19 September 1928.

334 **A Bite for the Biteless**
Pathé: "Sammy and Sausage"
D:S:A: Joe Noble
Included in *Eve's Film Review* No. 385; released 24 October 1928.

335 **Shooting Stars**
Pathé: "Sammy and Sausage"
D:S:A: Joe Noble
Included in *Eve's Film Review* No. 392; released 12 December 1928.

336 **'Orace the 'Armonious 'Ound in "The Jazz Slinger"** (500)
British Sound Film Productions
D:S:A: Joe Noble, D (live action): Bertram Phillips, C: George Noble
The first British cartoon film with synchronized sound. Premiered at the Tivoli Cinema, Strand, London, on Monday 15 December 1928. The artist Joe Noble appears as himself in the live action sequences.

337 **Mr. . . . Goes Motoring**
Shell Motor Spirit
A: David Barker, S:DES: H.M. Bateman
Advertising film for Shell Motor Spirit designed by the popular magazine cartoonist H.M. Bateman. A hearty motorist convinces less fortunate drivers that Shell is the right spirit for them. Print preserved in the National Film Archive.

338   The Boy Who Wanted to Make Pictures
PCT Pictorial
A: David Barker, S:DES: H.M. Bateman
Advertising film for Kodak cameras designed by the popular magazine cartoonist H.M. Bateman. A boy annoys his family with his badly
drawn pictures of them, a habit that is cured when his father presents him
with his own Kodak camera. Print preserved in the National Film Archive.

1929

339 Fire!
Pathé: "Sammy and Sausage"
D:S:A: Joe Noble, C: Monty Redknap
Included in *Eve's Film Review* No. 395; released 9 January 1929.

340 Meet Mr. York – A Speaking Likeness (584)
British Publicity Talking Pictures
D:S:A: Joe Noble, D (live action): Bertram Phillips, C: George Noble,
DES: Alfred Leete
The first British cartoon advertising film with synchronized sound, made for Rowntree's Chocolate through the S.H. Benson Agency. Joe Noble the cartoonist appears as himself in the live action sequences. Mr. York of York, Yorks, a famous advertising character created by Alfred Leete, comes to life on the drawing board and has several adventures involving chocolate. Print preserved in the National Film Archive.

341 The Second Adventure of 'Orace the 'Armonious 'Ound
British Sound Film Productions
D:S:A: Joe Noble, C: George Noble
Print preserved in the National Film Archive.

342 No Parking Here
Pathé: "Sammy and Sausage"
D:S:A: Joe Noble, C: Monty Redknap
Included in *Eve's Film Review* No. 404; released 14 March 1929.

343 Whatrotolis
Pathé: "Sammy and Sausage"
D:S:A: Joe Noble, C: Monty Redknap
Burlesque of the German science-fiction film *Metropolis.* Included in *Eve's Film Review* No. 410; released 17 April 1929.

344 **Ten Little Dirty Boys** (318)
Health and Cleanliness Council
Health propaganda cartoon: ten little dirty boys are forced to wash themselves. Print preserved in the National Film Archive.

345 **Tusalava** (589)
Film Society
P: Robert Graves, D:S:A: Len Lye
Experiment in abstract animation, drawn directly onto the film. Described by the maker, Len Lye, as "representing a self-shape annihilating an antagonistic element." Print preserved in the National Film Archive. Premiered at the London Film Society, December 1929.

1930

346 Call Me Speedy
Pathé: "Sammy and Sausage"
D:S:A: Joe Noble, C: Kenneth Gordon
Included in *Pathé Pictorial* No. 659; released November 1930.

347 Tropical Breezes (972)
Comedy Cartoon Sound Films
P:D:S:A: Sidney Griffiths, Brian White, A. Goodman, M: John Johnson, Sam Firman
Hite, a tall sailor, and Mite, a short sailor, are cast away on a desert island where they have varied adventures with its musical inhabitants, including a banjo-playing kangaroo and an orchestra of monkeys. Print preserved in the National Film Archive.

348 The Elstree 'Erbs
British International Pictures
P: John Maxwell, D:S:A: Joe Noble, M: Laurence Easson, the Innes Chicago Cabaret Twelve
Teddie goes fishing with Wanda the Worm, while Reggie tries to get some sausages from Poll's Polony Palace. No trace of public showing or release; an unedited print is preserved in the National Film Archive.

349 John the Bull
Empire Marketing Board
A: Len Kirley, Bill Whinney
Advertising cartoon film for the National Marked Beef Campaign. A prize-winning British bull leads a march by cows in protest against imported frozen beef. Print preserved in the National Film Archive.

350 Bingo Breaks Loose (830)
Shepherd – MGM
P: Horace Shepherd, D:S:A: Norman Cobb
First in a series of four cartoons featuring Bingo the dog. Released December 1930. Not reviewed.

351   Bingo in Circus Daze (820)
Shepherd — MGM
P: Horace Shepherd, D:S:A: Norman Cobb
"Bingo escapes from prison and helps a touring circus where his presence is anything but welcome to all but one, a maiden whose costume he borrows but whose heart he steals. Verily, Bingo is a wizard of the tightrope, where he flees to escape the attention of the owner of the circus. High above the auditorium, Bingo enchants the audience but, once again on earth, a jailer calls to take him back to the fold he left in such a hurry." (*Pathéscope Monthly* March 1935.) Released December 1930.

352   Bingo in Bahahula (881)
Shepherd — MGM
P: Horace Shepherd, D:S:A: Norman Cobb
Third in the series of cartoons featuring Bingo the dog. Released December 1930. Not reviewed.

353   Bingo the Battling Bruiser (683)
Shepherd — MGM
P: Horace Shepherd, D:S:A: Norman Cobb
Fourth in the series of cartoons featuring Bingo the dog. Released December 1930. Not reviewed.

1931

354 The Right Spirit (860)
Conservative and Unionist Films Association
Political propaganda cartoon. Stanley Baldwin gets John Bull's broken-down car going again, while Ramsay MacDonald is asleep: "Vote Conservative." Print preserved in the National Film Archive. Not reviewed.

355 Red Tape Farm
Conservative Central Office
Political propaganda cartoon. Mr. Nosey Parker, a Socialist official, interferes with farm workers: "Vote Conservative." Not reviewed.

1932

356 The Story of the Port of London
Nettlefold
P: Archibald Nettlefold, D:S:A: Anson Dyer, V: Eric Dunstan
Animated documentary. "Anson Dyer has made use of cartoons to present the history of the Thames, and the present-day views of the river with its picturesqueness and its busy docks and industries are beautifully photographed." (*The Era* 7 March 1932.)

1933

357 Colonel Capers
Raycol Films—ABFD
D: Adrian Klein, S: H.M. Bateman, A: Brian White, Sid Griffiths, M: Harold Willoughby
Raycol Colour
Colour cartoon based on the popular "fiery colonel" characters drawn in many magazines by H.M. Bateman. No trace of review or release date.

358 On the Farm (650)
Raycol Films—ABFD
D:A: Brian White, Sid Griffiths, Joe Noble, S:DES: H.M. Bateman
Raycol Colour
"This, the first of the new series of cartoons in colour by H.M. Bateman, is a little lacking in continuity, but original ideas are evident, and the development is accompanied by many laughs. Adequate fill-up." (*Kinematograph Weekly* 21 September 1933.)

1934

359   Treasure Island
Raycol Films – ABFD
D:S:A: Brian White
Raycol Colour
Introduced as "Barnacle Bill Series" No. 1, but no further episodes
made. "An amusing cartoon, the first of a new series, presented in natural
colour. Quite a useful fill-up." (*Kinematograph Weekly* 1 February 1934.)

360   The Lost Ball (547)
Champion Productions – MGM
P:D: Dennis Connolly (?)
"A British cartoon based on a neat idea, with 'spot' and 'plain' bil-
liard balls vieing for the love of dainty Miss 'Red.' Effectively drawn but a
trifle laboured." (*Daily Film Renter* 3 December 1934.)

361   The Eternal Triangle (515)
Champion Productions – MGM
P:D: Dennis Connolly (?)
"This British cartoon effort narrates the adventures of a golf ball in
search of its mate, who has got lost in the rough. A novel idea, but might
be better developed." (*Daily Film Renter* 3 December 1934.)

362   The Sleeping Beauty (650)
JWT Productions
D: George Pal, M: Bela Radici, Louis Levy and His Orchestra
Technicolor
Anglo-Dutch production: puppet film advertising Philips Radio, produced in Holland. Reissued without the commercial message and in
monochrome by DUK Films in July 1950. "Once upon a time there lived
in a lonely castle far from towns and people, a Princess. One day whilst
dreaming of the Prince who would come and fetch her, an old witch appears and distributes a powerful sleeping draught that puts the Princess and
the whole court into deep and lasting slumber. It is not until the 20th century when the Prince arrives and brings music to the castle, that the Princess
is awakened." (*Pathéscope Monthly* February 1951.)

1935

363 Morris May Day
Publicity Pictures
P: Herbert Hopkins, Reginald Wyer
A: Laurie Price, Christopher Millett
Advertising cartoon for Morris Motors. "How a crafty showman gets away with the cash leaving his company stranded. He drives off in a comic motor car which performs many laughable tricks as it plunges over hill and dale, and occasionally comes to pieces en route. But though a wizard of a car it cannot escape the pursuing Morris Oxford, which finally overhauls it, and the driver of which rescues the cash." (*Commercial Film* February 1935.)

364 The Midshipman
Publicity Pictures: "Cheery Chunes"
P: Herbert Hopkins, Reginald Wyer, A: Christopher Millett, Laurie Price, M: Leo Croke
Spectracolor
Advertising cartoon for Worthington beer. "A rollicking series of slapstick scenes aboard a ship which is engaged in a slapstick battle. Guns roar, the comic crew do miraculous stunts, the midshipman becomes a hero, the admiral becomes the butt of everybody, and – well, you haven't the slightest idea of what is in store!" (*Commercial Film* February 1935.)

365 The Baronial Beanfeast
Publicity Pictures
P: Herbert Hopkins, Reginald Wyer, A: Laurie Price, Christopher Millett
Spectracolor
Advertising cartoon for OK Sauce. "The chief figures are a fat old baron and a timid servitor. The latter, for some lapse of duty, is flung into a dungeon where he awaits death. A hungry mouse appears while he is munching his bread and cheese, and begs a portion of the meal. In return he turns into a kindly genii, who instructs the prisoner in the art of

96

preparing. At last a magic bottle appears and the delighted menial is released from the dungeon to present his lord with the OK Sauce! One taste of this and all is forgiven." (*Commercial Film* February 1935.)

366   Carnival Capers
Publicity Pictures – National Interest Films
P: Herbert Hopkins, Reginald Wyer, A: Laurie Price, Christopher Millett, M: Leo Croke
Spectracolor
Advertising cartoon; trade shown March 1935.

367   Dirty Bertie (420)
Central Council for Health Education
Propaganda cartoon. Clean Eugene, a schoolboy, teaches his grubby young chum, Dirty Bertie, the lesson that "Where there's dirt there's danger." Print preserved in the National Film Archive.

368   Woofy (794)
Zenifilms
"A feeble cartoon, the drawings are unoriginal and the sound effects are poor. Crude cartoon of a dog who rescues his sweetheart from a burning house. Poor drawings, animation and sound effects make it a doubtful attraction for minor halls." (*Kinematograph Weekly* 29 August 1935.)

369   See How They Won
Revelation Films
P: Charles Cochrane, D: Ub Iwerks
Brewstercolor
Advertising cartoon for Boots the Chemists, animated and filmed by American animators in Hollywood, from British script and designs. John Careless infects his family with disease, but the germs are routed by the Good Health Army. Released October 1935.

370   Sam and His Musket (850)
Anglia Films – Reunion
P: Archibald Nettlefold, D: Anson Dyer, Sup: Sid Griffiths, S: Marriott Edgar, A: Jorgen Myller, D. Mikkelson, Bob Privett, C: Charles Stobbart, V: Stanley Holloway, M: Wolseley Charles, Jose Norman
Dunningcolor
Based on the Stanley Holloway radio and recording success, a comic monologue by Marriott Edgar. The Duke of Wellington is unable to commence the Battle of Waterloo until an old Yorkshire soldier agrees to pick up his musket. "This, the first in a series of British cartoons in colour, is a clever and effective piece of work. Stanley Holloway delivers his famous

monologue, from which the film gets its title, in his own inimitable manner, and the drawings synchronize perfectly with the words. The gags are bright and the colour work flawless. This short has both novelty value and selling angles, and can be confidently recommended as a featurette." (*Kinematograph Weekly* 24 October 1935.)

371 Robin Hood (800)
  Champion – MGM
  P:D: Dennis Connolly
  Registered 4 November 1935, but not reviewed by the trade press. Presumably the adventures of the legendary outlaw and his Merrie Men.

372 Giro and His Enemies
  British Utility Films – Newhall Films
  Propaganda cartoon made for the Health and Cleanliness Council. "The attempts of Giro the Germ and his satellites to invade the model town of Healthiville, their subsequent defeat by the forces of household hygiene, polish, soap and electricity." (*Monthly Film Bulletin* November 1935.) One of a series of four episodes. Print preserved in the National Film Archive.

373 The Gay Cavalier
  Publicity Pictures – National Interest: "Cheery Chunes"
  P: Herbert Hopkins, Reg Wyer, A: Laurie Price, Ian Matherson, Christopher Millett, M: Leo Croke, ED: Marcus Samuel, C: G. Capper
  Spectracolor
  Advertising cartoon for Worthington's beer. Released November 1935. Not reviewed.

374 Kaleidoscope (360)
  PWP Productions
  P: Gerald Noxon, D:S:A: Len Lye, M: Don Marino Barreto and his Cuban Orchestra, SD: Jack Ellit
  Spicer Colour
  Abstract animation advertising Churchman's Cigarettes (Imperial Tobacco Co.), synchronized to the tune "Beguine d'Amour."

375 The Little Paper People (800)
  Jenkins – ABFD
  P:D: Cyril Jenkins, S:A: Margaret Hoyland, V: Philip Godfrey
  Animated puppets. "Ingenious novelty short which takes the form of a marionette show featuring paper dolls." (*Kinematograph Weekly* 9 January 1936.) "The cleverness of Margaret Hoyland's paper-made marionettes

cannot quite be appreciated in a featurette depicting seaside personalities of the Victorian and Edwardian periods. An amusing and original short with commentary having an appeal for the better class as well as the popular patron." (*Kinematograph Weekly* 30 April 1936.) Reissued 1949. "We see the prim young ladies, the minstrels, the old salt, and the dancers." (*NSTA Report.*)

1936

376 The Birth of the Robot (630)
Shell—Mex Films
P: Humphrey Jennings, D: Len Lye, S: C.H. David, DES: John Banting, Allen Farmer, M: Gustav Holst ("The Planets"), London Symphony Orchestra, C: Alex Strasser, SD: Jack Ellit, V: E.V.H. Emmett
Gasparcolor
Animated puppet film advertising Shell Petrol. Old Father Time makes the planets revolve by turning his ancient mangle. A motorist runs out of oil in a sandstorm and dies. Venus weeps tears of oil, the robot is born, and the world becomes mechanized. Premiered April 1936; print preserved in the National Film Archive.

377 Carmen (850)
Anglia Films—Reunion: "Colourtunes"
P: Archibald Nettlefold, D: Anson Dyer, SUP: Sid Griffiths, A: D. Mikkelson, Jorgen Myller, C: Charles Stobbart, S: Georges Bizet, M: Jose Norman
Dunning Color
Burlesque version of Bizet's opera "Carmen." "The highlight of the comedy is a bullfight in which Sam accidentally becomes a matador and lays out the bulls with a ball and chain. The cartoon seems to lose some of its appeal without the Stanley Holloway monologue accompaniment, but nevertheless the animation is quite good." (*Kinematograph Weekly* 22 April 1936.)

378 'Alt! 'Oo Goes There? (868)
Anglia Films—Reunion
P: Archibald Nettlefold, D: Anson Dyer, SUP: Sid Griffiths, S: Marriott Edgar, A: D. Mikkelson, Jorgen Myller, C: Charles Stobbart, M: Jose Norman, V: Stanley Holloway
Dunning Color
"The adventures of Sam when he dropped his musket at Buckingham Palace and went and had tea with the King. The monologue is delivered

in the characteristic Stanley Holloway manner and is cleverly synchronized with the drawings. The Northcountryman's popularity, the gags and the colour work contribute to make this an acceptable short subject for the majority." (*Kinematograph Weekly* 22 April 1936.)

379 On Parade
J.W.T. Productions
D:A: George Pal, C: Frank Hendrix, M: Debroy Somers Band, V: Malcolm MacEachern
Gasparcolor
Animated puppet film advertising Horlicks Malted Milk. Anglo-Dutch production made in Holland. A sleepy soldier is livened up by a cup of hot Horlicks. Released August 1936.

380 Beat the Retreat (810)
Anglia Films—Associated Producers
P: Archibald Nettlefold, D: Anson Dyer, SUP: Sid Griffiths, S: R.P. Weston, Bert Lee, A: D. Mikkelson, Jorgen Myller, C: Charles Stobbart, M: Jose Norman, V: Stanley Holloway
Dunning Color
"One of the Old Sam series pleasantly coloured by the Dunning process, with amusing Yorkshire dialect commentary by Stanley Holloway in the story of the private who defies Napoleon when asked to beat the retreat. The animation is very good, and the gags amusing, resulting in engaging entertainment of the type." (*Today's Cinema* 7 November 1936.)

381 Sam's Medal (835)
Anglia Films—Associated Producers
P: Archibald Nettlefold, D: Anson Dyer, SUP: Sid Griffiths, S: Mabel Constanduros, Michael Hogan, A: D. Mikkelson, Jorgen Myller, C: Charles Stobbart, M: Jose Norman, V: Stanley Holloway
Dunning Color
"Crazy story of how Sam comes to be handed a medal for alleged valour from a grateful monarch. Highlights of cartoon type already referred to also in evidence here, assuring very pleasant general entertainment." (*Today's Cinema* 7 November 1936.)

382 The Fox Hunt (716)
London Films—Denning—United Artists
P: Alexander Korda, D:S: Anthony Gross, Hector Hoppin, Laszlo Meitner, A: Anthony Gross, Hector Hoppin, Laszlo Meitner, Kathleen Murphy, Carl Giles, ED: Robert Compton Bennett, M: Mischa Spoliansky, MD: Muir Matheson
Technicolor

Anglo-French production. "This first colour cartoon created by Hector Hoppin and Anthony Gross, who were put under contract by Alexander Korda after he had seen their *Joie de Vivre,* is a stylised affair with rhythm in music and the use of colour. It has not a wide, popular appeal, but as an artistic achievement it certainly ranks high. The subject is a fox hunt, which takes place along a suburban arterial road, and in which the fox gets the better of his pursuers, who eventually include motor buses, steam rollers, cars and bicycles. The humour is of a whimsical variety, and the drawings more impressionistic than usual. Its great claim lies in its fantastic invention, its 'rhythmic flow,' and bold use of contrasting colour. As a novelty short it should be received well at all first class houses." (*Kinematograph Weekly* 5 November 1936.) The above review appeared following the film's trade show by the distributors, Denning Films. Six months later the film was trade shown for a second time, this time by United Artists. Commented *Kinematograph Weekly:* "There is nothing here to cause Walt Disney loss of sleep." (3 June 1937.) The film was reissued in 1948 by British Lion, but is currently believed to be lost.

383   A Colour Box (110)
GPO Films Unit
P: John Grierson, D:S:A: Len Lye, M: Don Marino Barreto and his Cuban Orchestra, SD: Jack Ellit
Dufaycolor
Abstract animation painted directly onto the film and synchronized to the beguine rhythm of "La Belle Creole." "Colour designs move in rhythm and end by advertising Post Office cheap parcel postage. The designs are painted directly onto the film. Ingenious in execution." (*Kinematograph Weekly* 28 January 1937.) The first British cartoon to win an award, the Special Prize at Brussells International Film Festival.

384   Rainbow Dance (357)
GPO Film Unit
P: Basil Wright, Alberto Cavalcanti, D:S:A: Len Lye, C: Frank Jones, M: Rico's Creole Band ("Tony's Wife"), SD: Jack Ellit, Dancer: Rupert Doone
Gasparcolor
Abstract animated film advertising the Post Office Savings Bank, featuring a live-action silhouette of a dancing business man performing against stylized backgrounds. "Very ingenious in design and execution, but its advertising denouement forms a bad anti-climax." (*Kinematograph Weekly* 28 January 1937.) Print preserved in the National Film Archive.

385   Steve Steps Out (714)
Roland Davies – Butcher: "Come On Steve" No. 1
P:D:S: Roland Davies, A: Carl Giles, C: John Rudkin-Hubbard, M: John Reynders

First in a series of six cartoons produced by the creator of the "Come On Steve" strip cartoon in *The Sunday Express*. Steve was an amiable old cart-horse, and the title of the strip came from the cry of the punters cheering jockey Steve Donoghue on to win. "When Steve espies a notice advertising a tight-rope walking competition, it is more than he can do to resist a little practice. It is great fun while it lasts, using the white line in the centre of the road as an imaginary rope, but the cars and buses which have to follow at almost a funeral march are loud in condemning the capers. With the police hot on his track, Steve has to bolt for safety, but finds it is safety of a perilous kind." (*Pathéscope Monthly* February 1938.) "Bright cartoon offering." (*Kinematograph Weekly* 17 December 1936.)

386   Steve's Treasure Hunt (854)
Roland Davies – Butcher: "Come On Steve" No. 2
P:D:S: Roland Davies, A: Carl Giles, C: John Rudkin-Hubbard, M: John Reynders

"Steve enters an ancestral home in the hope of finding buried treasure. He is in competition with a plunderer but demoralises him with the aid of the haunted chamber of the castle." (*Pathéscope Catalogue* 1941.) "Another ingenious and laughable cartoon in the new but potentially popular Steve series. Good short of its type." (*Kinematograph Weekly* 17 December 1936.)

1937

387 The Lion and Albert (692)
Anglia Films – Sound City: "Colourtunes"
P: Archibald Nettlefold, D: Anson Dyer, SUP: Sid Griffiths, S: Marriott Edgar, A: D. Mikkelson, Jorgen Myller, C: Charles Stobbart, M: Jose Norman, V: Stanley Holloway
Dunningcolor
"The sad story of the Ramsbottoms' visit to the Zoo at Blackpool, and how little Albert was eaten up by a lion. Rendered in cartoon style with colour, the entertainment appeals on the comedy narration of Stanley Holloway in rich dialect." (*Today's Cinema* 19 February 1937.)

388 Drummed Out (863)
Anglia Films – Sound City
P: Archibald Nettlefold, D: Anson Dyer, SUP: Sid Griffiths, S: Marriott Edgar, A: D. Mikkelson, Jorgen Myller, C: Charles Stobbart, M: Jose Norman V: Stanley Holloway
Dunningcolor
"Sam tells how he is drummed out of the regiment, accused of putting water in the Sergeant's beer, until the Colonel's daughter intervenes. Quite well drawn and fair as to colour and animation." (*Today's Cinema* 22 February 1937.)

389 Three Ha'Pence a Foot (840)
Anglia Films – Sound City
P: Archibald Nettlefold, D: Anson Dyer, SUP: Sid Griffiths, S: Marriott Edgar, A: D. Mikkelson, Jorgen Myller, C: Charles Stobbart, M: Jose Norman, V: Stanley Holloway
Dunningcolor
"Anson Dyer cartoon about Sam Small, the price he put on wood when Noah built his Ark in Bury. Typical Stanley Holloway tale-telling, enlivens slightly a coloured concoction which lacks unity and the essential qualities of humour, but which should pass muster with the average audience." (*Today's Cinema* 17 March 1937.)

390   Gunner Sam (802)
Anglia Films—Sound City
P: Archibald Nettlefold, D: Anson Dyer, SUP: Sid Griffiths, S: Marriott Edgar, A: D. Mikkelson, Jorgen Myller, C: Charles Stobbart, M: Jose Norman, V: Stanley Holloway
Dunningcolor
"Based on a famous Stanley Holloway monologue in which Sam, according to this film, dreams of the time when he was press-ganged and was present at one of Nelson's sea battles. By refusing to let go two cannonballs, he is nearly drowned but is saved by Nelson, who, according to draughtsmanship, is 'Stan Laurel' to Hardy's 'Oliver.' Up to the standard of previous cartoons in this series." (*Today's Cinema* 4 May 1937.)

391   Steve's Cannon Crackers (806)
Roland Davies—Butcher: "Come On Steve" No. 3
P:D:S: Roland Davies, A: Carl Giles, C: John Rudkin-Hubbard, M: John Reynders
"This effort shows how Steve and his master occupy a disused fort at the seaside, and accidentally come into cannon-ball conflict with the Fleet. Fairly well drawn, moderately animated and not very strong in laughs, this cartoon should nevertheless serve for family and juvenile audiences." (*The Cinema* 6 April 1937.)

392   Steve of the River (920)
Roland Davies—Butcher: "Come On Steve" No. 4
P:D:S: Roland Davies, A: Carl Giles, C: John Rudkin-Hubbard, M: John Reynders
Broad burlesque of the Alexander Korda film *Sanders of the River,* from the Edgar Wallace stories. "A horsey version of the late Edgar Wallace's *Sanders of the River,* but there is far more comedy than drama in this account." (*Pathéscope Monthly* October 1937.)

393   Steve in Bohemia (840)
Roland Davies—Butcher: "Come On Steve" No. 5
P:D:S: Roland Davies, A: Carl Giles, C: John Rudkin-Hubbard, M: John Reynders
"Another bright Roland Davies cartoon, well charged with novel and laughable gags." (*Kinematograph Weekly* 27 May 1937.) "Steve, endeavouring to find a suitable costume in which to go to the Artists' Ball, tastes the fun of nightlife. All sorts of costumes seem likely to come his way, but always something happens to bring his plans to nought. Eventually he does get to the ball, arriving through the roof of the hall, after falling from an inflated rubber figure Steve plans to filch." (*Pathéscope Monthly* December 1937.)

394 Steve Cinderella (752)
Roland Davies – Butcher: "Come On Steve" No. 6
P:D:S: Roland Davies, A: Carl Giles, C: John Rudkin-Hubbard, M: John Reynders
"Steve goes to the local horse show, sheds a hoof in making his midnight getaway, and wins a cup when the hoof is found to fit him. Genial fun of the cartoon type." (*The Cinema* 22 May 1937.) "Steve is left behind when the Farm Show, not the ball, takes place. To him comes a fairy Godmother, who makes it possible for him to go. Of course, Steve loses his slipper just like Cinderella, but, oh, what fun he has when he wins first prize in the show!" (*Pathéscope Monthly* November 1937.)

395/6 National News
National News Company – Sound City
P: Norman Loudon, D:S:A: Dennis Connolly, C: Leslie Murray, V: Thomas Woodrooffe
Topical animated cartoon segment as part of newsreel. "A cartoon sequence elaborating on a statement that a higher degree of comfort is promised in prisons." The first of what was to be a regular animated cartoon item of a new twice-weekly newsreel. Previewed Monday 11 October 1937 at the Monseigneur News Theatre, Piccadilly Circus. "The second feature of the newsreel will be a weekly animated cartoon based on a topical theme. It has been found possible, it is stated, to produce an animated cartoon for weekly distribution that can be based on the very latest world news. The cartoonist is Dennis Conelly [*sic*], who has had long experience of Fleet Street work, and a style which should adapt itself readily to film animation. It is hoped his caricatures will become a welcome and popular feature of *National News*." (Advertisement 12 October.) "Quite the worst cartoon I've seen to date, a cartoon that might have found favour 15 years ago. The cartoon sequence is not up to standard of modern animated drawings." (*Daily Film Renter* 12 October 1937.)

397 The Magic Seaplane
D. & W. Gibbs
Advertising cartoon. "The twins, Pat and Peter, are first seen busily cleaning their teeth, each with their own tube of Gibbs' Tooth Paste. Suddenly, Peter has an idea. Making a model seaplane out of the tube of paste and two tooth-brushes, he floats the model in the bath. Surprisingly the airscrew begins to turn and the Archer appears to invite them for a trip to the Land of Health and Happiness. They make a forced landing in front of a castle in Rack and Ruin Country. Here are a lot of miserable people, Giant Decay and Dragon Dirt, and a complete poison factory. The Archer and the Twins make their escape, thanks to the arrival of the Gibbs Fairies with more fuel." (*Pathéscope Monthly* November 1937.)

398 The King's Breakfast (970)

Facts and Fantasies — ABFD

D:A: Lotte Reiniger, Martin Battersby, DES: Ernest H. Shepherd, S: A.A. Milne, M: H. Fraser-Simpson, MD: Ernest Irving, V: Olive Groves, George Baker

Silhouette film. "Depicted entirely by characters in silhouette. The effect is unusual and fascinating, and certain to score with family audiences. Attractive novelty featurette." (*Kinematograph Weekly* 25 November 1937.) Print preserved in the National Film Archive.

399 All the Fun of the 'Air (272)

Publicity Films

P:D: Anson Dyer, A: D. Mikkelson, Jorgen Myller, C: Charles Stobbart, M: Jose Norman

Dunningcolor

Advertising cartoon for Bush Radio. "The body of this picture concerned a typical bank holiday crowd on Hampstead Heath. They ended up at the famous Old Bull and Bush tavern. A close-up was shown of the sign outside the inn. The bull got stung by a bee and rushed madly away, leaving only the bush, which then made an announcement on the merits of Bush Radio." (*Advertising World* August 1938.)

400 The King with the Terrible Temper (386)

Publicity Films

P:D: Anson Dyer, A: D. Mikkelson, Jorgen Myller, Len Kirley, S:V: Sutherland Felce, C: Charles Stobbart

Technicolor

Advertising cartoon for Bush Radio. "The King had three daughters, one very thin, one very fat, and one just perfect, each with appropriate music. The film dealt with the adventures of the perfect one, who married a handsome Prince, and the King relents from his terrible temper. He gives them as a wedding present a radio set, not one with a thin tone, not one with a fat tone, but a perfect tone." (*Advertising World* August 1938.) Print preserved in the National Film Archive.

401 Trade Tattoo (500)

GPO Film Unit

P: John Grierson, D:S:A: Len Lye, M: The Lecuona Band, SD: Jack Ellit

Technicolor

Abstract animation sponsored by the Post Office to advertise "Post Early." Lye included black-and-white offcuts from various GPO documentaries, processed in color, and avant-garde techniques including solarization and photo-montage, animated lettering and patterns.

402   Sky Pirates (600)
JWT Productions
D: George Pal, C: Frank Hendrix, M: Debroy Somers
Technicolor
Anglo-Dutch production; animated puppets advertising Horlicks
Malted Milk. "The sleepy little aerodrome is brought to life at the sound of
Reveille, and it is with the greatest effort that the planes manage to take the
air. The flight is attacked by bandits and all but one are destroyed. The sur-
vivor manages to get to the Palace where he unfolds his tale, and very soon
the royal planes take to the skies and proceed to destroy the bandits in their
hideout." (*Pathéscope Monthly* February 1951.) Reissued July 1950 by DUK
Films, in monochrome and with the commercial message removed.

403   Love on the Range (600)
JWT Productions
D: George Pal, C: Frank Hendrix, M: Debroy Somers
Technicolor
Anglo-Dutch production; animated puppets advertising Horlicks
Malted Milk. "The action takes place on the wide open spaces and features
all those characters to be found in ye olde fashioned melodrama. The
dashing, daring cowboy, the fair country maiden, with, of course, an in-
valid father, and the cruel, heartless villain. The villain, thwarted in his attempt to claim the father's ranch owing to non-payment of the mortgage,
kidnaps the daughter and rides away to his mountain hideout. The dashing
young hero, however, comes to the rescue after a struggle with the villain,
saves the heroine from a fate worse than death." (*Pathéscope Monthly*
March 1951.) Reissued July 1950 by DUK Films, in monochrome and
without the commercial message. Songs: "The Hilly Billy Band" and
"They're Tough Mighty Tough in the West."

404   What Ho! She Bumps! (700)
AKA: **Captain Kidding**
JWT Productions
D: George Pal, C: Frank Hendrix, M: Debroy Somers
Technicolor
Anglo-Dutch production; animated puppets advertising Horlicks
Malted Milk." Captain Kidding and his crew are seen here on the high seas
in HMS *Hopeless.* They are sighted and attacked by pirates and come off
second best in the battle, during which Captain Kidding sends a message
to his base and, in response to his call for aid, the shore batteries open up
on the pirates, thus driving them off. That night the crew celebrate their
rescue and rename their ship HMS *Hopeful.* The following day they put out
to sea again, rearmed, and again encounter the pirates, but this time the

boot is on the other foot and the pirates are wiped out and their ship taken in tow." (*Pathéscope Catalogue* 1952.) Reissued July 1950 under the new title *Captain Kidding* by DUK Films, in monochrome and without the commercial message.

1938

405   The King with the Terrible Hiccups (169)
Publicity Films
P:D: Anson Dyer, A: Len Kirley, Laurie Price, Kathleen Murphy,
S:V: Sutherland Felce, C: Charles Stobbart, M: Jose Norman
Technicolor
Advertising cartoon for Bush Radio. Print preserved in the National
Film Archive.

406   This Button Business (402)
Publicity Films
P:D: Anson Dyer, A: Len Kirley, Laurie Price, V: Vic Oliver, C:
Charles Stobbart
Technicolor
Advertising film for Bush Radio. The need for buttons is shown in a
series of humorous sequences featuring firemen, nudists, and the Pearly
Kings. The climax is a Bush-Button push-button radio. Print preserved in
the National Film Archive.

407   South Sea Sweethearts (600)
JWT Productions
D: George Pal, C: Frank Hendrix, M: Debroy Somers
Technicolor
Anglo-Dutch production; animated puppets advertising Horlicks
Malted Milk. "On a South Sea island some black puppets are carrying away
a girl puppet, another man's sweetheart. This man is lying on the ground
in a weak state and a doctor comes along and somehow peps him up, when
he chases the other puppets in a canoe, fights them all, and knocks them
into a volcano, and saves the girl who was about to be burnt as a sacrifice."
(*NSTA Review.*) Reissued July 1950 by DUK Films, in monochrome and
without the commercial message.

408   Philips Broadcast of 1938 (500)
AKA: **The Big Broadcast**
JWT Productions
D: George Pal, C: Frank Hendrix, M: Ambrose's Orchestra, V: Sam Browne, Evelyn Dall
Technicolor
Anglo-Dutch production: animated puppets advertising Philips Radio. "This shows a puppet orchestra with a man and a woman puppet dancing and a crooner singing 'Harbour Lights,' and a chorus dancing it after. The theme is a Harlem scene; an appropriate song is sung and you see black puppets putting their heads out of windows, playing dice in streets, etc." (*NSTA Review.*) Reissued July 1950 under the new title *The Big Broadcast,* by DUK Films, in monochrome and without the commercial message. The music track is by Ambrose and his dance orchestra, playing "She Wore a Little Jacket of Blue," "Harbour Lights" sung by Sam Browne, and "The Rhythm's Okay in Harlem" sung by Evelyn Dall.

409   Cavalcade of Music (500)
AKA: **Philips Cavalcade**
JWT Productions
D: George Pal, C: Frank Hendrix, M: Jack Hylton's Band
Technicolor
Anglo-Dutch production: animated puppets advertising Philips Radio. "In an old time Music Hall puppet performers play to a puppet orchestra. They dance to 'The Merry Widow' waltz, there are some Negro spirituals, and a girl puppet croons." (*NSTA Review.*) Reissued July 1950 by DUK Films in monochrome, and without the commercial message.

410   Love on the Wing (157)
GPO Film Unit
P: Alberto Cavalcanti, D:A: Norman McLaren, C: Fred Gamage, Jonah Jones, M: Jacques Ibert ("Divertissement")
Dufaycolor
Abstract animation advertising Empire Air Mail. "The action all takes place in front of one of those bare Chiricoesque settings that seem to have crept into the repertoire of even the commercial studios. When the action starts it looks like ballet broken loose from the laws of gravity. The little figures, drawn in simple flat white outline, grow and change with alarming and gay vitality. Probably the action is a little fast for the unsophisticated eye. Some of the allusion of the drawing is lost because such extreme simplification of idea (lovers kissing become two mouths kissing, and so on) requires a little interval for the idea to get across to the audience." (*Documentary News Letter* February 1940.) Print preserved in the National Film Archive.

411   How the Motor Works (630)
British Animated Films–Pamphonic Reproducers – Technique
P: Henry J. Elwis, A: Kathleen Murphy, V: Charles Spencer
Gasparcolor
"This diagrammatic cartoon in pleasing Gasparcolor explains, with the aid of excellent commentary, exactly how a car engine works, the functions of the petrol pump, carburettor, distributor, engine block, crankshaft, cooling system, etc. being personified by amusing little figures. Excellent draughtsmanship and animation are a feature of an astoundingly interesting and novel subject of wide general appeal." (*Today's Cinema* 8 September 1938.)

412   Music Man (776)
British Animated Films – Technique
P: Henry J. Elwis, A: John Halas, Joy Batchelor
Technicolor
"This technicolor cartoon shows how a small boy, plagued by violin lessons, falls asleep and dreams he enters the land depicted in a picture hanging in his room, meeting a little girl, watching flowers change into humans, and having a fight with his sinister music master. Of fair technical quality, this cartoon has a certain amount of quaint charm." (*Today's Cinema* 8 September 1938.) Historically important as the production on which John Halas met Joy Batchelor.

413   Red, White and Blue
Publicity Films
P:D: Anson Dyer, A: Len Kirley, Laurie Price, S: Harold Purcell, C: Charles Stobbart, V: Sutherland Felce, M: Jose Norman
Technicolor
Advertising cartoon for the Samuel Hanson company. "It tells the story of three Foreign Legionnaires, Beau Best, Beau West and Beau Zest, who are sent into the desert by a villainous sergeant, Beau Looney. Red, White and Blue coffee essence plays a stirring part in the eventual rescue. Red, white and blue are the predominant colours of the film, and the tune 'Three Cheers for the Red, White and Blue' is also featured." (*Advertiser's Weekly* 29 September 1938.)

414   The Road of Health (1099)
British Social Hygiene Council
D:A: Brian Salt, Advisers: Mary Field, L.W. Harrison
Health propaganda. "Representing the Road to Health and the by-roads from it, e.g., immorality, broken homes, prostitution, etc., which, if followed, lead into the bog of venereal disease. The propaganda work of the BSHC in spreading knowledge and fighting disease is symbolised in the

figure of a knight with a sword and torch lighting the way back to health over a bridge built through the work of the Government, local authorities, medical practitioners, nursing and almoning services." (*Monthly Film Bulletin* October 1938.)

1939

415   Around the World in Eighty Days
AKA: **Indian Fantasy**
London Films – British Film Institute
P: Alexander Korda, D:DES: Hector Hoppin, Anthony Gross, S: Jules Verne, A: Hector Hoppin, Anthony Gross, Laszlo Meitner, ED: Alan Lloyd, M: Tibor Harsanyi, V: Donald Pleasence
Technicolor
Intended as the first animated cartoon feature film to be produced in Britain, production was interrupted by the 1939 war, and the film was never completed. In 1955 the finished sequences were assembled by the British Film Institute and shown for the first time, under the new title of *Indian Fantasy*. Print preserved in the National Film Archive. Phileas Fogg makes a wager at his London club that he will traverse the world in eighty days. With his companion Passe-Partout he journeys through India.

416   The Tocher (455)
GPO Film Unit
P: Alberto Cavalcanti, D:S:A: Lotte Reiniger, M: Rossini, MD: Benjamin Britten
Silhouette animation. "Filmballet" advertising the Post Office Savings Bank. Princess Rhona is saved from marriage to a rich fat laird by the last minute arrival of the hero Angus with his Post Office Savings Bank Book. Print preserved in the National Film Archive.

417   The H.P.O. (340)
GPO Film Unit – ABFD
P: Alberto Cavalcanti, D:S:A: Lotte Reiniger, C: R.M. Harris, M: Brian Easdale
Dufaycolor
Animated silhouettes advertising the Post Office Greetings Telegram service. A cherub from the HPO delivers a series of Greetings Telegrams, concluding with the message: "It's Heaven to receive a Greetings Telegram. Be an Angel and send one." Lotte Reiniger's first silhouette film in color. Print preserved in the National Film Archive.

418   Colour Flight (360)
Imperial Airways
D:S:A: Len Lye, M: Red Nichols and his Five Pennies, SD: Ernst Meyer
Gasparcolor
Abstract animation advertising Imperial Airways. "A Len Lye synchronized colour music film. The treatment of this short is similar in theme to his previous films in that it gives unusual colour images set to the rhythm of swing music. It is well designed and makes an interesting novelty." (*Kinematograph Weekly* 15 June 1939.) Patterns painted directly onto the film and synchronized to the tune of "Honolulu Blues."

419   Paper People Land (1600)
Jenkins – ABFD
P:D:S: Cyril Jenkins, A: Margaret Hoyland, Cyril Jenkins, Peter Barker-Mill, M: Matyas Seiber, V: Philip Godfrey, Verses: Wilfred Rolfe
Animated cut-outs. "Decidedly interesting little novelty involving clever use of paper marionettes to real entertainment purposes, including skilful camera work and ingenious choral commentary." (*Today's Cinema* 25 October 1939.) "One of the figures is intended to be a cameraman at a television studio. He shoots a cabaret show which includes singers and dancers, all of whom are paper figures. Ingenious but not particularly entertaining." (*NSTA Review.*) Reissued September 1949.

420   You're Telling Me
G.B. Screen Services
D: A.G. Jackson, A: Anson Dyer, Sid Griffiths, Len Kirley, Laurie Price, Kathleen Murphy, M: Jose Norman
Technicolor
Live action and animation. A visit to the Anson Dyer animation studio to see how a cartoon film is made. The finished example shown at the end of the film is an animated advertisement for Messrs. W.D. and H.O. Wills' "Capstan Cigarettes." Print preserved in the National Film Archive.

421   Oh Whiskers!
GPO Film Unit
P: Alberto Cavalcanti, D:A: Brian Pickersgill
Live action and animated models. Propaganda cartoon for the Ministry of Health illustrating the importance of cleanliness. Print preserved in the National Film Archive.

422   The Obedient Flame
Science Films – British Commercial Gas Association
P: Arthur Elton, D:A: Norman McLaren, C: Frank Goodliffe

Live action and animated diagrams: how the flame of a gas cooker can be adjusted, the working of the modern gas stove, the use of the Regulo device, etc. "Some of the horrors of hand cooking are driven home by speeded-up action which gives an ordinary cake a new and refreshing aspect." (*Documentary Newsletter* January 1940.)

423   Swinging the Lambeth Walk (330)
Realist Films – T.I.D.A.
P: Basil Wright, D:A: Len Lye, M: Noel Gay, MD: Ernst Meyer
Dufaycolor
Abstract animation synchronized to the popular song "The Lambeth Walk," in a jazz rendition. Drawn and painted directly onto film, described on the credits as "Colour Accompaniment by Len Lye." Sponsored by the British Council for the Travel and Industrial Development Association. "This is one of Mr. Lye's screen experiments in setting colour to music. I have poor eyes. In giving me a headache this film may have robbed me of objectivity. I allow its technical interest. I don't see its cultural value at the moment." (*Documentary Newsletter* March 1940.)

424   The Queen Was in the Parlour
Publicity Films
D: Anson Dyer, A: Len Kirley, Laurie Price, Kathleen Murphy, C: Charles Stobbart, V: Albert Whelan
Technicolor
Advertising film for Rinso featuring "Jim Crow."

1940

425 Run Adolf Run
Pathé
D:A: Joe Noble, M: Noel Gay, V: George Elrick
Musical item in *Pathé Gazette* newsreel No. 2; released January 1940. An animated Adolf Hitler in a topical parody of the popular song "Run Rabbit Run." Not reviewed.

426 Follow Me Sing-Song Series
Kimberley — GFD
P: Paul Kimberley
1: The Washing on the Siegfried Line (452), **2: Run Rabbit Run** (564), **3: How Ashamed I Was** (488), **4: South of the Border** (530), **5: Down at the Hole in the Wall** (589), **6: Somewhere in France with You** (485)
Series of six Bouncing Ball sing-song shorts. "The words are shown on the screen, sung and played by a band, to a background of comic drawings. The presentation is bright and the films should be welcomed where community singing is popular." (*Film Report* 13 April 1940.)

427 Musical Poster No. 1 (225)
Crown Film Unit — T.I.D.A.–M.O.I.
D:S:A: Len Lye, M: Ernst Meyer
Technicolor
Abstract animation painted directly onto film and synchronized to jazz music. Propaganda cartoon sponsored by the Ministry of Information. "A fantastic but effective blending of color and sound to draw audience interest to a warning to the public. This message is outlined in bold titles carrying the idea to be careful, 'The Enemy is Listening to You, What you do, Where you live, Where you work.' Short runs less than three minutes, but is highly effective in cautioning the average citizen not to give the enemy any information, carelessly or indirectly." (*Variety* 1941.) Released July 1940.

428   Adolf's Busy Day (750)
Lance White Productions—Anglo American
P:D:S: Lance White (Lawrence Wright)
"The fun starts from the first ring of the alarm clock and continues till the final episode of Adolf's day of raging, parading, and ship-launching is complete. A cartoon of Haw-Haw propaganda with laughs enough to make an efficient counter-attack. Will be welcome everywhere except Germany." (*Kinematograph Weekly* 18 July 1940.) "Burlesque in cartoon form of Hitler's daily plans for world power. The drawings are clever and amusing." (*Film Report* 13 July 1940.)

429   Kitten on the Quay
Ealing Studios—MOF
P: Alberto Cavalcanti, D:S: Robert St. John Cooper, A: Jack Dunkley, Bernard Venables
Propaganda cartoon for the Ministry of Food. Seagull tries to steal a kitten's herring. Not reviewed.

430   I'm Forever Blowing Bubbles
Publicity Films
D: Anson Dyer, A: Len Kirley, Laurie Price, Kathleen Murphy, C: Charles Stobbart
Technicolor
Advertising cartoon for Rinso.

1941

431   The Pocket Cartoon (180)
JWT Productions
D:A: John Halas, Joy Batchelor, S: Alexander Mackendrick
Technicolor
Three-minute satire on the leading political figures of the day. No trace of release or reviews.

432   The Brave Tin Soldier
JWT Productions
D:S:A: John Halas, Joy Batchelor
Technicolor
Animated version of the old fairy story. No trace of release or review.

433   Carnival in the Clothes Cupboard
JWT Productions
P: William Larkins, D: John Halas, Joy Batchelor, S: Alexander Mackendrick, A: John Halas, Joy Batchelor, Vera Linnecar, Kathleen Murphy, Harold Mack, Wally Crook, M: Francis Chagrin
Technicolor
Advertising cartoon for Lever Brothers' Lux Soapflakes.

1942

434 The Fable of the Fabrics
JWT Productions
P: William Larkins, D: John Halas, Joy Batchelor, S: Alexander Mackendrick, A: John Halas, Joy Batchelor, Vera Linnecar, Kathleen Murphy, Wally Crook, M: Francis Chagrin
Technicolor
Advertising cartoon for Lever Brothers' Lux Soapflakes.

435 Filling the Gap (471)
Realist Films—MOI—NSS
P: Frank Sainsbury, Edgar Anstey, D:S: John Halas, Joy Batchelor, A: John Halas, Joy Batchelor, Vera Linnecar, Wally Crook, M: Ernst Meyer
Propaganda film for the Ministry of Agriculture and Fisheries. "It impresses upon the public the necessity of helping out by cultivating allotments and vegetables in their gardens." (*Film Report* 4 April 1942.) Released 6 April 1942.

436 Dustbin Parade (491)
Realist Films—MOI—NSS
P: John Taylor, D:S: John Halas, Joy Batchelor, A: John Halas, Joy Batchelor, Vera Linnecar, Wally Crook, Kathleen Murphy, M: Ernst Meyer
Propaganda film for the Ministry of Information. A bone, an empty tin, and a squeezed toothpaste tube enlist to be turned into a shell, illustrating the message: "Mobilize Your Scrap!" Released 5 October 1942; print preserved in the Imperial War Museum.

437 Digging for Victory (180)
Realist Films—MOI—NSS
D:S: John Halas, Joy Batchelor, A: John Halas, Joy Batchelor, Vera Linnecar, Wally Crook, Kathleen Murphy, M: Matyas Seiber
Propaganda film for the Ministry of Agriculture and Fisheries.

438   Save Your Bacon (125)
MacDougall & Mackendrick – MOI
P:D:S: Roger MacDougall, Alexander Mackendrick
Propaganda cartoon: a farmer appeals for kitchen waste to feed his hungry pigs. Item in *Pathé Gazette;* released 8 October 1942.

439   Little Annie's Rag Book (135)
Rotha Productions – MOI
P: Paul Rotha, D: L. Bradshaw
Animated puppets: propaganda film for the Ministry of Supply. Rubber puppets collect old rags and clothing to help the war effort. Item in *Pathé Gazette;* released 24 December 1942. Print preserved in the National Film Archive.

1943

440   Diphtheria No. 3 (135)
Larkins—MOI
P:D:A: William Larkins
Propaganda film. Animated diphtheria germs infect a child's body.
Item in *Pathé Gazette;* released 29 March 1943. Third in a series made for
the Ministry of Health (the first two contained no animation).

441   Abu Series
AKA: **Middle East Cartoons : Khalil Series**
Halas & Batchelor—MOI
P:D: John Halas, Joy Batchelor, A: John Halas, Joy Batchelor, Vera
Linnecar, Wally Crook, Kathleen Houston, S: Alexander Mackendrick, M:
Matyas Seiber
　　　1: Abu's Dungeon (819), **2: Abu's Poisoned Well** (730), **3: Abu's
Harvest/Khalil Builds a Reservoir, 4: Abu Builds a Dam**
Propaganda cartoons sponsored by the Ministry of Information for
distribution overseas in the Middle East; never shown in Britain. "A series
of cartoons in Arabic directing anti–Nazi propaganda to the peoples of the
Middle East." (*Halas & Batchelor List* 1962.) No. 1 released April 1943; No.
2 released September 1943; Nos. 3 and 4 released 1944.

442   Peak Load 135)
Film Traders—MOI
P: George Hoellering, D:A: Strausfeld
Propaganda cartoon for the Ministry of Fuel and Power. The effects
of using electricity between the peak hours of 8 am to 1 pm. Item in *Pathé
Gazette;* released 8 April 1943.

443   Salvage Saves Shipping (135)
Film Traders—MOI
P: George Hoellering, D:A: Strausfeld
Propaganda cartoon for the Ministry of Supply. How to save paper
and bones in the home, and the products such salvage makes. Item in *Pathé
Gazette;* released 3 June 1943.

444 Contraries (135)

MacDougall & Mackendrick — MOI

P:D:S: Roger MacDougall, Alexander Mackendrick, S: Lewis Carroll

Propaganda cartoon for the Ministry of Supply. Inspired by the poem "The Walrus and the Carpenter," these two characters collect waste paper and point the moral, "Sort Your Salvage." Item in *Pathé Gazette;* released 1 July 1943; print preserved in the National Film Archive.

445 Compost Heaps (135)

Halas & Batchelor — MOI

P:D:S: John Halas, Joy Batchelor, A: John Halas, Joy Batchelor, Vera Linnecar, Wally Crook, V: C.H. Middleton

Propaganda cartoon for the Ministry of Agriculture and Fisheries. Mr. Middleton, the BBC radio gardener, advises on the use of compost heaps. Item in *Pathé Gazette;* released 8 July 1943; reissued 11 May 1944.

446 Diphtheria No. 4 (135)

Larkins — MOI

P:D:A: William Larkins

Propaganda film for the Ministry of Health. Animated diagrams show the effect of diphtheria on small children. Item in *Pathé Gazette;* released 29 July 1943.

447 Model Sorter (135)

Halas & Batchelor — MOI

P:D:S: John Halas, Joy Batchelor, A: John Halas, Joy Batchelor, Vera Linnecar, Wally Crook, V: Cyril Ritchard

Propaganda cartoon for the Ministry of Supply. Released in newsreels, 5 August 1943.

448 I Stopped, I Looked (135)

Halas & Batchelor — MOI

P:D:S: John Halas, Joy Batchelor, A: John Halas, Joy Batchelor, Vera Linnecar, Wally Crook, M: Michael Carr

Propaganda film for the Ministry of War Transport. Released in newsreels, 14 October 1943.

449 Early Digging (135)

Halas & Batchelor — MOI

P:D:S: John Halas, Joy Batchelor, A: John Halas, Joy Batchelor, Vera Linnecar, Wally Crook, M: Matyas Seiber, Arthur Young

Propaganda cartoon for the Ministry of Agriculture and Fisheries. Thwart Jack Frost by digging over your garden earth before the winter. Item in *Pathé Gazette;* released 28 October 1943.

450   Calling Mr. Smith (800)
Polish Film Institute
P: Eugene Cekalski
Dufaycolor
Propaganda film combining live action and animation. "Considering what the Nazis have done one should have no qualms about wiping them out." (*Cambridge Film Festival* 1983.) Print preserved in the National Film Archive.

451   Skeleton in the Cupboard (135)
Film Traders – MOI
P: George Hoellering, D:A: Strausfeld
Propaganda film for the Ministry of Supply. A skeleton visits a cinema where he sees a trailer about bone salvage. He promptly offers himself as bone-meal. Item in *Pathé Gazette;* released 16 December 1943.

452   Bob in the Pound
GB Screen Services – NSS
Propaganda film for the National Savings Committee. A "bouncing ball" singalong cartoon. Print preserved in the National Film Archive.

453   Behind the Clock
JWT Productions
D:A: Anson Dyer
Print preserved in the National Film Archive.

1944

454 The Clothes Moth (135)
Elwis Films – MOI
P:D: Henry Elwis
Propaganda cartoon for the Ministry of Supply. German moth lays eggs marked with a swastika in people's clothes, and helmeted grubs hatch out and eat holes in them. Item in *Pathé Gazette;* released 30 March 1944.

455 Tim Marches Back (135)
Film Traders – MOI
P: George Hoellering, D:A: Strausfeld
Propaganda film for the Post Office. Irresponsible telephone users dance about on the wires, delaying important military calls. Item in *Pathé Gazette;* released 6 April 1944.

456 Leather Must Last (135)
"Make Do and Mend" No. 1
Films of GB – MOI
Propaganda film for the Board of Trade. How to take care of leather shoes. Item in *Pathé Gazette;* released 24 April 1944.

457 Cold Comfort (135)
Halas & Batchelor – MOI
P:D:S: John Halas, Joy Batchelor, A: John Halas, Joy Batchelor, Vera Linnecar, Wally Crook
Propaganda film for Ministry of Fuel and Power. Economize on electricity by not leaving lights or radio sets switched on. Item in *Pathé Gazette;* released 29 April 1944.

458 The Grenade (135)
Giles & Laurence – MOI
P: Lister Laurence, D:A: Carl Giles
Propaganda cartoon. A little hand grenade succeeds in destroying the Nazi Eagle. Item in *Worker and Warfront* No. 1; released April 1944. Print preserved in the National Film Archive.

125

459 From Rags to Stitches (135)
Halas & Batchelor – MOI
P:D:S: John Halas, Joy Batchelor, A: John Halas, Joy Batchelor, Vera Linnecar, Wally Crook
Propaganda film for Ministry of Supply. Factory converts pieces of old rag into uniforms for nurses. Item in *Pathé Gazette;* released 25 May 1944.

460 It Makes You Think (135)
Elwis – MOI
P:D: Henry Elwis
Propaganda film for the Fire Offices Committee. Careless smoker sets fire to a factory, while a farmer's discarded cigarette burns his own cornfield. Item in *Pathé Gazette;* released 29 May 1944.

461 A Ticket's Dream (135)
Elwis – MOI
P:D: Henry Elwis
Propaganda film for the Ministry of Supply. A lazy bus-ticket dreams how it could help to make a cartridge case. Item in *Pathé Gazette;* released 1 June 1944.

462 Blitz on Bugs (135)
Halas & Batchelor – MOI
P:D:S: John Halas, Joy Batchelor, A: John Halas, Joy Batchelor, Vera Linnecar, Wally Crook
Propaganda film for the Ministry of Agriculture and Fisheries. Garden pests devour growing vegetables until they are killed with a spray. Item in *Pathé Gazette;* released 8 June 1944.

463 Spending Money (135)
Propaganda film for National Savings Committee. A girl uses all her money to buy new clothes, while her friend invests in National Savings Certificates. Item in *Pathé Gazette;* released 10 July 1944.

464 Bristles and Brushes (135)
Elwis Films – MOI
P:D: Henry Elwis
Propaganda film for the Ministry of Supply. Neglected brushes are treated and revitalized at the Brush Hospital. Item in *Pathé Gazette;* released 13 July 1944.

465 Bones Bones Bones (135)
Elwis Films – MOI
P:D: Henry Elwis
Propaganda cartoon for the Ministry of Supply. Item in *Pathé Gazette;* released 24 August 1944.

466   One Pair of Nostrils (135)
Giles & Laurence – MOI
P: Lister Laurence, D:S:A: Carl Giles
Propaganda film for the Ministry of Health. Item in *Pathé Gazette;*
released 19 October 1944.

467   Mrs. Sew and Sew (135)
Halas & Batchelor – MOI: "Make Do and Mend" No. 2
P:D:S: John Halas, Joy Batchelor, A: John Halas, Joy Batchelor, Vera
Linnecar, Wally Crook
Propaganda film for the Board of Trade. How to renovate old
clothes. Item in *Pathé Gazette;* released 6 November 1944.

468   Christmas Wishes (135)
Halas & Batchelor – MOI
P:D:S: John Halas, Joy Batchelor, A: John Halas, Joy Batchelor, Vera
Linnecar, Wally Crook
Propaganda film for the General Post Office advising post early for
Christmas. Item in *Pathé Gazette;* released 7 December 1944.

469   A Cautionary Tale (135)
Rotha Productions – MOI
P: Paul Rotha, D:A: Carl Giles, S: E.C. Bentley, V: Stanley Holloway
Propaganda film for the Ministry of Health. A factory worker cuts his
finger and refuses to see a doctor about it. Item in *Worker and Warfront*
No. 8.

1945

470 More Hanky Panky (135)
Dufay Chromex — MOI
D:A: Henry Elwis
Propaganda film for Ministry of Health. Item in newsreels; released 5 February 1945.

471 Robbie Finds a Gun (806)
GB Instructional — GFD
P: Mary Field, D: Anson Dyer, A: Len Kirley
The first entertainment cartoon made specifically for release to Saturday morning Children's Clubs, commissioned by the Children's Film Foundation. "Amusing cartoon of a 'little Fellow' resembling a rabbit who has fun with a catapult. He is carried away by a crow which he has to shoot when he finds a gun, and is dropped into a pond. Good fare for youngsters." (*Today's Cinema* 4 April 1945.)

472 Summer Travelling (135)
Larkins — MOI
P:D: William Larkins, A: Denis Gilpin, DES: Peter Sachs
Propaganda film for the Ministry of War Transport. Item in *Pathé Gazette;* released 6 July 1945.

473 War in the Wardrobe (135)
Larkins — MOI: "Make Do and Mend" No. 3
P:D: William Larkins, A: Denis Gilpin, DES: Peter Sachs
Propaganda film for the Board of Trade. Advice on the destruction of moths. Item in *Pathé Gazette;* released 3 August 1945.

474 The Meco-Noose Power Loader (135)
AKA: **Joy Loader**
P:D: William Larkins
Propaganda film for the Ministry of Fuel and Power.

475   Tombstone Canyon (135)
Dufay Chromex – MOI
D:A: Henry Elwis
Propaganda film for the Ministry of War Transport. Item in newsreels; released 6 September 1945.

476   Writing's Worth While (135)
Dufay Chromex – MOI
D:A: Henry Elwis
Propaganda film for the War Office. Item in newsreels; released 20 December 1945.

477   How a Motor Car Engine Works
Verity Films
P: Sydney Box, D: Maxwell Munden, A: Theodore R. Thumwood
Instructional film for the Ford Motor Company. "It explains entirely by cartoon the function of the cylinders and pistons in making a motor car go. The animation is excellent, and the film is extremely clear and easy to understand." (*Documentary Newsletter* January 1946.)

478   The Big Top
Halas & Batchelor – JWT
D: John Halas, Joy Batchelor, A: John Halas, Joy Batchelor, Vera Linnecar, Wally Crook, M: Francis Chagrin
Dufaycolor
Advertising film for Rinso.

479   Tommy's Double Trouble
Halas & Batchelor – MOI
P:D: John Halas, Joy Batchelor, S: Roger MacDougall, A: John Halas, Joy Batchelor, Vera Linnecar, Wally Crook, Kathleen Houston, M: Matyas Seiber
Instructional film for the War Office. The problems of jungle warfare, and the danger of contracting food poisoning in the Far East.

480   Six Little Jungle Boys
Halas & Batchelor – MOI
P:D: John Halas, Joy Batchelor, S: Roger MacDougall, A: John Halas, Joy Batchelor, Vera Linnecar, Wally Crook, Kathleen Houston, M: Matyas Seiber
Instructional film for the War Office. The danger of soldiers contracting venereal disease in the Far East.

481   Handling Ships
Halas & Batchelor—Admiralty
P: John Halas, Joy Batchelor, D: John Halas, Robert E. Privett, S: Allan Crick, A: Rosalie Crook, Christine Jollow, Vera Linnecar, Elizabeth Williams, Freda Brown, Walter Beaven, Stanley Jackson, Stella Harvey, William Long, Rosalind Rogora, Richard Horn, Patricia Sizer, Edith Hampton, Victor Bevis, Marianne Zeisel, Brenda Phillips, C: Percy Wright, M: Ernst H. Meyer
Technicolor
Instructional film for the Admiralty. The first feature-length cartoon film made in Britain: running time, 65 minutes. "At first thought, animated drawings would seem the only means of showing precisely the right and wrong ways of bringing a ship into harbour. But if the pictures are really to work they must be very slow and smoother than is humanly possible by this method. Hence the technique is used here of combining models with drawings, so that the ships move smoothly, and the wind and tide are represented by symbols. Except for a few fancy feet at the start, every part of the film is insistently lucid. A first rate example of a training film technique." (*Documentary Newsletter* January 1946.)

1946

482 Old Wives' Tales (698)

Halas & Batchelor – MOI

P: John Halas, Joy Batchelor, D: John Halas, S: Joy Batchelor, A: Bob Privett, M: Matyas Seiber

Instructional film for the Ministry of Health. "Cartoon film on health exploding three popular fallacies: (1) Ne'er cast a clout; (2) A little dirt won't hurt you; (3) Night air is dangerous." (*Central Film Library Catalogue* 1961.) Released 15 March 1946.

483 Train Trouble

Halas & Batchelor – JWT

D: John Halas, Joy Batchelor, S: Alexander Mackendrick, A: John Halas, Joy Batchelor, Vera Linnecar, Kathleen Houston, Harold Mack, Wally Crook, DES: John Beavan, M: Francis Chagrin

Technicolor

Advertising film for Kellogg's Corn Flakes. Signalman Squirrel saves a bear from a nasty railway accident, thanks to eating a quick cornflake breakfast.

484 Radio Ructions

Halas & Batchelor – JWT

D: John Halas, Joy Batchelor, S: Joy Batchelor, M: Matyas Seiber, A: John Halas, Joy Batchelor, Vera Linnecar, Wally Crook

Technicolor

Advertising film for Kellogg's Cornflakes.

485 Pacific Thrust (135)

Larkins – MOI

P:D: William Larkins

Propaganda film for the Ministry of Information; item in newsreels.

486   Sparky Goes Shopping (180)
GB Animation/GB Screen Services
P:D: David Hand, S: Ralph Wright, A: John Reed, Bert Felstead
Technicolor
Advertising cartoon for Spa Toothbrushes; the first film made by Gaumont British Animation.

487   The Big Four or What to Eat (857)
Larkins – MOI
P:D: William Larkins, A: Denis Gilpin, DES: Peter Sachs, V: Fred Yule, M: Francis Chagrin
Propaganda film for the Ministry of Food. Man ("nature's masterpiece") requires four essentials: calcium, protein, iron and vitamins. Print preserved in the National Film Archive. Released 3 July 1946.

488   Bee Wise
Analysis Films
P:D: Anson Dyer, A: Len Kirley, M: W.L. Trytel, V: E.V.H. Emmett
Technicolor
Advertising film for Bush Radio. Life in a busy beehive, with the Queen Bee, the Workers, the Drones and the Wee Bees. Print preserved in the National Film Archive.

489   Britain Must Export (135)
Halas & Batchelor – MOI
P:D: John Halas, Joy Batchelor, A: John Halas, Joy Batchelor, Vera Linnecar, Wally Crook
Propaganda film; item in newsreels.

490   Export or Die (135)
Halas & Batchelor – MOI
P:D: John Halas, Joy Batchelor, A: John Halas, Joy Batchelor, Vera Linnecar, Wally Crook
Propaganda film; released 4 August 1946; item in newsreels.

491   Export! Export! Export! (135)
Halas & Batchelor – MOI
P:D: John Halas, Joy Batchelor, A: John Halas, Joy Batchelor, Vera Linnecar, Wally Crook
Propaganda film; item in newsreels.

492   Road Safety (135)
Halas & Batchelor – MOI
P:D: John Halas, Joy Batchelor, A: John Halas, Joy Batchelor, Vera Linnecar, Wally Crook
Propaganda film for the Ministry of Transport; item in newsreels.

493   Coco and the Bear (200)
GB Animation
P:D: David Hand, S: Ralph Wright, A: John Reed, Bert Felstead, Frank Moysey, M: Hans Ward, V: Elisabeth Welch, C: William Traylor
Technicolor
Advertising cartoon for Rowntree's Cocoa showing how Coco, a Negro boy, calms an angry bear with a cup of hot cocoa.

494   Brickmakers (135)
Dufay Chromex–MOI
D:A: Henry Elwis
Propaganda film for the Ministry of Labour; item in newsreels; released 19 August 1946.

495   Join the Army (135)
Larkins–MOI
P:D: William Larkins
Propaganda film for the War Office; item in newsreels; released 29 August 1946.

496   Watch the Fuel Watcher (135)
Dufay Chromex–MOI
D:A: Henry Elwis
Propaganda film for the Ministry of Fuel and Power. Item in newsreels; released 11 November 1946.

497   The King's Men (135)
Larkins–MOI
P:D: William Larkins
Propaganda film for the War Office. Item in newsreels; released 16 December 1946.

498   The Keys of Heaven (135)
Halas & Batchelor–MOI
P:D: John Halas, Joy Batchelor, A: John Halas, Joy Batchelor, Vera Linnecar, Wally Crook
Propaganda film for the P.M.'s Office; item in newsreels released 23 December 1946.

499   Good King Wenceslas
Halas & Batchelor
P:D: John Halas, Joy Batchelor, A: John Halas, Joy Batchelor, Vera Linnecar, Wally Crook
Technicolor
Advertising film for Rinso.

500   Roof Control (135)
Larkins – MOI
P:D: William Larkins
Propaganda film for the Ministry of Fuel and Power; item in newsreels.

501   Trouble in Toytown (546)
Blackheath Film Unit – ROSPA
D:S:A: Dudley Ashton, ED: Ralph Cathles, M: Beryl Price, V: Derek McCulloch
Color
Propaganda film for the Royal Society for the Prevention of Accidents: animated puppets and live action. A small boy sees his toys come to life and enact a drama involving a traffic accident. Narrated by "Uncle Mac" of the BBC radio *Children's Hour*.

502   A Modern Guide to Health (858)
Halas & Batchelor – COI – NSS
P: John Halas, Joy Batchelor, D: Bob Privett, John Halas, A:DES: Joy Batchelor, M: Matyas Seiber, C: Percy Wright
Propaganda film for the Central Council for Health Education. "Here are some first rate tips on good posture, fresh air and exercise, sensible clothing, and sound sleep, presented in a simple style which contrives to be both instructional and entertaining. Elementary but more the wise for that. We have had too many overstuffed films." (*Documentary Newsletter* June 1947.) Released 21 January 1947.

1947

503 Farmyard Rising
British Industrial Films
P: W. Erskine Mayne, John Curthoys, D: Anson Dyer, S: Francis Bieber, V: Mat Mulcaghy
Advertising film for E.T. Green Ltd., economically made with non-animated drawings. Print preserved in the National Film Archive. "Novel technique and a probable record in speedy production are two of the interesting features. The film was made by using over a hundred pencil sketches to illustrate the action." (*Advertiser's Weekly* 11 September 1947.)

504 Smokey Comes Clean (126)
G.B. Animation
P: David Hand, V: Stewart MacPherson
Technicolor
Advertising cartoon for Oxydol.

505 Puddle Trouble (135)
G.B. Animation
P: David Hand
Technicolor
Advertising cartoon.

506 Squirrel War
Analysis Films – GB Instructional – GFD
P:D: Anson Dyer, S: Helen Williams, SC: Mary Cathcart Borer, A: Len Kirley, Harold Whitaker, Laurie Price, Betty Smith, Mollie Zambra, DES: Allan Carter, William Carter, M: Jose Norman
Technicolor
1: The Doll's House (1105), **2: The Storm** (1100), **3: Springtime** (800)
The first cartoon serial, in three ten-minute episodes shown at weekly intervals. Specially made for showing in Saturday morning cinema clubs. Corky the Toymaker's assistant helps Rollo the Red Squirrel and his parrot pal save his nuts from Gringo the Grey Squirrel and his evil accomplice, Brown Rat. "It combines amusement with an instructional in-

sight into the habits of various woodland animals." (*Kinematograph Weekly* 10 April 1947.)

507   The Big City (638)
British Animated Productions—British Lion
"Bubble and Squeek" No. 1
P:S: George Moreno, Jr., D: Harold Mack, A: Harold Mack, Pamela French, Hugh Gladwish, Fred Thompson, M: Jose Norman, V: Jon Pertwee
Technicolor
First of a series starring Bubble the cockney driver and Squeek, his highly animated taxicab, created and designed by an American animator, George Moreno, Jr., a prewar member of the Max Fleischer cartoon studio. "The colour is extremely good, as is the drawing, and the animation and sound effects, if not quite up to the best American standards, are well calculated to please the general run of cartoon lovers." (*Today's Cinema* 30 April 1947.)

508   The Wraggle Taggle Gipsies-O (787)
Diagram Films—GFD: "Let's Sing Together" No. 1
M: Leslie Woodgate
Technicolor
Singalong cartoon made for showing in Saturday morning Children's Clubs. "The fine old songs, arranged and conducted by Leslie Woodgate. Each is sung twice, first with a coloured cartoon, then with the words on the screen so that the children can join in." (*GB Library Catalogue* 1961.)

509   One More River (765)
Science Films—GFD: "Let's Sing Together" No. 2
P: H. Bruce Woolfe, A: Mina Woolfe, Reg Jeffreys, Ken Hardy, M: Leslie Woodgate
Technicolor
Singalong cartoon made for Saturday morning Cinema Clubs. "Leslie Woodgate conducts and arranges the musical score, which is sung twice, first with a coloured cartoon, and then with the words superimposed on the screen so that all the children can join in." (*Watsofilms Catalogue.*)

510   Dashing Away with the Smoothing Iron (653)
Analysis Films—GFD: "Let's Sing Together" No. 3
P:D: Anson Dyer, M: Leslie Woodgate
Technicolor
Singalong silhouette cartoon made for Saturday morning Cinema Clubs. "The words of the old part song, 'Twas on a Monday Morning,' are thrown on the screen and the children are invited to join in the choruses. The song is repeated so often it becomes monotonous." (*Film Report* 27 June 1947.)

511 Heave Away My Johnny (840)
Halas & Batchelor – GFD: "Let's Sing Together" No. 4
P:D: John Halas, Joy Batchelor, S: Joy Batchelor, A: Vera Linnecar,
Wally Crook, Kathleen Houston, DES: John Beavan, C: Percy Wright, M:
Leslie Woodgate
Technicolor
Singalong series made for Saturday morning Cinema Clubs. Cartoon
based on the old-time sea shanty.

512 Who Robbed the Robins? (850)
Analysis Films – GB Instructional – GFD
P:D: Anson Dyer, A: Len Kirley, Harold Whitaker, Laurie Price, John
Garling, Tony Guy, DES: Allan Carter, William Carter
Technicolor
Children's cartoon made for Saturday morning Cinema Clubs. "A col-
oured cartoon introducing Detective Moley, who is called upon to in-
vestigate the stolen eggs from Mrs. Robin. After many exciting events Mr.
Jay is brought to justice." (*Watsofilms Catalogue.*) "The sound is not always
perfectly synchronised with the action." (*Today's Cinema* 15 October 1947.)

513 The Mail Goes Through (800)
Wright – Butcher
P:D:S: Lance White (Lawrence Wright)
"The Pride of Crewe, the famous Royal Mail, speeds along with fear-
less Fred at the controls, and Ernie the Fireman on the alert. Along slithers
a one-cylinder horseless chariot with Percy Vere, famous Eton boy, ex-
pelled, with his companion, the unshaven minion Bill Sykes. There's gold
in the van, and Percy and Bill spot the gleaming swag, as an aeroplane
hovers above with a dangling rope ladder. The climax, after feats of daring
unexampled in the history of banditry, is both amazing and thrilling."
(*Golden Films Catalogue.*) "Animation hardly up to familiar standards, and
gags lacking in humour." (*Today's Cinema* 5 November 1947.)

514 Fun Fair (650)
British Animated Productions – Pathé: "Bubble and Squeek" No. 2
P:S: George Moreno, Jr., D: Harold Mack, A: Harold Mack, Pamela
French, Hugh Gladwish, Fred Thompson, M: Jose Norman, V: Jon Pertwee
Technicolor
Bubble and his cab, Squeek, visit a fun fair and try the coconut shy to
win a new musical motor-horn. One tough nut refuses to fall, but on the
way home Bubble gets a magic ball from a conjurer's booth. Using it to
knock down the nut, the ball explodes, destroying the fun fair, except for
the precious horn! "This specimen registers as a considerable advance in
draughtsmanship and animation on the first one shown, and although its

tale of misfire prowess on the coconut shies of Hampstead Heath is not itself especially amusing, the personalities of Bubble and Squeek emerge as ingratiating and will doubtless develop their comedy appeal." (*Today's Cinema* 19 November 1947.)

515   Coco the Angler (200)
GB Animation
P:D: David Hand, S: Ralph Wright, A: John Reed, Bert Felstead, Frank Moysey, M: Hans Ward, V: Elisabeth Welch, C: William Traylor
Technicolor
Advertising cartoon for Rowntree's Cocoa, featuring "Coco," a Negro boy. One of the first films produced by Gaumont British Animation, set up by film financier J. Arthur Rank at Moor Hall, Cookham, Berkshire, in the charge of David Hand, former animator and director from the Walt Disney Studios.

516   The Cyclist
Larkins – COI
P:D: William Larkins
Propaganda film for the National Savings Committee.

517   The Lincolnshire Poacher (279)
Larkins – COI
P:D: William Larkins, A: Denis Gilpin, Richard Taylor, DES: Peter Sachs, M: Hubert Clifford
Animated version of the traditional song, made for release overseas by the British Council.

518   Widdicombe Fair (508)
Larkins – COI
P:D: William Larkins, A: Denis Gilpin, Richard Taylor, DES: Peter Sachs, M: Hubert Clifford
Animated version of the traditional song, made for overseas release by the British Council.

519   T for Teacher (480)
Larkins – UK Tea Bureau – Voice and Vision
P:D: William Larkins, A: Richard Taylor, Denis Gilpin, DES: Peter Sachs, S: Roger MacDougall, M: Francis Chagrin
Technicolor
Advertising film. "Humorous cartoon showing how to brew a good cup of tea. For training catering and domestic science students. A gay little animated film to instruct without offending." (*Film Sponsor* February 1949.) Released December 1947.

520 This Is the Air Force
Halas & Batchelor — COI
P:D:S: John Halas, Joy Batchelor, A: Vic Bevis, Brian Borthwick, Wally Crook, Kathleen Houston, Vera Linnecar, DES: Bob Privett, Douglas Low, C: Percy Wright, M: Francis Chagrin

521 How an Aeroplane Flies
Shell Film Unit
A: Frances Rodker, A.J. Shaw, C: Sidney Beadle
Instructional film: animated diagrams; sponsored by Shell Petrol.

1948

522 How What and Why Series
Basic Films – GB Instructional – GFD
P: R.K. Neilson-Baxter, D: Kay Mander, A: Cynthia Whitby, Alice Fenvyes, ED: Kitty Marshall
Series of short films including animation sequences, produced for Saturday morning cinema clubs. Sample item: "What Can the Elephant Do With its Trunk."

523 Oxo Parade
Halas & Batchelor
P:D: John Halas, Joy Batchelor, S: Joy Batchelor, A: Wally Crook, Kathleen Houston, Vera Linnecar
Technicolor
Advertising film for Oxo Cubes.

524 Honeybunch and the Giraffe (180)
Publicity Films
M: Hans Ward
Technicolor
Advertising film featuring Honeybunch, a little Negro child; one of a series. Included in the magazine film *Signs of the Times* No. 219. "An engaging cartoon interlude which insinuates that Rowntrees is the cocoa." (*Today's Cinema* 3 March 1948.)

525 Old King Coal (321)
Pinschewer Films – NSS
P:D:A: Julius Pinschewer
Propaganda cartoon for the National Coal Board.

526 Bound for the Rio Grande (970)
GB Animation – GFD: "Let's Sing Together" No. 5
P:D: David Hand, M: Leslie Woodgate, V: The BBC Singers
Technicolor

140

Singalong cartoon made for showing in Saturday morning cinema clubs. "Sung first by BBC vocalists for community singing, cartoons are then used for illustrations, words appear on the screen, and ultimately the children are invited to join in." (*Today's Cinema* 3 March 1948.)

527   Oh No John (675)
GHW Productions – GFD: "Let's Sing Together" No. 6
M: Leslie Woodgate, V: The BBC Singers
Technicolor
Animated puppets: singalong made for showing in Saturday morning cinema clubs. "The BBC Singers render this well-known song. The words are thrown on the screen to enable members to join in, and there is added novelty by the introduction of coloured puppets to illustrate the song." (*Today's Cinema* 10 March 1948.)

528   New Town (805)
Halas & Batchelor – COI: "Charley" No. 1
P:D: John Halas, Joy Batchelor, S: Joy Batchelor, A: Vic Bevis, Brian Borthwick, Wally Crook, Kathleen Houston, Vera Linnecar, C: Percy Wright, M: Matyas Seiber, V: Harold Berens, Jack Train, Dorothy Summers
Technicolor
First of the "Charley" series of propaganda cartoons, made for the Ministry of Town and Country Planning, designed to explain to the public new, postwar social reforms and innovations initiated by the Government. "Charley bicycles along the spacious boulevard of the New Town and con-jures up a picture of the way things used to be. Then he tells how he and his friends decided to put things right by planning and building a new town, which takes shape before our eyes. An inspiring film, amusingly pre-sented." (*NSTA Review.*) Released 15 March 1948.

529   Atomic Physics
GB Instructional – GB Animation
P: Frank Wells, D: Derek Mayne, AD: David Hand
Instructional film with animated sequences produced by the GB Animation Unit.

530   Your Very Good Health (806)
Halas & Batchelor – COI: "Charley" No. 2
P:D: John Halas, Joy Batchelor, S: Joy Batchelor, A: Vic Bevis, Brian Borthwick, Wally Crook, Kathleen Houston, Vera Linnecar, C: Percy Wright, M: Matyas Seiber, V: Harold Berens
Technicolor
Propaganda cartoon made for the Ministry of Health. "Charley has the workings of the Ministry of Health explained to him, and is shown how

the main services work. He is told of some of the many benefits of the scheme, including free medical treatment of all kinds, improved maternity and child welfare services, and the establishment of health centres as building allows." (*NSTA Review.*) Released April 1948.

531   Charley's March of Time (832)
Halas & Batchelor – COI: "Charley" No. 3
P:D:A: John Halas, Joy Batchelor, A: Vic Bevis, Brian Borthwick, Wally Crook, Kathleen Houston, Vera Linnecar, C: Percy Wright, M: Matyas Seiber, V: Harold Berens
Technicolor
Propaganda film for the Ministry of National Insurance. "Charley is told of the benefits which he and his family will derive after 1 July 1948. He dislikes the regular payment part of it and is taken back to the beginning of time when a helpless amoeba is chased by a large fish. It reaches land safely and finds security. Charley is next seen as a prehistoric man and once again finds security, this time in a cave. In the Middle Ages a castle spells safety to Charley and his family. So he journeys through the centuries. In the nineteenth century he is the recipient of an industrial accident but receives no compensation. The tempo quickens, 1911, the first National Insurance Act, the Beveridge Report, the 1948 Act. Charley decides it is a good thing after all." (*NSTA Review.*) Released May 1948.

532   The Thames (799)
GB Animation – GFD: "Musical Paintbox" No. 1
P: David Hand, D: G. Henry Stringer, S: Ralph Wright, R.A.G. Clark, A: Peter Jay, Brian O'Hanlon, Waclaw Machan, Andre Amstutz, Deryck Foster, M: Henry Reed
Technicolor
First entertainment cartoon produced by the J. Arthur Rank Gaumont British Animation studio under the Disney animator, David Hand. Described as a "Sketchbook Fantasy" this was a series of still drawings combined with limited animation. "The subject of this completely novel technicolor cartoon is the Thames, and the journey from the source to Southend Pier contains clever hand-painted impressions of the popular beauty spots and show places. These are bound by effective vocal and orchestral accompaniment. The new idea is neatly exploited, yet still leaves tremendous room for expansion." (*Kinematograph Weekly* 10 July 1948.) "We hear the song, 'Old Father Thames,' and pass from the trickling source to Magdalene Tower at Oxford. We glide on to Henley Regatta, meet the ghost of the Vicar of Bray, and then pass the playing fields of Eton. At Runnymede, King John signs the Magna Carta, at Hammersmith the Boat Race is won. Slowly the cartoon slides through London and ends up jovially on crowded Southend Pier. Charming and original." (*NSTA Review.*)

533 Wales (738)

GB Animation – GFD: "Musical Paintbox" No. 2

P: David Hand, D: C. Henry Stringer, S: Ralph Wright, Nicholas Spargo, A: Waclaw Machan, Brian O'Hanlon, Peter Jay, Andre Amstutz, Deryck Foster, M: Henry Reed, V: Trefor Jones

Technicolor

"The Land of the Leeks, needless to say, is the happy hunting ground of this cartoon. Here again still life drawings are employed, and the highlight is a clever satire on the famous legend of Devil's Bridge. The second of the series, it is an improvement on the first and is clear proof that the new Rank cartoon organisation is on its toes." (*Kinematograph Weekly* 7 October 1948.) "A typical Welsh public house which contains pictures around the walls of Welsh beauty spots. The Welsh legend of Devil's Bridge is brought to life with cartoon characters. Excellent, beautiful, humorous, the best of David Hand's to date." (*NSTA Review.*)

534 The Lion (756)

GB Animation – GFD: "Animaland" No. 1

P: David Hand, D: Bert Felstead, S: Pete Griffiths, Ralph Wright, A: Stan Pearsall, Ted Percival, Bill Hopper, John Wilson, Chick Henderson, M: Henry Reed, V: Richard Goolden

Technicolor

First of the Gaumont British Animation series, "Animaland." "Technicolor cartoon illustrating a hunter's treatise on the King of the Beasts. The hunter finishes up as Mr. Leo's main meat course, but before he does his observations are laughably illustrated. The only fault here, and that's slight, is facetious commentary." (*Kinematograph Weekly* 7 October 1948.)

535 The House Cat (707)

GB Animation – GFD: "Animaland" No. 2

P: David Hand, D: Bert Felstead, S: Ralph Wright, Reg Parlett, R.A.G. Clarke, A: Frank Moysey, Arthur Humberstone, Bill Hopper, Chick Henderson, Ted Percival, M: Henry Reed, V: Richard Goolden, the Radio Revellers

"Technicolor cartoon satirising the habits and love life of the common moggy. Animation good, gags neat, and colour work excellent, but commentary a trifle strained. Overall impression first rate." (*Kinematograph Weekly* 7 October 1948.)

536 Robinson Charley (930)

Halas & Batchelor – COI: "Charley" No. 4

P:D:S: John Halas, Joy Batchelor, A: Vic Bevis, Brian Borthwick, Wally Crook, Kathleen Houston, Vera Linnecar, M: Matyas Seiber

Technicolor

Propaganda cartoon for the Central Office of Information. "Charley develops the practice of trading produce he has grown for commodities from neighboring countries. He soon finds that it is easier to trade than to grow, and determines to make it his business. Charley becomes wealthy but two wars knock him completely over and he is broke. A relative, Uncle Sam, lends him money until he can pay his own way. He is told to put his back into it so that he can pay his own way in the future. Informative cartoon, timely and colourful." (*NSTA Review.*) "Familiar but effective propaganda." (*Film Report* 5 November 1948.)

537 Men of Merit (400)

Larkins – BEDA – NSS

P:D: William Larkins, S: Roger MacDougall, DES: Peter Sachs, Nancy Hanna, A: Richard Taylor, M: Francis Chagrin, V: Geoffrey Sumner

Technicolor

Propaganda cartoon. "In its mixture of drawings and puppetry the film is fresh and original, eschewing the Disney beaten track. The puppet professor, whose lecture on electricity forms the theme of the film, is particularly attractive, white-haired, purple-faced, dignified (a soupcon of Colonel Chinstrap here?). The commentary in rhymed couplets (of James Watt: "What he thought of – was a locomotof!") neatly ties up this engaging and witty little effort." (*Film Sponsor* January 1949.) Trade show 25 November 1948.

538 The Old Manor House (700)

British Animated Productions – Pathé: "Bubble and Squeek" No. 3

P:S: George Moreno, Jr., D: Harold Mack, A: Harold Mack, Pamela French, Hugh Gladwish, Fred Thompson, M: Jose Norman, V: Jon Pertwee

Technicolor

"A blimpish mouse lives in a two-centuries empty manor house, and tries to protect it against the intrusion of Bubble and Squeek. The usual ghosts and firing of cannons all created by the house protector successfully frighten the trespassers away." (*NSTA Review.*) "Animation is good and the ingenuity of the gags will amuse most audiences." (*Today's Cinema* 3 November 1948.)

539 The Cuckoo (659)

GB Animation – GFD: "Animaland" No. 3

P: David Hand, D: Bert Felstead, S: Ralph Wright, Reg Parlett, M: Henry Reed, V: Richard Goolden, the Radio Revellers

Technicolor

"A cuckoo is seen robbing a nest and inserting her own egg in the home of a house sparrow. The bird when hatched is very ugly and a bully. It ventures abroad and gets into mischief, meanwhile the small sparrow is caught by a weasel and put into his soup pot to boil. The greedy cuckoo steals the pot from the fire, and discovers the sparrow who escapes. The weasel returns, finds the cuckoo with the pot, and a chase ensues to the joy of the little sparrow. About average. These Hand cartoons lack good humour." (*NSTA Review.*) Trade show 3 November 1948. Shown March 1948.

540   Old English Cartunes Series
GB Animation – Technical & Scientific Films
P: David Hand, S: Ralph Wright, V: the Radio Revellers
Technicolor
1: Oh Dear What Can the Matter Be? (193), **2: Tavern in the Town, 3: A Lover and His Lass**
Series of three advertising cartoons for Esso Petrol, made for the Anglo-American Oil Company, set to a background of Old English songs sung by the popular broadcasting group, the Radio Revellers. "The theme running through them is that of a demure little she-cat in love with a peculiar long-eared dog (!) who loves his car best. This car keeps breaking down until the cat has the bright idea of filling it up with Esso, which sends her stock up enormously." (*Film Sponsor* February 1949.) Shown September 1947.

541   The Platypus (713)
GB Animation – GFD: "Animaland" No. 4
P: David Hand, D: Bert Felstead, S: Ralph Wright, Reg Parlett, A: Stan Pearsall, Bill Hopper, Arthur Humberstone, George Jackson, M: Henry Reed, V: Dick Bentley
Technicolor
"The platypus, a native of Australia, is chosen to be portrayed in David Hand's new series. The animals' various habits are explained and pictures before a male and female of the species form an affection for each other, and we watch the amorous pursuit by the male. Delightfully produced but lacking in humour." (*NSTA Review.*) Trade show 8 January 1949.

542   Timber!
Publicity Films – Stratford Abbey: "Adventures of Soupy" No. 1
P:D: Anson Dyer, A: Len Kirley, Laurie Price, Harold Whitaker, John Garling, M: Jose Norman
Technicolor
First in a series of advertising cartoons for Symington's Soups. "Series of colour cartoons in which Soupy gets himself into various difficult situations but always gathers enough strength from a good draught of Symington's Soup to extricate himself. Soupy himself, who originated in the film, has now been made the central figure of the firm's advertising in all

media, and plastic figures have been made of him for display purposes."
(*Film Sponsor* February 1949.)

543 Jump to It
    Publicity Films – Stratford Abbey: "Adventures of Soupy" No. 2
    P:D: Anson Dyer, A: Len Kirley, Laurie Price, Harold Whitaker, John
Garling, M: Jose Norman
    Technicolor
    Advertising cartoon for Symington's Soups. Soupy fails at pole vault-
ing and tightrope walking until a bowl of hot soup gives him renewed
strength. Print preserved in the National Film Archive.

544 Loch Ness Legend (663)
    British Animated Productions – Pathé
    P:S: George Moreno, Jr., D: Harold Mack, A: Fred Thompson,
Pamela French, Harold Mack, M: Jose Norman
    Technicolor
    "Warned at breakfast by a squirrel, the Colonel finds people and
even the hills running away in a panic, and decides to catch the Loch Ness
Monster himself. Frenzied and grotesque technique, lacking American
standards of mobility, but possibly acceptable by uncritical and juvenile
audiences." (*Kinematograph Weekly* 3 January 1957.) Reissued December
1956 by Butcher's Films.

545 Home Sweet Home (673)
    British Animated Productions – Pathé: "Bubble and Squeek" No. 4
    P:S: George Moreno, Jr., D: Harold Mack, A: Hugh Gladwish,
Pamela French, Jimmie Holt, Harold Mack, M: Jose Norman
    Technicolor
    "Tramp spaniel shown compassion arouses Squeek's jealousy and is
kicked out, but returns to share home comfort. What animal or object
Squeek is based on is puzzling, and the feverish speed and lack of subtlety
do not help the distortion of the characters. Handy for children, but well
below the creative slickness of today's average cartoon fare." (*Kinematograph Weekly* 3 January 1957.) Reissued December 1956 by Butcher's Films.

546 Just Janie (200)
    Larkins
    P:D: William Larkins
    Advertising cartoon for Halex Toothbrushes. "Chief character is Janie
who doesn't like her bristly toothbrush which scratches her mouth, but
loves brushing her teeth with the new kind with rondated bristles. Commentary is rhymed couplets and winds up with the following: 'Brush,
brush, brush your teeth,/ On top and underneath,/A Halex brush in very
truth,/ Safeguards every tiny tooth.'" (*Film Sponsor* February 1949.) Released August 1948.

1949

547 Somerset (733)

GB Animation – GFD: "Musical Paintbox" No. 3

P: David Hand, D: Pat Griffin, S: Nicholas Spargo, Pete Griffiths, M: Henry Reed, V: Bernard Miles, Ian Wallace

Technicolor

"This musical cartoon deals with the beauty and fables of Somerset. Several of the county's famous songs, including 'Strawberry Fair,' 'Somerset Farmer,' 'What Shall We Do With the Drunken Sailor,' and 'Up From Somerset' provide cheerful accompaniment for local legends and colourful characters." (*Kinematograph Weekly* 17 March 1949.) "We see a typical Somerset landscape and travel along to a gypsy encampment, where a woman is crystal gazing. A number of sequences in the crystal are recalled and include shots of Bath to the music of 'Strawberry Fair,' parallels between humans and animals to the words of 'Somerset Farmer,' the Wookey Hall Hole Caves, the local legend being related, Cabot Tower, Bristol Docks . . . Attractively presented but desires humour." (*NSTA Review.*) Trade Show 28 February 1949.

548 Going Up

Publicity Films – Stratford Abbey: "Adventures of Soupy" No. 3

P:D: Anson Dyer, A: Len Kirley, Harold Whitaker, John Garling, Tony Guy, M: Jose Norman

Technicolor

Advertising cartoon for Symington's Soups. "Soupy is climbing a mountain but gets into terrible difficulties. He comes down to earth long enough to drink soup, then hares up to the top with extreme rapidity." (*Film Sponsor* March 1949.)

549 No Fishing 198)

Publicity Films – Stratford Abbey: "Adventures of Soupy" No. 4

P:D: Anson Dyer, A: Len Kirley, Harold Whitaker, John Garling, Tony Guy, M: Jose Norman

Technicolor

Advertising cartoon for Symington's Soups. "Soupy blows a hole in the ice with a fuse and sits fishing. A huge fish comes out of the hole and pursues him, actually chasing him into the hole. Soupy comes out pale green with cold to find the Symington waiter in charge of plates of soup. He drinks it and gradually his colour returns to normal." (*Film Sponsor* March 1949.) Released October 1947.

550   Dolly Put the Kettle On (207)
Halas & Batchelor
P:D: John Halas, Joy Batchelor, S: Joy Batchelor, A: Wally Crook, Kathleen Houston, Vera Linnecar, M: George Ranky, V: Neal Arden
Technicolor
Advertising cartoon for Brooke Bond Tea. "Colour cartoon on pretty rather than comedy lines. Two dolls, Jane and Gwen, are rivals for the hand of a Teddy Bear. Jane woos him with tea and shows him her dividend card, full except for one coupon which is on the packet. Gwen, wild with jealousy, cuts it off the packet and is overwhelmed by the avalanche of tea which bursts out. Her guilt is discovered and the card completed. 'So Jane and Ben forgive their friend,/ And bring you to the Divid- End!'" (*Film Sponsor* April 1949.)

551   Charley's Black Magic (800)
Halas & Batchelor – COI: "Charley" No. 5
P:D:S: John Halas, Joy Batchelor, A: Douglas Low, Vic Bevis, Brian Borthwick, Wally Crook, Kathleen Houston, Vera Linnecar, M: Matyas Seiber, V: Harold Berens
Technicolor
Propaganda cartoon for the Central Office of Information. "Coal is again the subject of this propaganda film. It explains the reason for the present high prices of coal and how the long-term policy of reorganization and mechanization of industry will ultimately result in cheaper coal, which in turn will mean cheaper goods for the home and export markets." (*Film Report* 15 April 1949.)

552   The Ostrich (741)
GB Animation – GFD: "Animaland" No. 5
P: David Hand, D: Bert Felstead, S: Ralph Wright, Reg Parlett, A: John Wilson, Frank Moysey, Chick Henderson, Ted Percival, M: Henry Reed, V: Radio Revellers
Technicolor
"The adult ostrich is said to be a stupid bird, but when young it appears to be quite sensible. The cartoon depicts the nightmare adventures of a foolish father bird and his new offspring in an Ancient Egyptian setting. Quite amusing. This series is improving." (*NSTA Review.*) "This presents a

laboured recital of the antics of an ostrich in the Egyptian desert. Animation, music and colour are first rate, but the basic idea lacks vitality." (*Today's Cinema* 27 April 1949.)

553   Fantasy on Ireland (737)
GB Animation – GFD: "Musical Paintbox" No. 4
P: David Hand, D: G. Henry Stringer, A: Brian O'Hanlon, S: Anthony Benton, M: Henry Reed, V: Ian Wallace
Technicolor
"David Hand cartoon presenting amiable caricatures of the Hibernian scene further enlivened by a variety of national airs. Pleasant of its type." (*Today's Cinema* 27 April 1949.) "Abstract cartoon impressions on popular Irish melodies, using colour and rhythm to great effect. Mainly for aesthetic tastes." (*Film Report* 29 April 1949.)

554   What's Cooking? (220)
Halas & Batchelor
P:D: John Halas, Joy Batchelor, S: Joy Batchelor, A: Wally Crook, Kathleen Houston, Vera Linnecar, C: Percy Wright, M: Francis Chagrin, V: Fred Yule
Technicolor
Advertising cartoon for Bovril. "A housewife comes out of a cookery book and wonders what she is going to have for dinner. The vegetables come to life and start marching across the kitchen. They are stopped by the potato who asks, 'Where's the flavour?' All search round the kitchen. The potato finds the Bovril in the cupboard and fetches the others. We see the housewife stirring a large stew saying, 'Remember Bovril stands for flavour!'" (*Film Sponsor* May 1949.) Released October 1947.

555   Doolittle Makes Good (198)
Signal Films – JWT
P: Gerard Holdsworth, C: Frank Hendrix
Technicolor
Animated puppets; advertising film for Horlicks Malted Milk. First of several British films made by this company, who brought a number of George Pal's former animators and technicians to England to make the films. "Rather reminiscent of George Pal's films. Doolittle is a character born too tired to get anything done until, in his middle age, he discovers Horlicks and at once becomes a great success." (*Film Sponsor* May 1949.) Released March 1948.

556   Top o' the Morning (200)
Signal Films – JWT
P: Gerard Holdsworth, C: Frank Hendrix
Technicolor

Animated puppets; advertising film for Horlicks. "A Swiss mountain setting with Hansel, an extremely tired mountaineer, unable to cope with his job until a glass of Horlicks every night sends him dashing to the heights." (*Film Sponsor* May 1949.) Released August 1948.

557 Mousewife's Choice (200)
Signal Films – JWT
P: Gerard Holdsworth, C: Frank Hendrix
Technicolor
Animated puppets; advertising film for Persil. "Mother Mousey does her washing, hangs it up, then goes off to do shopping. She goes into a human kitchen to pick up crumbs, then passes some washing on a clothes-line which is dazzling white, putting her own clothes to shame. She is thoroughly depressed until she finds a packet of Persil, then reads what is on it. Next we see her back in her own little house, where her four children are all dressed in dazzling white aprons. The soundtrack is sung on *Silly Symphony* lines." (*Film Sponsor* May 1949.)

558 A Change for the Better
Signal Films
P: Gerald Holdsworth, D: Frank Hendrix, V: Stanley Holloway
Technicolor
Animated puppets: advertising film for the Cooperative Wholesale Society.

559 Long Long Ago (900)
Basic Films
P: R.K. Neilson-Baxter, S:A: Cynthia Whitby, M: Francis Chagrin, V: Harold Reese
Technicolor
Propaganda film for the British Gas Council. "Cartoon story of the very early days of the world, its strange monsters and primeval forests that gave rise to the coal seams of today. Mildly amusing for young children but not recommended otherwise." (*Film Sponsor* June 1949.)

560 A Yorkshire Ditty (785)
GB Animation – GFD: "Musical Paintbox" No. 5
P: David Hand, D: C. Henry Stringer, S: Ralph Wright, A: Waclaw Machan, Peter Jay, Andre Amstutz, John Woodward, M: Henry Reed
Technicolor
"A series of colourful drawings depicting the county of Yorkshire, representing the light and shade between the countryside and the rather grim mill towns. The story, which is suggested by the song 'On Ilkley Moor Baht 'At,' is brought to life and we see the romance of Mary Jane. Artistic, colourful and clever, but lacking in popular entertainment value." (*NSTA Review.*) Trade show 10 June 1949.

561   A Clean Sweep (200)
GB Animation
P: David Hand, V: Stewart MacPherson
Technicolor
Advertising cartoon for Oxydol, featuring "Smut and Snowy." Released June 1949.

562   Snowy Cleans Up (200)
GB Animation
P: David Hand, V: Stewart MacPherson
Technicolor
Advertising cartoon for Oxydol, featuring "Smut and Snowy." Released September 1949.

563   Willie Does His Stuff (352)
Pinschewer Films — NSS
P:D:A: Julius Pinschewer
Technicolor
Propaganda film for National Savings. "It was an excellent notion to use Willie, the famous white elephant of the posters, as a film character, but it was a pity to reform him straight away into a sterling, right living, everyday grey elephant bereft of his coy charm, leading the youth of Britain in a triumphant chorus on to ever-increasing savings. Nevertheless, the film is very pleasing, and both colour and animation are excellent. Also it has one other merit which renders it outstanding, there is no commentary but it achieves its effect by music." (*Film Sponsor* July 1949.) Print preserved in the National Film Archive.

564   Farmer Charley (886)
Halas & Batchelor — COI: "Charley" No. 6
P:D:S: John Halas, Joy Batchelor, A: Douglas Low, Bob Privett, Wally Crook, Vera Linnecar, Vic Bevis, Brian Borthwick, Kathleen Houston, Elizabeth Williams, John Beavan, ED: Jack King, C: William Traylor, M: Matyas Seiber, V: Harold Berens, Stephen Jack
Technicolor
Propaganda film for the Ministry of Agriculture. "Charley is left a half interest in his uncle's farm, and he leaves his job as a garage mechanic for the land. His cousin takes him around various jobs on his first day. It is a long day, and he has to work very hard. That evening Charley decides that he is better fitted for his old job, and that farming is after all a skilled job, particularly as agriculture has a target to maintain so that people can be adequately fed." (*NSTA Review.*) Released 11 July 1949.

565   It's a Lovely Day (740)
   GB Animation – GFD: "Animaland" No. 6
   P: David Hand, D: Bert Felstead, S: Ralph Wright, Pete Griffiths, R.A.G. Clarke, A: Stan Pearsall, Bill Hopper, Arthur Humberstone, George Jackson, M: Henry Reed
   Technicolor
   "First of a new series of David Hand *Animaland* cartoons in technicolor, this amusing whimsy presents the piscatorial pranks of Ginger Nutt, the little red squirrel, who falls foul of Corny Crow, Dusty Mole, and Loopy Hare. Although it breaks no new ground, either in comedy or cartoon craft, the material has a certain inventiveness in imagination narration and quite definite skill in animation and colour treatment, indicating light-hearted cartoon fare of established pattern." (*Today's Cinema* 10 August 1949.) "Dusty is given the dirty work to do and burrows underground, emerging in the stream underwater, where he ties an old boot in Ginger's line. A large fish intervenes and upsets the plan. Dusty, in trouble, cries for help, and finally he, together with Loopy and Corny, are carried downstream, leaving Ginger in peace to carry on with his fishing." (*NSTA Review.*)

566   Sketches of Scotland (823)
   GB Animation – GFD: "Musical Paintbox" No. 6
   P: David Hand, D: G. Henry Stringer, S: Nicholas Spargo, A: Peter Jay, John Woodward, Deryck Foster, John Worsley, M: Henry Reed, V: John Laurie
   Technicolor
   "This issue of the Musical Paintbox series goes to the Scottish Highlands to the tune of 'Annie Laurie,' which changes to 'A Hundred Pipers and A,' played by a band of Scottie dogs and a comical Scotsman. The Scotty dog has a macabre dream and we see him leading a batallion of other dogs against a fort, the front of which resembles a nightmarish cat. Weird figures spring out at him and he rushes back to his kennel. An old crofter shows us his home and reminisces before finally he and his friends leave us with the singing of 'Auld Lang Syne.' Attractive and arty, but this series is not slick enough to please everyone." (*NSTA Review.*) Trade show 15 September 1949.

567   Cornwall (724)
   GB Animation – GFD: "Musical Paintbox" No. 7
   P: David Hand, D: Pat Griffin, S: Anthony Benton, A: Waclaw Machan, M: Henry Reed
   Technicolor
   "This cartoon opens in a typical Cornish fishing village. Passing a tin mine and china clay works, we follow a rainbow down to the little town of Helston. The characters in an antique shop's window come to life and

dance the Helston Furry Dance. We go to the church of St. Neot and the legend of St. Neot and the Well is related. Visiting the Cornish coast, ghost smugglers appear to the tune of 'Blow the Man Down.' The last scene shows a signpost at sunset pointing to Lands End." (*NSTA Review.*) Trade show 14 October 1949.

568   The Birth of Local Government
AKA: **Local Government, a History in Pictures**
Larkins – COI
P:D: William Larkins, A: Denis Gilpin, Richard Taylor, DES: Peter Sachs, V: Geoffrey Sumner
Technicolor
Propaganda cartoon for the Ministry of Health. "A cartoon sketching the growth of local government in England. A procession of still pictures in cinematograph treatment. The story opens in early Saxon England and shows how the community gather round the local well to discuss their problems and needs. From such gatherings emerged the common assembly of burgesses. Not animated. Very dull." (*NSTA Review.*) Trade show 2 November 1949.

569   Ginger Nutt's Bee Bother (727)
GB Animation – GFD: "Animaland" No. 7
P: David Hand, D: Bert Felstead, S: Reg Parlett, R.A.G. Clarke, A: Stan Pearsall, Frank Moysey, John Wilson, Bill Hopper, M: Henry Reed
Technicolor
"Ginger Nutt receives a letter from his girl friend Hazel, which arranges a meeting. He tears up the letter but Corny Crow puts it together and reads it. He calls Loopy Hare and Dusty Mole and they read that Hazel asks for flowers. Ginger goes to gather some but a bee is disturbed by Dusty who pulls all the flowers through the earth from under ground. The bee chases Dusty up and down his burrows, but the mole evades his pursuer and joins his friends in time to watch Ginger about to present a bouquet to Hazel. Dusty burrows again and snaps off the flower heads. The bee at this moment again finds and stings Dusty, who shoots into the air scattering the flowers which fall around the delighted Hazel." (*NSTA Review.*) Trade show 25 November 1949.

570   R.A.F. – First Line of Defence (490)
Halas & Batchelor – COI – NSS
P:D:S: John Halas, Joy Batchelor, A: Bob Privett, Vic Bevis, Brian Borthwick, Wally Crook, Kathleen Houston, Vera Linnecar, DES: Douglas Low, M: Francis Chagrin, Central Band of the RAF
Technicolor
Propaganda film for the Air Ministry. "This brief little effort intended for Royal Air Force recruiting, which describes flying from its earliest days,

shows the producers to have everything they need in the way of wit (Icarus comes to grief under the boiling sun to the tune of 'If I Only Had Wings'!), style, and originality. They are among the very few of their kind who are not influenced by Walt Disney." (*Film Sponsor* February 1950.) Trade show 5 December 1949.

571 Ginger Nutt's Christmas Circus (660)
GB Animation – GFD: "Animaland" No. 8
P: David Hand, D: Bert Felstead, S: Pete Griffiths, Reg Parlett, A: Stan Pearsall, Frank Moysey, John Wilson, Arthur Humberstone, M: Henry Reed
Technicolor
"Boko the parrot gatecrashes the circus by using Willie Weasel's ticket. Ginger is ringmaster and has all the animals in the ring. Willie finally manages to get in without a ticket and chases Boko who has been interrupting the show. The parrot escapes and chases into Corny Crow's human cannonball, hotly pursued by Willie. The gun is fired and they both hurtle through space and land in the snow outside. Dusty Mole pops up and plants a notice saying 'Peace on Earth.' Willie is determined on revenge and grabs it to hit Chester Cat. One of David Hand's best efforts to date, quicker and more humorous." (*NSTA Review.*) Trade show 6 December 1949. It reintroduced all the characters from the *Animaland* series including the Cuckoo, Digger and Dinkum the platypusses, Zimmy Lion and Oscar Ostrich.

572 Canterbury Road (770)
GB Animation – GFD: "Musical Paintbox" No. 8
P: David Hand, D: Brian O'Hanlon, M: Henry Reed
Technicolor
"This opens to the tune of 'Greensleeves' and a book is shown dealing with the road from Winchester to Canterbury, and the pilgrims who followed it. Then the pages seem to be missing and the narrator turns to his inspiration to show the history. The first legend is about a maiden, her lover, and a wicked king. The narrator then produces Titus, a pilgrim, who tells the story of Alfred the barrel-maker and Nicholas the astrologer. They both love Alison, the only girl for miles around, who in turn loves both men. Finally we see a view of Canterbury cathedral." (*NSTA Review.*) Trade show 9 December 1949.

573 Water for Firefighting (4850)
Halas & Batchelor – COI
P: John Halas, Joy Batchelor, D: John Halas, Allan Crick, S: Allan Crick, Bob Privett, DES: Bob Privett, A: Bob Privett, Vic Bevis, Brian Borthwick, M: Ernst Meyer
Technicolor

Feature-length instructional film for the Home Office and the Fire Brigade. "Here we have model fire appliances combined with diagram to explain the behaviour of water and help the firefighter in calculating resistances and pressures so that he can direct the right supply of water to the right spot." (*Monthly Film Bulletin* January 1950.)

574 Charley Junior's Schooldays (820)
Halas & Batchelor—COI: "Charley" No. 7
P:D: John Halas, Joy Batchelor, S: Joy Batchelor, A: Vic Bevis, Brian Borthwick, Wally Crook, Kathleen Houston, Vera Linnecar, M: Matyas Seiber
Technicolor
Propaganda film for the Ministry of Education. "Charley junior, waiting in the clouds to be born, is told about his future schooldays by a celestial nursemaid. He hears about the different types of school that will be available for him, and about the differences in education between his own day and that of his father. A separate edition is issued in Scotland, adapted in cooperation with the Scottish Education Department." (*Central Film Library Catalogue* 1961.) "This is perhaps the best and unhappily, looks like being the last of a lively series." (*Monthly Film Bulletin* January 1950.)

575 Fly About the House (778)
Halas & Batchelor—COI—NSS
P:D: John Halas, Joy Batchelor, S: Joy Batchelor, A: Bob Privett, Wally Crook, Vera Linnecar, Brian Borthwick, Vic Bevis, C: William Traylor, M: Francis Chagrin, ED: Jack King
Technicolor
Propaganda film for the Ministry of Health. "Humorous cartoon fable about the dangers of leaving food or garbage where flies can get to it. The lesson is a little hard to follow, but technically this is the most mature of Halas-Batchelor propaganda films and quite entertaining." (*Film Sponsor* April 1950.) "The character given to the film by viewing everything from fly level is neat and effective. But the overall story is a bit muddled. One fly, even in cartoon, tends to look very much like another fly." (*Monthly Film Bulletin* January 1950.)

576 The Magic Canvas (835)
Halas & Batchelor—Apex
P:D:S: John Halas, Joy Batchelor, DES: Peter Foldes, A: Wally Crook, M: Matyas Seiber, Blech String Quartet
Technicolor
Halas and Batchelor's first nonsponsored entertainment film. "A symbolistic film of the creative spirit and its liberation from the forces that stifle free expression." (*Halas & Batchelor Catalogue*.) "It is a courageous attempt by the makers to please themselves." (*Monthly Film Bulletin* January 1950.)

577   A Well Kept Machine (90)
Halas & Batchelor – COI
P:D: John Halas, Joy Batchelor, M: George Ranky
Propaganda film for the Central Office of Information designed to encourage productivity.

578   A Little Forethought (90)
Halas & Batchelor – COI
P:D: John Halas, Joy Batchelor, M: George Ranky
Propaganda film for the Central Office of Information designed to encourage productivity.

579   A Better Spirit (90)
Halas & Batchelor – COI
P:D: John Halas, Joy Batchelor, M: George Ranky
Propaganda film for the Central Office of Information designed to encourage productivity.

580   Start with What Is Under Your Nose (90)
Halas & Batchelor – COI
P:D: John Halas, Joy Batchelor, M: George Ranky
Propaganda film for the Central Office of Information designed to encourage productivity.

581   And Now Today (900)
Basic Films
P: R.K. Neilson-Baxter, S:A: Cynthia Whitby, M: Francis Chagrin, V: Harold Reese
Technicolor
Educational film for the British Gas Council, the sequel to *Long Long Ago* (1948) and released in tandem with it under the overall title of *The ABC of Gas*. "Designed primarily for the younger age groups. A brief introduction explains in a simple way the evolution of coal from the giant prehistoric forests. The film then shows how modern industry transforms coal into gas, coke and other valuable products." (*Central Film Library Catalogue* 1951.)

582   Cartoonland (1600)
AKA: **Make Believe**
Chalfont Productions – New Realm
P: Bill MacDonnell, D:S:C: Eric Owen, A: Anson Dyer, Harold Whitaker, Len Kirley, M: Paxtons, V: John Blythe
Live action with animated sequences. "The production of animated cartoons in the Anson Dyer studios is briefly but clearly explained. Of interest to most general audiences." (*Film Sponsor* February 1950.) Filmed at

the Anson Dyer studio in Stroud, Gloucester, where his story man, key animators, in-betweeners, and inkers are shown at work. The veteran animator tells "The Tale of Ronnie Rabbit" to a small girl, Christine Anne. Shown April 1948.

583   Cherry the Boots (180)
   Stratford Abbey Films
   P:D: Anson Dyer, A: Tony Guy, Harold Whitaker, S: Ronald Neilson, M: Jose Norman
   Technicolor
   Advertising cartoon for Cherry Blossom Boot Polish. "It tells the amusing story of a 'boots' in a large hotel who has hundreds of boots to clean. He is chased by them in a fantastic dream sequence. In the end he falls at the feet of the 'There's Nothing Like' creature used by Chiswick Products to advertise their Cherry Blossom Boot Polish." (*Film Sponsor* February 1950.)

1950

584 Save Baby Save (270)
Pinschewer Films
P:D:A: Julius Pinschewer
Technicolor
Propaganda film for the National Savings Committee. "This one opens with a baby in a cot and, with a general background of song and savings stamps, shows him as a sprightly young scholar, then a dapper bridegroom, leading an attenuated blonde to the altar; finally full circle with a stork delivering a baby clutching some more savings stamps. It has a pleasing musical background and no commentary – lovely!" (*Film Sponsor* March 1950.)

585 Very Good Sergeant (180)
Stratford Abbey Films
P:D: Anson Dyer, A: Harold Whitaker, Tony Guy, M: John Bath, S: Ronald Neilson
Technicolor
Advertising cartoon for Cherry Blossom Boot Polish. Released June 1951.

586 River of Steel (903)
Larkins – ABFD
P:D: William Larkins, A: Denis Gilpin, Richard Taylor, DES: Peter Sachs
Technicolor
Propaganda film for the British Iron and Steel Federation. "A lighthearted colour cartoon emphasising the vital part played by steel in the modern world. From the drama of steel production the film goes on to picture a world suddenly bereft of steel: cars without engines or bodies, bridges without girders, kitchens without knives or stoves. But a river of steel pours back into this steel-less world, restoring transport, industry and the people's homes." (*Central Film Library Catalogue* 1951.)

587   Devon Whey (719)

GB Animation – GFD: "Musical Paintbox" No. 9

P: David Hand, D: G. Henry Stringer, S: Nicholas Spargo, Graeme Phillips, A: Norman Abbey, Deryck Foster, Peter Jay, John Woodward, Brian Ward, Alan Gray, Andre Amstutz, M: Henry Reed, V: Jon Pertwee, Ian Wallace

Technicolor

Scenes and short stories set to the songs of Devon. Trade show February 1950.

588   A Fantasy on London Life (728)

GB Animation – GFD: "Musical Paintbox" No. 10

P: David Hand, D: G. Henry Stringer, M: Henry Reed

Technicolor

"A parody on the life of London including the Billingsgate Fish Market, flower sellers, Covent Garden Opera House and its surroundings, the pin-striped gentlemen of the City travelling to work on the Underground, St. Paul's, glimpses of suburbia, and other facets of life in the city. About the best of the Musical Paintbox series, more humour than usual." (*NSTA Review.*) "It is well designed, agreeably coloured, has touches of humour, some sardonic comments on City workers, and a delightful musical accompaniment. Excellent addition to any programme." (*Today's Cinema* 29 March 1950.)

589   Ginger Nutt's Forest Dragon (600)

GB Animation – GFD: "Animaland" No. 9

P: David Hand, D: Bert Felstead, S: Pete Griffiths, Reg Parlett, A: Stan Pearsall, Bill Hopper, Arthur Humberstone, Chick Henderson, M: Henry Reed

Technicolor

Last of the "Animaland" and Ginger Nutt series, and the last entertainment cartoon produced by J. Arthur Rank's animation unit. It was closed down having proved uneconomical. "Ginger Nutt the little squirrel is subjected to a practical joke by three other forest dwellers who pretend to be a dragon. Good colour and animation but poor vocal effects." (*Today's Cinema* 11 April 1950.) "Corny Crow overhears Ginger boasting to Hazel that he is a hero. The birds and animals decide to play a trick on him, and Loopy Hare dons a piece of hollowed out tree bark which makes him look horrible. Ginger is petrified and runs home leaving Hazel to fend for herself. He soon feels ashamed and decides to hunt the terror. He discovers something wrong with it and catches the jokers." (*NSTA Review.*)

590   Mr. H.C. Andersen (5612)
British Foundation Pictures
P:D: Ronald Haines, A: Joe Noble, C: W.R. Hutchinson (Ronald Haines), M: W.L. Trytel
Live action feature film with animated sequences. Hans Christian Andersen (Ashley Glenn) was born in Denmark in 1805, the son of a cobbler. His early life was full of struggle and disappointment, but his ambition was to become a poet. One of his poems attracted attention and he was helped to become educated and continue his writing. He attained success and died at the age of 70. "This is a poor production and fails to do anything like justice to the subject. Instead of telling the story straight, many lengthy and irrelevant cartoon sequences are introduced. They contain a few amusing moments but on the whole are very crude. There is very little dialogue, the story being mostly narrated in an ingenious manner." (*Film Report* 30 June 1950.)

591   The Fox and the Crow (365)
Sadfas – GFD
Experimental cartoon using stills and limited animation, made for Saturday morning Children's Clubs. "Charming black-and-white cartoon with spoken narrative telling Aesop's fable about a crow and a piece of cheese. Simple moral, 'Beware of flatterers,' neatly pointed. Excellent child fare." (*Today's Cinema* 7 July 1950.)

592   As Old as the Hills (1048)
Halas & Batchelor – Apex
P: John Halas, Joy Batchelor, D: Bob Privett, S: Allan Crick, A: Bob Privett, Vic Bevis, DES: Bob Privett, Digby Turpin, ED: Jack King, M: Matyas Seiber
Technicolor
Instructional cartoon for the Anglo-Iranian Oil Company. "Its object is to show the origins and nature of oil in terms both scientifically accurate and easily understandable, and by clear and pleasing use of what are in effect animated diagrams, this aim is achieved. The film shows the gradual development of the substance of oil, together with the changes in rock formation which led to its accumulation in the Persian mountains." (*Monthly Film Bulletin* November 1950.) Trade show 18 October 1950.

593   Fowl Play (950)
Halas & Batchelor – Apex
P: John Halas, Joy Batchelor, D: Anson Dyer, Len Kirley, A: Harold Whitaker, Len Kirley, John Garling, Dennis Purchase, M: Jose Norman
Technicolor
"A fox tells how he got into his present plight, which seems to consist of sitting in an armchair floating in a river. The story is that he is hungry

and goes after a chicken which, after a fight in a coop, is carried uncon-
scious to the fox's house. The fox, having read a chicken recipe, goes off
to get the firewood, and by some typical cartoon inefficiency, trips up and
gets himself tied to a post and set on fire. The chicken turns the hose on
from the house, the house floods, the fox climbs in and is carried out on
the water in an armchair, and into the river. At the end of the story he disap-
pears underwater." (*NSTA Review.*) Trade show 30 October 1950. Attempt
at a cartoon closer to the American style, originally designed for a sponsor.
When the finance ran out, Halas and Batchelor took over the production
from Anson Dyer.

594   **The Magic Chalks** (946)
Sadfas – GFD
Live action with superimposed animation, made for Saturday morning Children's Clubs. "This one-reel fantasy is in a completely original technique, the actuality being in black-and-white and the fantasy figure in coloured cartoon. It took Sadfas years to perfect this technique, which is more
economical than ordinary cartoon and accepted by children because of its
magicality." (Mary Field *Good Company* 1952.) "Combines black and white
photography and colour animation to achieve pointless story of young girl
and chalk-drawn animal. May get by with younger children on novelty appeal. Disappointing offering." (*Today's Cinema* 3 November 1950.)

595   **The British Army at Your Service** (540)
Halas & Batchelor – COI
P:D: John Halas, Joy Batchelor, S: Douglas Low, A: Vic Bevis, Brian
Borthwick, Wally Crook, Kathleen Houston, Vera Linnecar, M: Francis
Chagrin
Technicolor
Propaganda film for the War Office. "A film cartoonist's impression of
the British soldier in his most famous campaigns of the last 250 years, from
the time of Marlborough to that of the second World War, matched in
sound with the marching songs of the various periods." (*Film Sponsor*
December 1950.)

596   **Bread**
Pinschewer Films
P:D:S:A: Julius Pinschewer
Technicolor
Advertising film for Harry Ferguson tractors. "The history of farming
through the ages, from the Garden of Eden to the present day, is ably traced
in this clever colour cartoon film. It shows how the forces of nature have
been influenced by man to work for him instead of against him, and then
gives the basic principles of the Ferguson system." (*Film Sponsor* January
1951.)

1951

597 Once Upon a Time
Kinocrat
Technicolor
Animated puppets. "The fairy tale of the Tinderbox told in abbreviated form by puppet actors, with a road safety message. Children of 10-minus will enjoy it and students of puppetry will be interested." (*Film User* March 1951.)

598 Submarine Control
Halas & Batchelor
P: John Halas, Allan Crick, D: Allan Crick, Bob Privett, S: Allan Crick, A: Bob Privett, Vic Bevis
Instructional film made for the Admiralty. "Animated diagrammatic description of the hydrostatics of submarine movement. Simple demonstrations of neutral, positive and negative buoyancies. The basic principles are made clear enough for grasping by children of thirteen-plus. As with so many Halas and Batchelor cartoons, a touch of humour is discernible, and the whole film is a delight to watch." (*Film User* June 1951.)

599 Poet and Painter Series No. 1 (750) (A)
Halas & Batchelor – BFI
P: John Halas, Joy Batchelor, D: John Halas, S: John Halas, Joan Maude, Michael Warre, C: William Traylor, Roy Turk, ED: Jack King, M: Matyas Seiber
1: Twa Corbies A: Michael Rothenstein, V: John Laurie; **Spring and Winter** S: William Shakespeare, A: Mervyn Peake, V: Peter Pear
First in a series of four eight-minute art films made for the British Film Institute, for showing at the Telekinema of the Festival of Britain. Minimal animation, all movement being produced by camera work. "As a whole the artists have produced attractive illustrations to poems excellently narrated. The camera movement seems sometimes to lack smoothness and flow, perhaps because, when working on this relatively small scale, it is difficult to sustain an atmospheric impression." (*Monthly Film Bulletin* June 1951.)

600   Poet and Painter Series No. 2 (502) (A)
   Halas & Batchelor— BFI
   P: John Halas, Joy Batchelor, D: John Halas, S: John Halas, Joan
Maude, Michael Warre, C: William Traylor, Roy Turk, ED: Jack King, M:
Matyas Seiber
      2: Winter Garden S: David Gascoigne, A: Barbara Jones, V: Michael
Redgrave; **Sailor's Consolation** S: Francis Dibdin, A: John Minton, V:
Stanley Holloway; **Check to Song** S: Owen Meredith, A: Michael Warre,
V: Eric Portman

601   Poet and Painter Series No. 3 (500) (A)
   Halas & Batchelor— BFI
   P: John Halas, Joy Batchelor, D: John Halas, S: John Halas, Joan
Maude, Michael Warre, C: William Traylor, Roy Turk, ED: Jack King, M:
Matyas Seiber
      3: In Time of Pestilence S: Thomas Nashe, A: Michael Ayrton,
V: Robert Harris; **The Pythoness** S: Kathleen Raine, A: Henry Moore, V:
Mary Morris

602   Poet and Painter Series No. 4 (880)
   Halas & Batchelor— BFI
   P: John Halas, Joy Batchelor, D: John Halas, S: John Halas, Joan
Maude, Michael Warre, C: William Traylor, Roy Turk, ED: Jack King, M:
Matyas Seiber
      4: John Gilpin S: William Cowper, A: Ronald Searle, V: Cecil
Trouncer

603   We've Come a Long Way (922)
   Halas & Batchelor— Regent
   P: John Halas, Allan Crick, D: Bob Privett, Allan Crick, S: Bob
Privett, Allan Crick, Joy Batchelor, A: Bob Privett, DES: Digby Turpin, M:
Matyas Seiber
   Technicolor
   Instructional film made for the Anglo-Iranian Oil Company. "Devel-
opments in the building of oil tankers during the last 100 years, from the
time when oil casks were lashed in the hold. Notably clear and simple
models and diagrams show how the problems of dealing with the danger
of escaping gas, and of increasing the weight of the cargo without imposing
too great a strain, were solved." (*Monthly Film Bulletin* July 1951.)

604   The Flu-ing Squad (211)
   Halas & Batchelor
   P:D: John Halas, Joy Batchelor, M: Francis Chagrin
   Technicolor
   Advertising cartoon for Aspro. Released October 1951.

605   Enterprise
Larkins Studio
P: William Larkins, D: Peter Sachs, A: Denis Gilpin, Richard Taylor,
C: Theodore Thumwood
Technicolor
Promotional film for ICI. "Brilliant colour cartoon linking the business acumen of a potter in Ancient Egypt with the adventures of the ICI
today. The rhymed commentary combined with the admirable visuals
make this one of the year's wittiest films. Never has the case for a vast semi-
monopoly been more happily put." (*Film User* December 1951.) A revised
edition of this film was issued in 1954, which included additional material
from the film *Balance 1950* (No. 606).

606   Balance 1950
Larkins Studio
P: William Larkins, D: Peter Sachs, A: Denis Gilpin, Richard Taylor,
C: Theodore Thumwood
Technicolor
Promotional film for ICI. "ICI's balance sheet for 1950. Animated
drawings describe how the organization spends its money and keeps its ac-
counts. Vivacious little matchstick men aided by an ever-active '£' and
other devices act before a back-cloth of ledgers. The witty commentary in
rhyme and the pictorial brilliance make a fascinating film out of a dull subject." (*Film User* April 1952.)

607   Mary's Birthday
Crown Film Unit — COI
D:A: Lotte Reiniger
Technicolor
Animated silhouettes; propaganda film for the Ministry of Health.
"Showing by a simple story the dangers of fly contamination and the spread
of disease by germ in the home, and how these dangers can be overcome."
(*Central Film Library Catalogue* 1961.)

1952

608　The Shoemaker and the Hatter (1539)
Halas & Batchelor – UA
P:D: John Halas, Joy Batchelor, S: Joy Batchelor, Philip Stapp, A: Stan Pearsall, Bob Privett, Wally Crook, Kathleen Houston, ED: Jack King, M: Matyas Seiber, V: Lionel Gamlin
Technicolor
Propaganda film for the Economic Cooperation Administration. "The hatter and the shoemaker are neighbours; the hatter makes one hat which he intends to sell at a high price; he secures a ban on the importation of hats. The shoemaker, on the contrary, believes in mass production, but finds that trade restrictions and tariff barriers prevent him from paying with shoes for the machinery he has acquired from a neighboring country. In his travels he discovers that each country is unable to sell what it produces to buy what it needs. Thanks to his initiative, action is taken to bring this state of affairs to an end, and the result is general prosperity." (*Monthly Film Bulletin* June 1952.)

609　Animated Genesis (2013) (A)
Foldes – British Lion
XP: Alexander Korda, P:D:S:A: Peter Foldes, Joan Foldes, M: Thomas Henderson, V: Edric Connor
Technicolor/Kodachrome
Amateur production by a husband and wife, filmed on 16mm kodachrome, released on 35mm technicolor by Alexander Korda. "An allegory of the creation of the world and man's enslavement by the machine, motivated by Greed, personified as an enormous and menacing spider. The spider is eventually overthrown by the intervention of Goodness, but not before atomic warfare has occurred." (*Monthly Film Bulletin* September 1952.) First cartoon to win a British Film Academy Award: 1952.

610   Service: Garage Handling (900)
Halas & Batchelor
P: John Halas, Joy Batchelor, D: Allan Crick, Bob Privett, S: Allan Crick, Joy Batchelor, M: Matyas Seiber
Technicolor
Promotional film for the Anglo-Iranian Oil Company. The benefits of giving good garage service. Print preserved in the National Film Archive.

1953

611 The Figurehead (710)

Halas & Batchelor – British Lion

P: John Halas, Joy Batchelor, D: Allan Crick, S: Crosbie Garstin, SC: Joy Batchelor, A: Digby Turpin, Allan Crick, Bob Privett, ED: Jack King, C: William Traylor, Roy Turk, M: Matyas Seiber, V: Robert Beatty

Technicolor

Animated puppets. A carving of a saint is accidentally changed into a sailor and sold as a figurehead for a sailing ship. A mermaid falls in love with him and when the ship is wrecked he joins her under the sea. Unhappily, under his paint, the sailor is still a saint. "The colour and design are beautifully coordinated, the underwater scenes are very attractive, and the sad little story is suitably described by Robert Beatty." (*Monthly Film Bulletin* March 1953.) Shown at the 1953 Royal Film Performance.

612 The Owl and the Pussycat (550)

Halas & Batchelor – Stereo Techniques – EFC

P: John Halas, Joy Batchelor, D:SC: John Halas, Brian Borthwick, S: Edward Lear, A: Vic Bevis, Reg Lodge, DES: Brian Borthwick, Digby Turpin, M: Matyas Seiber, V: Maurice Bevan

Technicolor/3D

The first British cartoon in three dimensions. Edward Lear's famous nonsense verse about the Owl and the Pussycat who put to sea in a Beautiful Peagreen Boat, for the Land where the Bong Tree grows. "His realisation of the famous characters should win approval from most Lear lovers, and the poem is most attractively sung. The extra dimension, the colour and the design are all utilised with discretion and taste." (*Monthly Film Bulletin* July 1953.)

613 Bouncer Breaks Up (833)

Sadfas – ABFD

D: Donald Chaffey, S: Winifred Holmes, A: Donald Goulding, Jennifer Grey, Robert Lumley, Kathleen Tremewan, Harry Wheeler, William Winney, C: Norman McQueen, M: Ken Morrison

Technicolor/monochrome

Combined live action (monochrome) and animation (technicolor), made for the Children's Film Foundation. John (Bunny May) and Mary (Mavis Sage) find a scrapbook and a music box in the attic. When they play the music box, the drawing of a dog, Bouncer, springs into life. "Pleasant little picture for children under nine." (*Kinematograph Weekly* 29 October 1953.)

614   The Moving Spirit (1800)
Halas & Batchelor
P: John Halas, Joy Batchelor, D: Bob Privett, Allan Crick, S: Bob Privett, Allan Crick, Joy Batchelor, DES: Bob Privett, Digby Turpin, M: Benjamin Frankel
Technicolor
Promotional film for the Petroleum Films Bureau, Anglo-Iranian Oil Company. "The development of the motor car from the horseless carriage of the 1880s to the modern streamlined automobile. The discovery of petrol is stressed, and later changes, such as mass production and the new and improved methods of design, are shown." (*Monthly Film Bulletin* December 1953.)

615   Full Circle
Larkins Studio
P: William Larkins, D: Peter Sachs, A: Denis Gilpin, Richard Taylor, Beryl Stevens
Promotional film for the Anglo-Iranian Oil Company. Print preserved in the National Film Archive.

616   Without Fear
Larkins Studio
P: William Larkins, D: Peter Sachs, A: Denis Gilpin, Richard Taylor, Beryl Stevens
Promotional film for the Mutual Security Agency.

617   Coastal Navigation and Pilotage (4000)
Halas & Batchelor
P: John Halas, Joy Batchelor, D: Louis Dahl, S: Allan Crick
Feature-length (45 minutes) instructional film made for the Admiralty, using animation and animated models. Print preserved in the National Film Archive.

1954

618 Watch the Birdie
Biographic Films
P:D:S:A: Bob Godfrey, Keith Learner, Vera Linnecar, Richard Taylor
Colour
Amateur cartoon made on 16mm at a cost of £20, but a watershed in the history of British animation. A breakaway in style and humour by professional animators from Halas & Batchelor and Larkins, it sewed the seed for a new and successful school of animation. "A cartoon natural history in the style of Edward Lear, of an engaging bird called Ungle Wungle by the vulgar, or Kodachromus Panchromaticus by science. A witty and polished amateur production that should on no account be missed." (*Film User* July 1956.)

619 Early Days of Communication
Halas & Batchelor
P: John Halas, Jack Seward, D: John Halas, S: Jack Seward, Bob Privett, DES: Digby Turpin, A: Arthur Button
Eastmancolor
Promotional film for Insulated Cable Company and Automatic Telephone Company. "The history of man's system of communication through sound up to the invention of the telephone through the researches of Faraday." (*Halas & Batchelor List* 1962.)

620 Linear Accelerator
Halas & Batchelor
P: Allan Crick, D: Bob Privett, S: Allan Crick, Bob Privett, A: Vic Bevis, Brian Borthwick, Bob Privett
Instructional film for Mullard. "An advanced science instructional film demonstrating the principles of the linear accelerator by means of animated sectional drawings and diagrams." (*Halas & Batchelor List* 1962.)

169

621 The Power to Fly (1784)
Halas & Batchelor
P: John Halas, Allan Crick, D: Bob Privett, S: Allan Crick, Bob Privett, Joy Batchelor, A: Bill Mevin, Vic Bevis, Reg Lodge, DES: Digby Turpin, C: William Traylor, Roy Turk, Vic Hodgkiss, ED: Jack King, M: Benjamin Frankel, V: Maurice Denham
Technicolor
Advertising film for Anglo-Iranian Oil Company. "Cartoon history of aviation, beginning with early experiments in levitation following the achievements of famous pioneers, and concluding with a survey of modern developments, showing the effect on the world of transport." (*Monthly Film Bulletin* February 1955.)

622 The House That Jack Built
Larkins Studio
P: William Larkins, D: Peter Sachs, A: Denis Gilpin, Richard Taylor, Beryl Stevens
Technicolor
Promotional film for the British Iron and Steel Federation. "Cartoon parody of the nursery rhyme – 'This is the steel that came from the scrap' – to encourage the public to send scrap iron to the local iron merchant. There are more words than wit in the commentary but the animation is amusing, the colour delightful." (*Film User* March 1954.)

623 The Little Chimney Sweep
Primrose Productions – BFI
P: Louis Hagen, Richard Kaplan, D: Vivian Milroy, A: Lotte Reiniger, Carl Koch
Animated silhouettes. "Lotte Reiniger's shadow figures in a story set in the London of Queen Anne. Beautiful heiress abducted by wicked nobleman is rescued by the small boy who sweeps the chimney. The animation is expert and the musical accompaniment delightful, but the rather jerky continuity may puzzle very young audiences." (*Film User* March 1954.)

624 Puss in Boots
Primrose Productions – BFI
P: Louis Hagen, Richard Kaplan, D: Vivian Milroy, A: Lotte Reiniger, Carl Koch
Animated silhouettes. "Traditional story told by a commentator and Lotte Reiniger's shadow figures against pleasant, drawn backgrounds. Smooth animation and a most delightful cat make very good entertainment." (*Film User* March 1954.)

625 **Snow White and Rose Red**
Primrose Productions—BFI
P: Louis Hagen, Richard Kaplan, D: Vivian Milroy, A: Lotte Reiniger, Carl Koch
Animated silhouettes. "Nearly all the Lotte Reiniger fairy tales are enjoyable, this one is particularly so." (*Film User* January 1955.)

626 **The Magic Horse**
Primrose Productions—BFI
P: Louis Hagen, Richard Kaplan, D: Vivian Milroy, A: Lotte Reiniger, Carl Koch
Animated silhouettes. "Cartoon on a story from the Arabian Nights. Delightful." (*Film User* March 1955.)

627 **Animal Farm** (6515)
Halas & Batchelor—Associated British Pathé
XP: Louis de Rochemont, P:D: John Halas, Joy Batchelor, S: George Orwell, SC: Lothar Wolff, Borden Mace, Philip Stapp, John Halas, Joy Batchelor, AD: John Reed, DES: John Halas, Joy Batchelor, Digby Turpin, Bernard Carey, A: Harold Whitaker, Edrick Radage, Arthur Humberstone, Ralph Ayres, Frank Moysey, C: Sid Griffiths, William Traylor, J. Gurr, Roy Turk, ED: Jack King, M: Matyas Seiber, V: Maurice Denham, Gordon Heath
Technicolor
The first feature-length (73 minutes) entertainment cartoon film made in Britain, and the first feature cartoon made for an adult audience. The production was financed from the USA by the producers of the *March of Time* series of documentaries. Napoleon and Snowball, two cunning pigs, lead the oppressed animals of Manor Farm in a revolution against the tyrannical Farmer Jones. They set up an animal republic and organise the farm work, successfully repelling Jones and his cronies' attempt to regain the farm. Napoleon has Snowball liquidated and becomes dictator. Boxer the cart-horse supervises the building of a windmill for generating electricity but Jones dynamites it. Conditions deteriorate rapidly for all animals except the pigs. Napoleon amends their Seventh Commandment to read, "All animals are equal but some animals are more equal than others." One night when Napoleon and his pigs are carousing, the animals rebel and march on the farmhouse. "As a considerable feat of animation (there are 750 scenes and 300,000 drawings) the production must be deemed a landmark in the history of the British cartoon, but the generally unadventurous nature of the design and the persistent lack of depth in the backgrounds make the achievement less satisfying than one might have hoped." (*Monthly Film Bulletin* February 1955.)

1955

628 Thirteen Cantos of Hell
BFI Experimental Committee
P:D:A:S: Peter King
Experimental animation. "The inferno seen through machine age eyes to an accompaniment of music concrete. The imagery is powerful and the technique interesting, but these are not enough to prevent the film seeming overlong." (*Film User* August 1958.) Print preserved in the National Film Archive.

629 The World That Nature Forgot (540)
Halas & Batchelor
P: John Halas, Joy Batchelor
Eastmancolor
Promotional film for Monsato Chemicals, live action with animated sequences. "The arrangement and composition of molecules in relation to the development of plastics." (*Halas & Batchelor List.*)

630 Basic Fleetwork (3000)
Halas & Batchelor
P: John Halas, Joy Batchelor
Instructional film for the Admiralty. How to manoeuvre ships in groups.

631 Refinery at Work (1800)
Halas & Batchelor
P: John Halas, Joy Batchelor
Eastmancolor
Instructional film for Esso Petroleum. "Monochrome scenes of Fawley Refinery dissolve into animated diagrams in colour on the process of distillation, catalytic cracking, and polymerisation. To those educated on Petroleum Film Board films the treatment will seem elementary." (*Film User* August 1955.)

632   Down a Long Way
Halas & Batchelor
P: John Halas, Allan Crick, D: Bob Privett, S: Bob Privett, Allan Crick,
Joy Batchelor, A: Vic Bevis, Brian Borthwick, Reg Lodge, DES: Alison De
Vere, Tom Bailey, Ted Pettingell, M: Matyas Seiber
Technicolor
Promotional film for British Petroleum. "History of an oil well in
light-hearted but accurate animation. Origin of oil deposits, prospecting
and drilling. By ending just before the oil comes to the surface this
sequence leaves a feeling of anti-climax." (*Film User* August 1955.)

633   The Sea of Winslow Homer (900)
Halas & Batchelor
P: John Halas, D: Edrick Radage, DES: Winslow Homer, SC: John
Halas, A: Edrick Radage, M: Franz Reisenstein, V: Burgess Meredith
Eastmancolor
Animated compilation of the sea paintings of Winslow Homer, spon-
sored by the Ford Foundation.

634   Gas Fuel Turbine Systems
Larkins Studio
P: William Larkins, D: Peter Sachs
Instructional film made for the Admiralty.

635   Strictly Instrumental
Larkins Studio
P: William Larkins, D: Peter Sachs, A: Denis Gilpin, Richard Taylor,
Beryl Stevens
Technicolor
Advertising cartoon made for Crompton Parkinson.

636   Shippam's Guide to Opera
Larkins Studio
P: William Larkins, D: Peter Sachs, A: Denis Gilpin, Richard Taylor,
Beryl Stevens
Technicolor
Advertising cartoon for Shippam's Pastes. "Snatches from popular
operas sung by potted meats and their ingredients, the high spot being a
romantic duet realised by a pilchard and a tomato. (*Film User* August 1956.)
Winner of the First Prize at the 1955 International Festival of Advertising
Films.

637   Hansel and Gretel
Primrose Productions – GB
. P: Louis Hagen, Richard Kaplan, D: Vivian Milroy, A: Lotte Reiniger, Carl Koch
Animated silhouettes. "Silhouette cartoon following tradition, except for the greater but agreeable stress laid on animals. The tale is charmingly told, and the witch, though obviously wicked, is not likely to cause nightmares." (*Film User* January 1956.)

638   Sleeping Beauty
Primrose Productions – GB
P: Louis Hagen, Richard Kaplan, D: Vivian Milroy, A: Lotte Reiniger, Carl Koch
Animated silhouettes. "All eyes will enjoy it and for children it is strongly recommended." (*Film User* January 1956.)

639   Three Wishes
Primrose Productions – GB
P: Louis Hagen, Richard Kaplan, D: Vivian Milroy, A: Lotte Reiniger, Carl Koch
Animated silhouettes. "As a reward for helping a fairy, a woodman is allowed to make three wishes. Enjoyable for all ages." (*Film User* January 1956.)

640   Thumbelina
Primrose Productions – GB
P: Louis Hagen, Richard Kaplan, D: Vivian Milroy, A: Lotte Reiniger, Carl Koch
Animated silhouettes. "The fairy tale executed with charm and delicacy." (*Film User* January 1956.)

641   The Caliph Stork
Primrose Productions – Pathé
P: Louis Hagen, Richard Kaplan, D: Vivian Milroy, A: Lotte Reiniger, Carl Koch
Animated silhouettes. "Beautifully designed and animated and accompanied by pleasant music." (*Film User* February 1956.)

642   The Frog Prince
Primrose Productions – Pathé
P: Louis Hagen, Richard Kaplan, D: Vivian Milroy, A: Lotte Reiniger, Carl Koch
Animated silhouettes. "For the very young children, probably the best choice." (*Film User* February 1956.)

643   The Gallant Little Tailor (966)

Primrose Productions – Pathé

P: Louis Hagen, D: Vivian Milroy, A: Lotte Reiniger, Carl Koch, M: Freddie Phillips

Animated silhouettes. "How a medieval tailor captures two giants and so wins the hand of a princess." (*Monthly Film Bulletin* July 1956.)

644   The Grasshopper and the Ant

Primrose Productions – Pathé

P: Louis Hagen, Richard Kaplan, D: Vivian Milroy, A: Lotte Reiniger, Carl Koch

Animated silhouettes. "Should be the most successful for all age groups. Its stern moral is softened by a charming happy ending." (*Film User* February 1956.)

645   Jack and the Beanstalk (1070)

Primrose Productions – Pathé

P: Louis Hagen, D: Vivian Milroy, A: Lotte Reiniger, Carl Koch, M: Freddie Phillips

Eastmancolor

Animated silhouettes with backgrounds in color. "Technical ingenuity and charm, engaging music score." (*Monthly Film Bulletin* July 1956.)

1956

646 Tam O' Shanter
Campbell Harper
D: W.J. Maclean, A: Elizabeth Odling, Edward Odling, S: Robert Burns
Limited animation film; made for the Scottish Joint Production Committee. "Illustrated reading of the poem with black-and-white drawings full of robust humour. Except for a few rolling eyeballs the pictures are static, and quick cutting and a tracking camera are effective substitutes for animation." (*Film User* April 1956.)

647 Speed the Plough (1454)
Halas & Batchelor
P: Allan Crick, D: Bob Privett, S: Allan Crick, Bob Privett, Joy Batchelor, DES: Digby Turpin, A: Vic Bevis, John Williams, M: Matyas Seiber
Technicolor
Promotional film for British Petroleum Film Board. "Cartoon analysis of the evolution of agricultural implements. It describes the medieval farming year, the inefficiency of the period's methods of sowing seed, the development of the plough, the advent of mechanical aids. The early part of the film, designed in the style of the Luttrell Psalter, is visually most attractive." (*Monthly Film Bulletin* June 1956.)

648 A Short Vision (600) (X)
Foldes – BFI Experimental Fund – Intercontinental
P:D:S:A: Joan Foldes, Peter Foldes, M: Matyas Seiber, V: James McKechnie
Eastmancolor
"The vision depicted in this short cartoon is that of atomic destruction. A 'thing' suddenly appears in the sky, flying over countryside and cities, and destroys all living things. All that finally remains is a single flame with a moth fluttering around it; and, after a moment, the flame devours the moth." (*Monthly Film Bulletin* July 1956.) The first British cartoon to be awarded an "X" Certificate (Adults Only).

649   To Your Health (892)
Halas & Batchelor
P: John Halas, E.M. Jellineck, D: Philip Stapp, S: Philip Stapp, Joy
Batchelor, A: Brian Borthwick, John Smith, DES: Philip Stapp, M: Matyas
Seiber
Eastmancolor
Propaganda film for the World Health Organisation. "The problems
of the chronic alcoholic, emphasising the deterioration in standards of
health and human dignity resulting from excessive drinking. It shows the
effect of alcohol on the brain and the senses, to the detriment of both
physical and mental control." (*Central Film Library Catalogue* 1961.) "The
colour and animation are exceptionally good." (*Monthly Film Bulletin*
August 1956.)

650   The Battle of Wangapore
Grasshopper Group
D:A: John Daborn
Color
Amateur cartoon. "A tribal war on the outposts of the Empire, and
the activities therein of the little Daughter of the Regiment. In animation
and draughtsmanship it shows traces of its amateur origin. The script is
often funny and occasionally inventive, but the basic idea is thin and the
tempo sometimes faulty; parts of the commentary too are indistinct.
Judged as a part-time effort made with improvised equipment, it is a
remarkable achievement, well worth the three years' work that went into
its production." (*Film User* August 1956.) Winner of the Grand Prix in the
Cannes Amateur Film Festival.

651   Calling All Salesmen (950)
Pearl & Dean
D: David Hilberman
Eastmancolor
Promotional film for *Life Magazine*. British Film Academy Award
1956.

652   New King Coke
Film Workshop
Color
Animated puppets; promotional film for the Gas Council. "Medieval
woodcutter who recommends charcoal for the smoking palace fire is flung
into the royal moat. He takes a trip into the future in search of a cheaper
smokeless fuel. There Mr. Therm explains the nature of coke and gas appliances for the home. The woodcutter then returns to his own era and
trades a sack of coke for the hand of the King's daughter. Good marks for

the skilful puppetry and the sponsor's determination to promote gas in an original way." (*Film User* October 1956.)

653   Cartoons and Cartoonists (1375)
Panoramic Films—UA
P:D:S: Harold Baim, A: George Moreno, Jr., C: Eric Owen, V: Franklin Engelmann
       Live action with animation sequences; a survey of British cartoonists including W.A.S. Herbert, George Sprod, John Taylor, Brockbank, "'Fougasse," Rowland Emmett and Michael Cummings. "This witty material is not always seen to the best advantage, being subjected to an animation device in which the drawings are gradually filled in against a white background, instead of being shown in full at the outset." (*Monthly Film Bulletin* November 1956.)

654   The History of the Cinema (700)
Halas & Batchelor—British Lion
P: John Halas, Joy Batchelor, D: John Halas, S: John Halas, Nicholas Spargo, DES: Ted Pettingell, A: Harold Whitaker, John Smith, C: William Traylor, Roy Turk, ED: Jack King, V: Maurice Denham
Eastmancolor
       "A lively, irreverent interpretation of the history of the cinema which, in design and characterization, strongly reflects the influence of UPA (United Productions of America). Early pioneers, the work of the censor, the arrival of the talkies, the coming of television and recent widescreen developments are neatly satirised in a series of economically animated episodes." (*Monthly Film Bulletin* December 1956.)

655   Cool Custom
Larkins Studio
P: William Larkins, D: Denis Gilpin, A: Richard Taylor, Beryl Stevens
Color
       Promotional film for B.E.D.A. "Ten minute colour cartoon on the advantages of electric refrigerators in the kitchen. A most successful combination of attractive drawing, amusing talk, and persuasive salesmanship." (*Film User* January 1957.)

656   Think of the Future
Halas & Batchelor—COI
P: John Halas, Joy Batchelor
Technicolor
       Propaganda film for the European Productivity Agency. "Modern factory worker, transported to the 'good old days' of a century ago, finds that low productivity meant only long hours, sweat and scanty rations. The

moral being that better methods are the stepping stones to a better life. The pictures will entertain but the commentary does not perhaps make its point with enough emphasis." (*Film User* October 1956.)

657   Invisible Exchange
Halas & Batchelor
P: John Halas, Joy Batchelor
Eastmancolor
Promotional film for Shell Petroleum. Cartoon to encourage better service in the garage.

658   Peak Period
World Wide Films – COI
Propaganda film for the Ministry of Transport. "Every day many children face death on the roads. This animated cartoon brings attention to the real time of danger, the peak period of four to six o'clock in the afternoon." (*Central Film Library Catalogue* 1961.)

659   Star of Bethlehem (1600)
Primrose Productions – Archway
P: Louis Hagen, Richard Kaplan, D: Vivian Milroy, A: Lotte Reiniger, Carl Koch, ED: Reginald Spragg, M: Peter Gellhorn, V: Anthony Jacobs
Eastmancolor
Animated silhouettes. "Legendary and apocryphal account of the wanderings of the three kings and the star which led them to Bethlehem. The kings are visited by various dangers – shipwreck, devils, desert sandstorms – but finally make their way to the stable where, alongside the shepherds, they make their offerings to the infant Jesus." (*Monthly Film Bulletin* March 1957.)

1957

660 Quick Freeze
RHR Films
P: Ronald H. Riley, D: R. Potter
Color
Promotional film for Unilever. "A cartoon prologue makes fun of man's early attempts to preserve food, then the camera illustrates that food, sold as fresh, is far from that by the time it reaches the kitchen." (*Film User* April 1957.)

661 Animal Vegetable or Mineral
Halas & Batchelor
P: John Halas, Allan Crick, D: Louis Dahl, S: Allan Crick, Bob Privett, Joy Batchelor, A: Vic Bevis, Bob Privett, DES: Alison De Vere, Tom Bailey, Ted Pettingell, M: Matyas Seiber, V: Maurice Denham
Technicolor
Promotional film for Petroleum Film Board. "Cartoon history beginning in Ancient Egypt, of man's attempts to reduce friction. With the arrival of motor cars the film slows down to explain the various problems solved by the modern detergent multigrade engine oil. It is amusing, to some extent instructive, but also mildly irritating." (*Film User* October 1957.)

662 The Candlemaker
Halas & Batchelor
P:D: John Halas, Joy Batchelor, S: Joy Batchelor, Philip Stapp, A: Brian Borthwick, Reg Lodge, Vic Bevis, DES: Philip Stapp, M: Matyas Seiber
Eastmancolor
Propaganda film for the United Lutheran Church (USA). "Called away from home, a candlemaker gives his son responsibility for making an altar candle for Christmas. The boy, having spent too long playing with his mouse, works in a hurry and leaves out the wick. During the service the candle will not light. Aware now that he has failed not only his father, but Christ, he tries again. The sponsor's object is to convey to children the notion that there is more to Christian stewardship than the giving of tangible gifts." (*Film User* February 1958.)

663   All Lit Up
Halas & Batchelor
P: John Halas, Joy Batchelor, D: John Halas, S: Joy Batchelor, A: Vic Bevis, Reg Lodge, John Williams, DES: Tom Bailey, Ted Pettingell, ED: Jack King, C: William Traylor, M: Francis Chagrin, V: Frank Holder
Eastmancolor
Advertising film for the Gas Council. "Since Roman times man has tried to heat his rooms without fuss or mess. At last with a gas poker it can be done. Delightful drawings are accompanied by a calypso that plugs the product hard without seeing it. The formula may not bear repetition, but on this occasion success is complete. Gas pokers are about to boom." (*Film User* February 1958.)

664   Mr. Finlay's Feelings
Larkins Studio
P: William Larkins, D: Richard Taylor, A: Richard Taylor, Beryl Stevens
Technicolor
Advertising film for Metropolitan Life Insurance. "Given a job to do at home, office worker displaces his anger towards the boss onto his family, and then onto his car, which results in a crash. In gaol he is visited by a friend who delivers a sermon on the text, 'Don't blow your top.' The sponsor's object is presumably to reduce the number of gastric ulcers and thus of claims from prematurely bereaved wives." (*Film User* February 1958.)

665   Pan-Tele-Tron
Pearl & Dean
D: Digby Turpin
Color
Promotional film for Philips Electrical. "Cartoon history of tele-communications, a slight sales message put over with wit and imagination." (*Film User* April 1958.) Print preserved in the National Film Archive. British Film Academy Award 1957.

666   Put Una Money for There
Larkins Studio
P: William Larkins, D: Denis Gilpin, S: Richard Taylor, DES: Trevor Bond, A: Richard Taylor, Beryl Stevens, Karlis Smiltens, Pat Wicks, M: Samuel Akbot
Color
Advertising film for Barclays Bank, for release in Nigeria.

667   Earth Is a Battlefield (980)
Larkins – Film Producers Guild – Renown
P: William Larkins, D: Richard Taylor, A: Richard Taylor, Beryl
Stevens
Eastmancolor
Promotional film for British Iron and Steel Federation. "The story in animated cartoon form of steel in the service of agriculture from medieval times to the present day. Dialogue is in verse parody, and ranges from Chaucerian English to Canterbury Cockney, with the little characters simplified almost into abstractions of human beings." (*Kinematograph Weekly* 3 April 1958.)

1958

668 All Aboard
World Wide Pictures
D: Ken Woodward
Eastmancolor
Promotional film for Bowaters. "A harassed mayor is nobody's friend until he meets the Bowaters logger, who shows him his building board magic transforming the town and all the people in it so that they live happily ever after. This is an excellent example of modern animation technique. The opening was perhaps a little too fast and subtle, but one soon settled down for a good laugh." (*Film User* August 1958.)

669 The First 99 (900)
Halas & Batchelor – de Rochemont Associates
XP: Louis de Rochemont, P: John Halas, Joy Batchelor, D: Joy Batchelor, S: Joy Batchelor, Tom Orchard, DES: George Him, A: Harold Whitaker, Vic Bevis, Brian Borthwick, M: Matyas Seiber
Eastmancolor
Promotional film for Seagram; live action and animation sequences. The history of whisky distillation in the USA.

670 Sir Patrick Spens
Campbell Harper Films
D: W.J. Maclean, A: Elizabeth Odling, Edward Odling
Limited animation cartoon for Educational Films of Scotland. "The old ballad about a sailor who perished on a voyage from Norway is illustrated by a series of still drawings 'animated' by camera movements and optical work. The technique is good, but though less of a foreign language film than *Tam O'Shanter*, this also would make excessive demands on young Sassenach ears." (*Film User* May 1958.)

671 Helene la Belle (1350)
Phantasia Productions – Mondial
P: Peter Shankland, D:A: Lotte Reiniger, Carl Koch, Gerry Lee, S:M: Jacques Offenbach
Eastmancolor

Animated silhouette version of the opera *La Belle Helene*. "Here the lightness of the music is admirably matched by the gaily frivolous silhouette figures, and the satirical touches in the story suit her style perfectly." (*Monthly Film Bulletin* January 1959.) Print preserved in the National Film Archive.

672 A Night in a Harem (1260)
Phantasia Productions – Mondial
P: Peter Shankland, D:A: Lotte Reiniger, Carl Koch, Gerry Lee, S:M: Wolfgang Mozart
Eastmancolor
Animated silhouette version of the opera *Il Seraglio*. "The music, more subtle and dramatic, needs finer playing than the limited resources available to the producers can give, while the vitality and expressiveness of Mozart's invention tend to leave the visual story-telling and paper-thin characters behind." (*Monthly Film Bulletin* January 1959.) Print preserved in the National Film Archive.

673 The Little Island (1995)
Williams Animated Films – RFD
P:D:S:A: Richard Williams, M: Tristram Cary
Eastmancolor/Cinemascope
The first British cartoon in Cinemascope, it took Canadian animator Richard Williams three and a half years to make this personal production. He won the 1958 British Film Academy Award. "Three men land on a tiny deserted island. One believes in Truth, one in Goodness, and one in Beauty. For several days they are content to sit in the sun and get brown. Then each indulges in a long private vision, to the mystification of the other two. Truth's vision is the most abstract, a patterned medley of hints from many philosophies. Beauty favours flowers and flute solos, the manias of critics and the snobberies of blabbering intellectuals. Goodness sees life as a crusade for the soul, with a sharp sword ready for anyone slow to respond to the attractions of church and choirboys. Beauty taunts Goodness, who prepares for war. Truth watches as the others fight, growing to unrecognisable monsters. He tots up the score on a vast ticking bomb. It explodes. The three men leave the island in panic." (*Monthly Film Bulletin* February 1959.) Print preserved in the National Film Archive.

674 Follow That Car
Halas & Batchelor
P: John Halas, Joy Batchelor, D:A: Gerry Potterton, S: Gerry Potterton, Joy Batchelor, DES: Tom Bailey, M: Don Banks
Eastmancolor
Promotional film for Shell Petroleum. The service required by new car owners.

675 Best Seller
Halas & Batchelor
P: John Halas, Joy Batchelor, D: Gerry Potterton, S: Gerry Potterton,
Joy Batchelor, DES:A: Gerry Potterton, M: Don Banks
Eastmancolor
Promotional film for Shell Petroleum. "The two main characters are
the Shell dealer and the motorist represented as abstractions. The humour
is not allowed to overshadow the real purpose of the film which is to create
well-informed dealers who know how to sell Shell X100 Motor Oil." (*Industrial Screen* March 1959.)

676 Paying Bay
Halas & Batchelor
P: John Halas, Joy Batchelor, D: Gerry Potterton, S: Gerry Potterton,
Joy Batchelor, DES:A: Gerry Potterton, M: Don Banks
Eastmancolor
Promotional film for Shell Petroleum. How to keep a garage up to
date.

1959

677 Sales Promotion: The Key to Efficiency
Allan Crick Productions
P:D: Allan Crick
Technicolor
Promotional film for Shell Mex. "The object of sales promotion and the methods used: Market research; publicity; selecting and training the sales force; selling directly, and helping the dealer to sell. An amusing little essay appropriate as a visual aid for a sales conference, but hardly able to stand up on its own." (*Film User* March 1959.)

678 Ship Husbandry Part Two: Painting
Associated British Pathé
DES: Ronald Searle
Instructional film for the Admiralty. "Cartoon characters by Ronald Searle stress the susceptibility to corrosion of bare metal exposed to salt water. Though far from subtle, the humour is apposite and the commentary has authority." (*Film User* April 1959.)

679 The Story of the Motor Car Engine
Industrial Animation Films
P: George Dunning, D: Edwin Bronner, Richard Williams, S: Richard Williams, George Dunning, A: Bill Sewell, M: Tristram Cary
Technicolor
Instructional film for Ford Motors. "Two cartoon characters, encouraged by the results of applying a lighted match to a pot containing petrol and air, add a piston, crank, hand-operated valves, and so forth. They end up with a four-cylinder, four-stroke engine driving a car. As entertainment this ingenious experiment cannot fail. As instruction its value will be hotly debated." (*Film User* April 1959.)

680 The Christmas Visitor (662)
Halas & Batchelor – Eros

186

P: John Halas, Joy Batchelor, D: John Halas, S: Joy Batchelor, A: Harold Whitaker, Tony Guy, DES: Ted Pettingell, M: Matyas Seiber
Eastmancolor
Based on the poem "The Night Before Christmas." Father Christmas comes down the chimney, fills the children's stockings, and enjoys a supper that has been left for him. The toys in his sack unwrap and come to life. The sailor boy falls for the glamorous doll, who is kidnapped by the jack-in-the-box. Toy soldiers fail to save her and she is tied to a railway line. The sailor saves her in the nick of time. "This entertaining Christmas fantasy cartoon, charmingly made in this studio's usual style, is one to please children of almost any age." (*Monthly Film Bulletin* June 1959.)

681   The World of Little Ig (740)
Halas & Batchelor – Eros
P: John Halas, Joy Batchelor, D: John Halas, S: Joy Batchelor, A: Harold Whitaker, Reg Lodge, George Singer, DES: Tom Bailey, Alison De Vere, M: Steve Race
Eastmancolor
Made for the National Broadcasting Company (USA) but released to British cinemas. The Solar Eye scans the universe to discover a new planet, Iglandia, and focus on the life of a small prehistoric boy, Ig. "Perhaps the standard of invention, high in the opening phases, is not maintained; certainly it peters out into a sudden and lame finish." (*Monthly Film Bulletin* June 1959.)

682   The Energy Picture
Halas & Batchelor
P: John Halas, Joy Batchelor, D: Gerry Potterton, S: Joy Batchelor, A: Gerry Potterton, DES: Austin Campbell, M: Matyas Seiber, V: Maurice Denham
Eastmancolor
Promotional film for British Petroleum. "Half of this is sheer entertainment, an amusing summary of man's methods of harnessing sources of energy from prehistoric times to the present. The second part, though scarcely less entertaining, carries a message: that the oil industry, if given political stability and a flow of new capital, can contrive to keep pace with the world's growing demands." (*Film User* October 1959.)

683   Dam the Delta
Halas & Batchelor
P: John Ferno, D: John Halas, Joy Batchelor, S: Joy Batchelor, A: Vic Bevis, Reg Lodge, DES: Beserik, M: Don Banks, V: Patrick Allen
Propaganda film for the Netherlands government. "The long-term struggle against the encroachment of the sea along the Netherlands coast that led to the Delta Plan." (*Halas & Batchelor List* 1962.)

684 Your Skin
World Wide Animation
D: Ken Woodward
Technicolor

Instructional film for Unilever. "Describes the structure of the skin, including the intricate system of nerves, blood vessels, sweat glands, and sebaceous glands; the skin's mode of renewal and maintenance; and response to various stimuli and climatic change." (*Central Film Library Catalogue* 1961.)

1960

685 The Marriage (270)
Larkins Studio
P: William Larkins, D: Richard Taylor, A: Richard Taylor, Beryl Stevens
Advertising cartoon for Barclays Bank, West Africa.

686 Piping Hot
Halas & Batchelor
P:D: John Halas, Joy Batchelor, S: Joy Batchelor, A: Vic Bevis, Reg Lodge, John Williams, DES: Tom Bailey, Ted Pettingell, M: Francis Chagrin
Technicolor
Advertising film for the Gas Council. "Domestic hot water through the ages, culminating in the modern home with insulated supplies heated by gas. The well-tried historical formula provides some amusing scenes, but even animated cartoons should stick to the point." (*Film User* May 1960.)

687 Polygamous Polonius (887)
Biographic — British Lion
P: Bob Godfrey, Keith Learner, D:S: Bob Godfrey, A: Bob Godfrey, Steve Hill, Ann Scott, Keith Learner, John Carter, Dorothy Mead, Trevor Bond, Joan Wilson, Ron Coulter, ED: Keith Learner, Peter Hearn, M: Temperance Seven
Eastmancolor
First professional animated cartoon by a group of breakaway animators under the leadership of Australian-born Bob Godfrey. A lady tries to lecture on classical art but she is continually interrupted by a determined gentleman who woos her in sundry disguises with ever-increasing ardour. "The style of this frequently inspired cartoon is refreshingly different to that of any better known group. Conventions are treated with splendid contempt, and the humour has an original, bawdy, music-hall tang. More discipline could have made the joke still more effective, as the deliberate lunacy sometimes gets out of control." (*Monthly Film Bulletin* May 1960.) Premiered at the 1960 Royal Film Performance.

688   Power Train (486)

Industrial Animation Films

XP: Robert Adams, P: George Dunning, D: Teru Murakami, S: Richard Williams, Stan Hayward, George Dunning, A: Bill Sewell, Richard Williams, George Dunning, C: John Williams, Charles Pithers, ED: Steve Cox, M: Tristram Cary

Technicolor

Instructional film for Ford Motors. "Like its predecessors this cartoon by Dick Williams uses a couple of cavemen for light relief. In the course of various comic adventures, they develop a vehicle with the power train of a modern car: at each stage, clutch, gearbox and differential, humour gives way to straightforward and effective animated diagrams explaining the purpose of these concepts and how they work. As entertainment this is excellent. The credits, sound effects and cartooning are refreshingly original and very good fun." (*Film User* November 1960.)

689   The Wardrobe (180)

TV Cartoons – Crispin

P:D:A: George Dunning, S: Stan Hayward

Eastmancolor

Short comedy cartoon. A man wearing old shoes climbs into a wardrobe. A second man wearing new shoes follows him. The first man then emerges wearing the new shoes. "Whimsical, simply drawn against a white background, and punctuated by loud noises on the soundtrack ." (*Monthly Film Bulletin* August 1970.)

690   Fanta the Elephant Series

Shell – BP Films

Five three-minute cartoons on road safety, originally made for television but released in 1965. "Crossing the road; playing ball in the road; zebra crossings; keeping to the right when walking in the road. Shown without a break instead of separately as on television, they could be the basis of an amusing and instructive memory game." (*Film User* October 1965.)

691   Guilty or Not Guilty

Technical and Scientific Films

A: Allan Crick

Eastmancolor

Instructional film for the General Dental Council. "Advice to mothers on correct habits of dental hygiene and suitable diet for their children. The central part of the film is a lightly handled animation sequence presenting the dream of a young boy under anaesthetic for an extraction, in which his mother, on trial for neglecting his teeth, receives valuable instruction from the judge." (*Central Film Library Catalogue* 1961.)

1961

692　The History of Inventions (895)

Halas & Batchelor – Bozetto – Eros

P: John Halas, Bruno Bozetto, D:S: Bruno Bozetto, A: Sergio Chesani, C: Roberto Scarpa, M: Pier Emilio Bassi

Eastmancolor

Anglo-Italian coproduction. "Ironic cartoon history of Man's quest for knowledge which claims that lightning first showed him the wonders of fire and set him on the hazardous path of invention. Today, his eyes on space, he yearns for other worlds to obtain the peace and quiet he needs to go on inventing." (*Monthly Film Bulletin* April 1961.)

693　The Do-It-Yourself Cartoon Kit (514)

Biographic – British Lion

P:D: Bob Godfrey, S: Colin Pearson, A: Vera Linnecar, Nancy Hanna, Bob Godfrey, Keith Learner, C: Gerry Walters, M: Arthur Dulay, V: Michael Bentine

Eastmancolor

Burlesque commercial for Biographic Films' animation outfit for beginners. "This goon cartoon defies synopsis, paying only lip-service to any normal concept of continuity. Much of the lunatic humour derives from the rude treatment of certain Victorian engravings and from sly digs at the British. A scene to describe the difficulties of animation features a rather disjointed woman's arm jerkily waving a Union Jack. The arm itself falls off (into the sea, for some reason) but the flag rights itself and goes on waving." (*Monthly Film Bulletin* April 1961.)

694　Holy Willie's Prayer

Educational Films of Scotland

D:A: Edward Odling, Elizabeth Odling, V: Harold Wightman, S: Robert Burns

Limited animation interpretation of the Robert Burns poem. "Drawings are in character and quite amusing. In the effort to recreate, Harold Wightman makes it very difficult to hear the words, many of which are, in any case, unknown to the unenlightened Sassenach." (*Film User* June 1961.)

695   Higher Profit for the Small Dairy Farm
Fisons
Promotional film for Fisons. "More than half of this film is an animated cartoon on the economics of the smaller farm. The animation is simple but neat, and it helps not only to brighten but also to add emphasis to a talk on economics that is necessarily rather long (16 minutes)." (*Film User* June 1961.)

696   For Better . . . for Worse (1080)
Halas & Batchelor
P:D: John Halas, Joy Batchelor, D: John Halas, Peter Sachs, S: Joy Batchelor, A: Harold Whitaker, Jeffrey Loynes, Tom Bailey, John Smith, DES: George Him, M: Matyas Seiber, V: Maurice Denham
Eastmancolor
Promotional film for Philips. The average viewer discovers how television can be a pleasure and useful information source if taken in sensibly small doses. "Contains some inventive gags, lively animation and genial humour. Its main drawback, however, is a certain diffuseness of treatment and the absence of a firm visual style. The colour is boldly used in the parodies of various television programmes, and the advertising plug is restricted to the last shot." (*Monthly Film Bulletin* August 1961.) Print preserved in the National Film Archive.

697   The Wonder of Wool
Halas & Batchelor
P: John Halas, Joy Batchelor, D: John Halas, S: Roger Manvell, A: Vic Bevis, Reg Lodge, Brian Borthwick, DES: Digby Turpin, M: Tristram Cary, V: Maurice Denham
Eastmancolor
Promotional film for the International Wool Secretariat. "Demonstration of the chemical properties of the wool fibre which reveal the unique quality of woollen fabrics for clothing." (*Halas & Batchelor List* 1962.) Print preserved in the National Film Archive.

698   Hamilton the Musical Elephant (834)
Halas & Batchelor – British Lion: "Hamilton" No. 1
P: John Halas, Joy Batchelor, D: John Halas, S: John Halas, John Cooper, A: Harold Whitaker, Tony Guy, DES: John Cooper, Ted Pettingell, ED: Jack King, M: Johnny Dankworth, V: Lionel Murton
Eastmancolor
First in a series (of two) of entertainment cartoons featuring Hamilton the Elephant. Hamilton is trained to take part in a circus but is always forgetting the tricks he has been taught. He hears a barrel-organ play and discovers he can blow music from his trunk like a trumpet. His trainer tries to exploit his new-found talent, but at the crucial moment Hamilton forgets again.

1962

699 The Ever-Changing Motor Car (992)
TV Cartoons
XP: Robert Adams, P: George Dunning, D: George Dunning, Alan Ball, S: Stan Hayward, Richard Williams, A: Mike Stuart, Alan Ball, Bill Sewell, Tony Gearty, Jack Stokes, David Rich, Charles Jenkins, DES: Richard Williams, ED: Steve Cox, C: John Williams, M: Ron Goodwin, V: Peter Cook, Dudley Moore, Jonathan Miller, Deryck Guyler, Dick Emery, Gordon Harrison
Technicolor
Promotional film for the Ford Company. Traces the design of the motor car through history, with the influence of fashion, technology and psychology on its development. "The humour is, for the most part, of the kind to cause smiles rather than outright laughter. However the presentation is surefire and the end product quite entertaining." (*Film User* November 1962.)

700 Lecture on Man (360)
Williams Films – ABC
P:D: Richard Williams, S: Christopher Logue, A: Bill Sewell, Richard Williams, C: Charles Pithers, M: Tristram Cary
Color
"Deliciously witty mixture of stock shots, cutouts, anatomy charts and cartoons." (*Variety* 11 July 1962.)

701 Spaghetti Varieties
World Wide – Sound Services
P: Hindle Edgar, D: Ken Woodward
Color
Promotional film for the British Macaroni Industry. "Combination of live action and animation in which a cartoon character called Cyril discovers how British pasta is manufactured from wheat germ in Canada. The film concludes by giving some tips on cooking." (*Film User* June 1962.)

193

702   The Redemption of a Retailer
TV Cartoons
P:D: George Dunning
Technicolor
Promotional film for Gillette razor blades. "Successful retailing, some advice on the subject given by a scissors-and-paste type of cartoon about a shopkeeper whose business languishes because he stocks the wrong lines. Of slight value for training, at any rate outside the ranks of Gillette stockists." (*Film User* August 1962.)

703   The Commonwealth
Halas & Batchelor
P: John Halas, Joy Batchelor, D:S: Joy Batchelor, A: Vic Bevis, DES: Tom Bailey, V: Huw Wheldon
Technicolor
Propaganda film for the Nuffield Foundation and the Commonwealth Institute. "The Commonwealth's size, distribution and trade. The way of life and the freedom of thought, speech, press, and worship that are common to all its members. Parliamentary systems and civil services modelled on Westminster. Cooperation in the teaching of skills. The animated cartoon treatment is particularly effective because so much of the message is delivered symbolically." (*Film User* September 1962.)

704   The Colombo Plan (917)
Halas & Batchelor—COI
P: John Halas, Joy Batchelor, D:S: Joy Batchelor, A: Harold Whitaker, Vic Bevis, DES: Tom Bailey, M: Don Banks, ED: Jack King, V: Huw Wheldon
Eastmancolor
Propaganda film made for the Tenth Anniversary of the Colombo Plan for Cooperative Economic Development in South and South East Asia sponsored by the Foreign Office, the Colonial Office, and the Commonwealth Relations Office. "How the plan works in principle, how technical assistance and capital aid are being applied in the area, and the progress already made." (*Central Film Library Catalogue* 1962.) "It is the kind of thing Halas and Batchelor can do on their heads (one notes the little man with a white moustache who has appeared in several of their oil films), and it is their very technical ability which betrays them." (*Monthly Film Bulletin* October 1962.)

705   Hamilton in the Music Festival (850)
Halas & Batchelor—British Lion: "Hamilton" No. 2
P: John Halas, Joy Batchelor, D: John Halas, S: John Halas, John Cooper, A: Harold Whitaker, Tony Guy, DES: John Cooper, Ted Pettingell, ED: Jack King, M: Johnny Dankworth, V: Lionel Murton

Eastmancolor

Hamilton, a circus elephant, is fired because he cannot do any tricks except turn his trunk into various musical instruments. After a job as a baby-sitter he substitutes for a trumpeter at an Albert Hall concert. When the entire orchestra walks out, Hamilton takes over alone. "This is an unimaginative film with only one basic idea which is not adequately worked out. As with many of Halas and Batchelor's entertainment cartoons there is no subtlety; and the gags are all rushed so quickly that they lose their effect." (*Monthly Film Bulletin* October 1962.)

706   Mr. Know-How in Hot Water

Industrial Animation: "Mr. Know-How" No. 1

P: George Dunning, D: Bill Sewell, M: Tristram Cary

Technicolor

Promotional film for the Gas Council. "Humorous but factual account of what goes on inside a gas water heater to give the 'endless hot water' one keeps hearing about in the cinema commercials. Its own live action commercial at the end of one version has been amputated in another version prepared for schools." (*Film User* October 1962.)

707   Love Me, Love Me, Love Me (765)

Williams Films – British Lion

P:D: Richard Williams, S: Stan Hayward, A: Richard Williams, Charles Jenkins, Tony Gearty, ED: John Bloom, C: Charles Pithers, Graham Orrin, M: Pete Shade, V: Kenneth Williams

Technicolor

Squidgy Bod does everything wrong and is loved by everyone; Thermus Fortitude does everything right and is loved by nobody – except Charlie, his stuffed alligator. Thermus takes a correspondence course in loveableness and succeeds in becoming loved by everybody – except his stuffed alligator. He slings Charlie through the window, whereupon he is stepped on by the passing Squidgy. Moral: "When it comes to love, no-one really has it good, especially stuffed alligators named Charlie." "Thurberesque fairy tale which benefits enormously from having its narrative delivered by Kenneth Williams in his richest plummy-idiot voice. The animation is kept to a minimum, the characterisation is excellent and witty, the linking words and sub-headings are elaborately drawn in and decorated, all giving the effect of a far out Victorian picture-book." (*Monthly Film Bulletin* February 1963.)

708   The Flying Man (248)

TV Cartoons – Connoisseur

P:D: George Dunning, S: Stan Hayward, A: George Dunning, Jeremy Hibbert, Roy Evans, C: John Williams, M: Ron Goodwin

Technicolor

Experimental cartoon using loosely painted figures lacking firm out-lines. A man takes off his jacket and flies while another man watches, tries, and fails. "The competent international jury of the Annecy Animation Festival selected this two-minute film for its mobility of animation, its astonishing three-dimensional depth, glorious pastel colouring, and the most important point of all, George Dunning has deposed the conventional outline figure that has for so long dominated the form of animated drawing. This is truly a sensational and impressive film." (*Industrial Screen* September 1962.)

709   The Apple (630)
TV Cartoons – Connoisseur
P:D: George Dunning, S: Stan Hayward, A: Alan Ball, Jack Stokes, Bill Sewell, Mike Stuart, Charlie Jenkins, Tony Gearty, ED: Alex Rayment, C: John Williams, M: Ernst Naser
Technicolor
A man in a park tries repeatedly to pick an apple off a tree. "A perfect comic tale taken at an apparently leisurely pace but with split-second timing. It uses music, natural sound, colour (and non-colour), perspective and line drawing to brilliant effect, but it is the masterly sense of timing throughout which gives this film its effortless superiority." (*Monthly Film Bulletin* March 1963.) British Film Academy Award 1962.

709a   The Plain Man's Guide to Advertising (1800)
Biographic Four – British Lion
P:D: Bob Godfrey, S: Colin Pearson, A: Bob Godfrey, Keith Learner, ED: Peter Hearn, C: Geoffrey Gurin, Roy Pointer, M: Johnny Johnston, V: David de Keyser, Dick Emery, Vernon Grieves
Live action with animation sequences. The Plain Man (Ronnie Brody) visits a cinema and is bombarded by advertisements of various kinds, including one for the Biographic Do-It-Yourself Advertising Kit. "Irrelevant, unfunny cartoon characters, who intend to boycott future cartoons, slow up the film alarmingly after a witty, well-paced opening." (*Monthly Film Bulletin* November 1962.)

1963

710 House Warming
De La Rue Films
Color
Promotional film for Thomas Potterton Ltd. "Home heating through the ages. A cartoon beginning with cave dwellers and ending with the efficient Potterton boilers of today." (*Film User* June 1963.)

711 A Short Spell
Grasshopper Group
D:S:A: Stuart Wynn Jones
Color
Experimental amateur cartoon. "An animated alphabet (e.g. H equals hat equals a picture of a hat) drawn directly on film and accompanied by electronic sound. Ingenious, witty, highly entertaining, recommended." (*Film User* October 1963.)

712 Your Digestion
World Wide
P: Hindle Edgar, D: John Reed
Technicolor
Instructional film for Unilever. "Animated drawings with a high but not necessarily excessive element of humour, describe the mineral constituents of the body (very amusingly) and the functions of the mouth, stomach, duodenum, small intestine, and colon." (*Film User* December 1963.)

713 Your Hair and Scalp (1254)
World Wide
P: Hindle Edgar, D: Ken Woodward, S: Glyn Jones, A: Alan Green, C: James Allen, ED: Arthur Stevens, M: Roberto Gerhard, V: John Grahame
Technicolor
Instructional film for Unilever. The physiology of the human hair, how it forms inside the follicle, how it grows, and why it falls out. Live action with animated sequences.

197

714   **Pulmonary Function** (1075)
Halas & Batchelor
P: John Halas, Joy Batchelor, D: John Halas, S: Dr. Howell, A: Brian Borthwick, Vic Bevis, ED: Jack King, V: Richard Baker
Instructional film for Boehringer-Ingelheim. "New methods for the diagnosis and treatment of pulmonary diseases in diagrammatic explanation." (*British National Film Catalogue* 1963.)

715   **Mr. Know-How in All Round Comfort**
Industrial Animation: "Mr. Know-How" No. 2
P: George Dunning, D: Bill Sewell, ED: Steve Cox, M: Tristram Cary
Technicolor
Promotional film for the Gas Council. How a radiant convector gas heater works.

716   **The Showing Up of Larry the Lamb**
Halas & Batchelor: "Toytown" No. 1
P: John Halas, Hendrik Baker, D: Harold Whitaker, S: S.G. Hulme Beaman, SC: Hendrik Baker, Terry Harrison, A: Terry Harrison, Harold Whitaker, DES: Ted Pettingell, M: Jack King, V: Dorothy Gordon, Wilfred Babbage, Redvers Kyle, Derek Nimmo
Eastmancolor
First in a series (of two) adapted from the popular stories for children broadcast in the BBC *Children's Hour* programmes.

717   **The Tale of the Magician**
Halas & Batchelor: "Toytown" No. 2
P: John Halas, Hendrik Baker, D: Harold Whitaker, S: S.G. Hulme Beaman, SC: Hendrik Baker, Terry Harrison, A: Terry Harrison, Harold Whitaker, DES: Ted Pettingell, M: Jack King, V: Dorothy Gordon,, Wilfred Babbage, Redvers Kyle, Derek Nimmo
Eastmancolor
Second in series of adaptations of the popular stories for children.

718   **Automania 2000** (872)
Halas & Batchelor – British Lion
P: John Halas, Joy Batchelor, D: John Halas, S: Todor, Gyorgyei, SC: Joy Batchelor, A: Harold Whitaker, DES: Tom Bailey, M: Jack King, V: Edward Bishop
Eastmancolor
The world's great cities have ground to a halt, thanks to the motor car. A new civilization of car-dwellers has arisen, spending their entire lives in their immobilized cars, piled in layers one above the other. The continuing demand for cars leads scientists to create a car that can reproduce

itself. Unhappily, once started there is no way of stopping it. "In effect this is the first film from Halas and Batchelor which shows signs of real imaginative invention. The basic idea is developed with some fine touches, and the image of mountains of cars with exhausted survivors crawling painfully to the peaks like dying dinosaurs surpasses anything that this team has yet done." (*Monthly Film Bulletin* January 1964.) Print preserved in the National Film Archive. First British cartoon film to be nominated for an Academy Award (1963). British Film Academy Award 1963.

719 The Rejected Rose
Grasshopper Group
D:S:A: Stuart Wynn Jones
Color
Amateur cartoon. "Rivals for the same girl, a painter and a musician, vie to impress her with their artistic achievements." (*Film User* January 1964.)

720 Victoria's Rocking Horse
Grasshopper Group
D:S:A: Errol le Cain
Color
Amateur cartoon. "A little girl who wants a rocking horse so much that she takes one from a fairground roundabout. The commentary, spoken by a four year old, needs attentive ears, but is charming." (*Film User* January 1964.)

721 Bumble Bee Fair (560)
Moreno Cartoons—Saxon: "Merry Music Shop" No. 1
P:A: George Moreno, Jr., D: Fred Thompson, V: Mike Sammes Singers
Eastmancolor
Community song cartoon for children.

722 Bunty the Bouncing Bassoon (570)
Moreno Cartoons—Saxon: "Merry Music Shop" No. 2
P:A: George Moreno, Jr., D: Fred Thompson, V: Mike Sammes Singers
Eastmancolor
Community song cartoon for children.

723 The Land of Birthday Toys (470)
Moreno Cartoons—Saxon: "Merry Music Shop" No. 3
P:A: George Moreno, Jr., D: Fred Thompson, V: Mike Sammes Singers
Eastmancolor
Community song cartoon for children.

724   Little Mr. Robin (470)
  Moreno Cartoons—Saxon: "Merry Music Shop" No. 4
  P:A: George Moreno, Jr., D: Fred Thompson, V: Mike Sammes
Singers
  Eastmancolor
  Community song cartoon for children.

725   The Little Swiss Whistling Clock (430)
  Moreno Cartoons—Saxon: "Merry Music Shop" No. 5
  P:A: George Moreno, Jr., D: Fred Thompson, V: Mike Sammes
Singers
  Eastmancolor
  Community song cartoon for children.

726   Thunderclap Jones (566)
  Moreno Cartoons—Saxon: "Merry Music Shop" No. 6
  P:A: George Moreno, Jr., D: Fred Thompson, M: Thunderclap Jones
  Eastmancolor
  "The peculiar jazzy patterns the piano playing of Thunderclap Jones
suggests to a listener." (*British National Film Catalogue* 1963.)

727   Jack O' Diamonds (360)
  Moreno Cartoons—Saxon: "Merry Music Shop" No. 7
  P:A: George Moreno, Jr., D: Fred Thompson, M: Lonnie Donegan
  Eastmancolor
  Cartoon synchronized to the popular recording of a traditional song,
played by Lonnie Donegan and his Skiffle Group.

1964

728 A Productivity Primer (1620)
Biographic Films
P:D: Bob Godfrey, S: Paul Fletcher, A: Trevor Bond, C: Gerry
Walters, Alan Marshall, ED: Peter Hearn, M: Harry South, V: John Warren
Eastmancolor
Propaganda film for the British Council. "The meaning of produc-
tivity and the economic ideas which lie behind it. The difference between
productivity and production." (*British National Film Catalogue* 1964.)

729 The Rise and Fall of Emily Sprod (845)
Biographic Four – British Lion
P:D:A: Bob Godfrey, S: Stan Hayward, ED: Peter Hearn
Technicolor
Emily Sprod, a vigorously amorous female, emerges from a block of
stone and chases her sculptor through several startling situations. "The
comic detail is wittily contrived, and a sequence where the sculptor rides
his bicycle through ornate palaces and across skies is quite stunning in its
effect. Now that the resurgence of British animation in the world scene has
been firmly established, this bright little film will serve to bolster its reputa-
tion still further." (*Monthly Film Bulletin* April 1964.)

730 Alf, Bill and Fred (700)
Biographic Four – Contemporary
P:D:A: Bob Godfrey, S: Stan Hayward, ED: Peter Hearn, M: Arthur
Dulay
Eastmancolor
Alf (a duck), Bill (a man), and Fred (a dog) bounce happily through
life until Bill becomes a man of means. He abandons Alf and Fred, leaving
them sad until he loses all his money, and returns. All three begin their
happy bouncing again. "Bob Godfrey tells this little story in a much quieter
fashion than his previous films. The narrative is unfurled partly through
charming silent film–type titles (by Ron Coulter). The animation is limited
in style, but not restricted in ability successfully to interpret the story."
(*Monthly Film Bulletin* June 1964.)

731   The Insects (450)
TV Cartoons – Contemporary
P: George Dunning, D:S:A: Teru Murakami, C: John Williams, ED: Alex Rayment, V: Paul Whitsun-Jones
Technicolor
A man writing at his desk is pestered by insects, who finally carry him off. "This little fable has all the hallmarks of the studio which produced *The Apple* – crunchy sound, simplicity, and humour based on perfect timing of pauses both visually and aurally." (*Monthly Film Bulletin* June 1964.) British Film Academy Award 1964.

732   The Sure Thing (1260)
Larkins – Film Producers Guild
P:D:S: Richard Taylor, C: D. Hall, R. Pearce, ED: William Leach, M: Tristram Cary, V: Patrick Cargill, Kenneth Cope, Lance Percival, Paul Whitsun-Jones
Eastmancolor
Promotional film for the British Insurance Association. After an historical sequence showing how insurance began, the film demonstrates what insurance is and why it is good. "Excellent draughtsmanship with a perceptive understanding of the importance of key images (such as the Puritan costume, which is carried on in the use of the hat as a symbol of insurance cover) creates a context in which the swift-moving exposition never loses interest." (*Monthly Film Bulletin* June 1964.)

733   Aquarius
Biographic One
D:A: Nancy Hanna, M: Harry South
Technicolor
Abstract patterns to modern jazz simulating a trip through space.

734   Demonstration
Taylor Cartoons
P:D: Richard Taylor, A: Richard Taylor, Ray Jackson, Tony Cuthbert
Color
"Humorous quip about Sixties demonstrators." (*Cambridge Animation Festival* 1983.)

735   The Polyolefins (2354)
Shell Film Unit – Film Centre
P: Michael Clarke, D: Alan Pendry, A: Francis Rodker, ED: Philip Gordon, C: Ronald Whitehouse, M: Johnny Hawkesworth
Eastmancolor
Instructional film for Shell International Petroleum; animation and live action. The use of plastics for polythene bags, beer barrels and

chairs. "The film shows clearly and very interestingly the factors involved, reasons for change, and problems to be overcome." (*Monthly Film Bulletin* August 1964.)

736   Be Careful Boys (900)
Biographic – Public Relations Associates
P: Oliver Lawson Dick, D:A: Vera Linnecar, Nancy Hanna, Keith Learner, S: Colin Pearson, ED: Peter Hearn, M: Johnny Johnston, V: Wallas Eaton
Technicolor
Instructional film for the Fruit Producers Council. Charlie Burke, a careless fruit porter, is cured of dropping crates after dreaming, on a psychiatrist's couch, that everyone, everywhere, is dropping things. "A new and hopeful style of industrial safety film, and has a good chance of slipping under the guard of those used to the more solemn type of warning." (*Monthly Film Bulletin* September 1964.) British Film Academy Award 1965.

737   Man in Silence (720)
Halas & Batchelor – Contemporary
P: Leopoldo Maler, D: Leopoldo Maler, John Halas, S: Leopoldo Maler, A. Ciria, Marcos Ana, DES: Augustin Ibarrola, C: Sid Griffiths, M: Manuel Nazareno, John Williams, V: John Justin
Art film featuring the drawings of Augustin Ibarrola, a political prisoner in Spain, which were smuggled out of Burgos Prison, brought to England, and here assembled to poems by Marcos Ana and the guitar music of John Williams. "Rather similar in style to Alain Resnais' *Guernica*, which is unfortunate since this production does not on the whole have the same good basic material." (*Monthly Film Bulletin* December 1964.)

738   Goldwhiskers (764)
Biographic Two – British Lion
D:S:A: Keith Learner, DES: Irene Guillaumet, ED: Peter Hearn, C: Gerry Walters, V: Peter Hawkins
Eastmancolor
Burlesque on the James Bond 007 feature *Goldfinger*. James Burk, Secret Agent 00, is assigned to capture the notorious mouse, Goldwhiskers, who covers his girlfriends with cheese. After a chase through a giant cheese, Burk saves the girl from the master criminal's clutch. "Insufficiently clever or inventive to come off, and it emerges as a weak piece of burlesque. Chases and general activity are not far removed from the conventions of the stereotyped American cartoon (Bugs Bunny ilk), though disguised by a more original brand of design and draughtsmanship." (*Monthly Film Bulletin* January 1965.)

739   Midsummer Nightmare (770)
Halas & Batchelor
P: John Halas, Joy Batchelor, D: John Halas, S: Hazel Townson, SC: Joy Batchelor, A: John Smith, Ralph Ayres, Reg Lodge, DES: Ted Pettingell, M: Jack King, C: William Traylor, V: Max Adrian
Eastmancolor
Puck visits the Twentieth Century and is amused by our obsession with television. His sense of mischief gets the better of him as he tries to persuade people to mix together socially as of old.

740   The Banking Game
Larkins Studio
P: Beryl Stevens, D:S: Richard Taylor, A: Richard Taylor, Douglas Jensen, DES: Shirley Rahman, V: Charles Hodgson
Technicolor
Promotional film for Barclays Bank.

741   Uhuru
Taylor Cartoons
P:D: Richard Taylor, A: Richard Taylor, Ray Jackson, Tony Cuthbert
Color
"Crack at British Colonialism." (*Cambridge Animation Festival* 1983.)

742   Discovery Penicillin (1105)
TV Cartoons – COI
P: George Dunning, D: Denis Rich, C: John Williams, ED: Alex Rayment, V: David Attenborough
Eastmancolor
Instructional film for the Foreign Office. The discovery of the drug penicillin by Sir Alexander Fleming, and its use during World War Two.

743   The First Adventure of Thud and Blunder (126)
TV Cartoons: "Thud & Blunder" No. 1
P:D: George Dunning, A: Bill Sewell
Eastmancolor
Instructional film for the National Coal Board. Two clumsy miners disobey the safety rules for working underground.

744   Knock Off Time (197)
TV Cartoons: "Thud & Blunder" No. 2
P:D: George Dunning, A: Alan Ball
Eastmancolor
Instructional film for the National Coal Board safety campaign.

745 Haulage Hazards
TV Cartoons: "Thud & Blunder" No. 3
P:D: George Dunning, A: Bill Sewell
Eastmancolor
Instructional film for the National Coal Board. Mishaps of clumsy miners illustrating dangers connected with haulage.

746 Universal Circle
Phillips
P:D:S:A: Derek Phillips, V: Laurence Baker
Color
Amateur cartoon: "In which the universe is put forward as one large circle." (*British National Film Catalogue* 1978.)

747 Work of Art
Phillips
P:D:S:A: Derek Phillips, V: Clive Burrell
Color
Amateur cartoon. "Two politicians talk about their parties and policies while the person in need is ignored." (*British National Film Catalogue* 1978.)

1965

748 The Axe and the Lamp (625)
Halas & Batchelor – BFI
P:D: John Halas, S: Paul Dehn, C: Ron Taylor, M: Jack King, V: Robert Robinson
Color
Art film examining in detail Peter Breughel's 16th century painting illustrating over one hundred proverbs and allegories. "It attacks sin with the axe of satire; it illustrates folly with the lamp of pity." (*Film User* May 1965.)

749 The Right Knight
Derek Stewart
P: Derek Stewart, D: Terry Trench, S: Leslie Mallory, A: Peter Sachs, V: Sir Brian Horrocks
Promotional film for Bovis. "The pros and cons of contract procedures in the building industry." (*British National Film Catalogue* 1965.)

750 The Loco
TV Cartoons: "Thud & Blunder" No. 4
P:D: George Dunning
Eastmancolor
Instructional film for the National Coal Board. Everyday hazards in coal mining.

751 The Bargain
Larkins Studio
P:D: Beryl Stevens, V: Richard Wattis, Bernard Cribbins
Eastmancolor
Promotional film for Barclays Bank. "The treatment is mainly a dialogue between an off-screen narrator and a likeable semi-nincompoop who puts up objections to the banking system, all of which, needless to say, are finally disposed of." (*Film User* February 1966.)

752 Charley
TV Cartoons
P:D: George Dunning, A: Teru Murakami, Ron Wyatt, Alan Ball, ED: Alex Rayment, C: John Williams, M: Ron Goodwin, V: Noel Picarba

Eastmancolor

Adventures of a small boy who can turn himself into anything. He becomes an airplane, flies to an island, becomes an explorer, entangles with a fierce underground creature, and when a policeman arrives out of the sea, Charley turns himself into a car and drives away.

753   Springtime for Samantha
Biographic Three
D:S: Vera Linnecar, V: Wallas Eaton
Technicolor
Adventures of a small girl in the Spring.

754   The Fan (360)
Phillips – BFI
P:D:S:A: Derek Phillips, V: Roger Sturm
Color
Amateur cartoon. "A flat dweller whose ambition is to play the piano like his neighbour downstairs. He practices hard with an unexpected and sad result. But for the word 'amateur' on the British Film Institute box, nobody would guess that this was anything but a fully professional cartoon." (*Film User* November 1968.)

755   A Fable (360)
Phillips – Concord
P:D:S:A: Derek Phillips
Amateur film. Satire on the problem of over-population.

756   Dream Sound
Larkins Studio
P: Beryl Stevens, D: Denis Gilpin, M: Tristram Cary
Color
Promotional film for Shell Petrol. "The music concrete track backed with arresting visuals gives this advertising short a strong yet subtle impact." (*Cambridge Animation Festival* notes 1965.)

757   Clever
Phillips
P:D:S:A: Derek Phillips
Color
Amateur cartoon. "A figure piles articles on top of each other." (*British National Film Catalogue* 1978.)

758   Simple Simon
Scottish Educational Film Association
Eastmancolor
Traditional nursery rhyme intended as a reading exercise for infants.

1966

759 Johnny and the D.K. Robot
Larkins Studio
P: Beryl Stevens, D: Douglas Jensen, C: David Norton, Robert Grey,
ED: William Leach
Eastmancolor
Instructional film for the Oral Hygiene Service. The importance of brushing the teeth before going to bed.

760 Titi and the Woodman
Larkins Studio
P:S: Beryl Stevens, D: Denis Gilpin, M: Samuel Akbot
Promotional film for Barclays Bank aimed at West African audiences.

761 Genius Man (135)
Nicholas Cartoons—COI
P:D:S:A: Nicholas Spargo, C: Jane Aldous
Eastmancolor
Informational film for the Central Office of Information.

762 Square
Phillips
P:D:S:A: Derek Phillips, V: Michael Lines
Color
Amateur cartoon: "Considers the square as a symbol of man's intelligence." (*British National Film Catalogue* 1978.)

763 The Greater Community Animal
Phillips
P:D:S:A: Derek Phillips
Color
Amateur cartoon.

764 A Passing Phase
Phillips
P:D:S:A: Derek Phillips
Color
Amateur cartoon: "Suggesting that the formation of the Earth, the creation of life, man's squabbles and the eventual destruction of the Earth, are all just a passing phase in universal evolution." (*British National Film Catalogue* 1978.)

765 In Popular Demand
Phillips
P:D:S:A: Derek Phillips
Amateur cartoon: "Demonstrating that the public knows what it likes." (*British National Film Catalogue* 1978.)

766 The Line (540)
Phillips – BFI
P:D:S:A: Derek Phillips
Color
Amateur cartoon: "Semi-serious essay advancing the proposition that everything in life is either above or below the line, a kind of 'principle of oppositeness,' the good always (in toto) equalling the bad." (*Film User* November 1968.)

767 The Helmet
TV Cartoons: "Thud & Blunder" No. 5
P:D: George Dunning
Eastmancolor
Instructional film for National Coal Board. Protective clothing in coal mines.

768 Safety Boots
TV Cartoons: "Thud & Blunder" No. 6
P:D: George Dunning
Eastmancolor
Instructional film for the National Coal Board. Importance of wearing safety boots.

769 The Roof
TV Cartoons: "Thud & Blunder" No. 7
P:D: George Dunning
Eastmancolor
Instructional film for National Coal Board. Everyday hazards in coal mines.

770   Materials Handling
TV Cartoons: "Thud & Blunder" No. 8
P:D: George Dunning, A: Bill Sewell
Eastmancolor
Instructional film for National Coal Board. Two miners ignore the safety rules and suffer the painful consequences.

771   The Rise of Parnassus Needy
Taylor Cartoons
P:D:S: Richard Taylor, A: Denis Rich, Bill Sewell, M: Fitzroy Coleman, V: George Benson, Derek Nimmo
Eastmancolor
Promotional film for Barclays Bank. "Parnassus is an impoverished poet whose rise to success begins with a bank loan which enables him to open a Do It Yourself Poetry Shop. Soon faced with stiff competition from a cut-price store, he joins forces with Gertie Gracious, a folk singer, whose songs lack words." (*Film User* December 1966.)

772   Barbarota
World Wide Pictures
D: Reg Lodge
Color
Promotional film for Philips Electrical. "Make believe history of shaving methods from the stone age onwards, ending with a good humoured puff for the rotary head electric shaver of today." (*Film User* September 1966.)

1967

773   A Mug's Game
British Transport Films
Color
Animated puppets. "Made to deter young people from putting ob-
structions on the railway track." (*Film User* November 1967.)

774   The Ladder
Dunning
P:D:S:A: George Dunning, ED: Alex Rayment, Torquil Stewart
Eastmancolor
"Dunning takes the brush-stroke technique of The Flying Man
several stages forward and introduces a storyline loosely founded on the
eternal triangle." (*Cambridge Festival Programme* 1967.)

775   The Professor
Rank Short Films
D:S:DES: Peter See, A: George Jackson, M: Cliff Adams
Technicolor
"A botanist, a caterpillar and a butterfly in a foolish pursuit in the
great tradition of British absurdity." (*Annecy Festival Programme* 1967.)

776   Rope Trick (270)
Godfrey Films – Connoisseur
P:D: Bob Godfrey, S: Stan Hayward, A: Bob Godfrey, Ron Coulter,
Ian Gordon, C: Bev Roberts, ED: Tony Fish
Eastmancolor
A man climbs a rope and comes down with a box of jewels. The
watching crowd take off their coats and climb the rope. The man collects
their coats and sets fire to the rope. "This mildly amusing cartoon is rather
uncharacteristic of Bob Godfrey's recent films in that it is a single idea rather
than a string of Goonish illogicalities. The animation is refreshingly simple."
(*Monthly Film Bulletin* May 1968.)

777 What Ever Happened to Uncle Fred (450)
Godfrey Films — Connoisseur
P:D:A: Bob Godfrey, S: Stan Hayward, C: Bev Roberts, ED: Tony Fish, DES: Claire Godfrey, M: Johnny Hawkesworth, V: Tessa Godfrey
Eastmancolor
A small girl's view of adultery in the home. "With artwork and sound-track produced by his children, our own Bob Godfrey has produced a devastating insight into the adult world from the child's viewpoint." (*Cambridge Festival Programme* 1967.)

778 Ruddigore (4814)
Halas & Batchelor — Gala
P: John Halas, Joy Batchelor, AP: James H. Lawrie, D: Joy Batchelor, AD: Harold Whitaker, S: William S. Gilbert, Arthur Sullivan, A: Tony Guy, Tony Whitehouse, A. Derrick, D. Knight, J. Perkins, J. Richards, D. Salter, T. Williams, DES: John Cooper, Ted Pettingell, M: Arthur Sullivan, MD: James Walker, Royal Philharmonic Orchestra, SD: Jack King, V: Ann Hood (Rose Maybud), John Reed (Robin Oakapple), Donald Adams (Sir Roderic Murgatroyd), David Palmer (Richard Dauntless), Jennifer Toye (Zorah), George Cook (Old Adam), Gillian Knight (Dame Hannah), Kenneth Sandforth (Sir Despard Murgatroyd), Peggy Ann Jones (Mad Margaret)
Eastmancolor
Feature-length (54 minutes) cartoon made for WBC-TV (USA) but shown theatrically in UK. Animated version of the operetta by Gilbert and Sullivan. In 1450 the Murgatroyd family of Ruddigore is cursed by a burning witch. In 1820 the new heir, Ruthven Murgatroyd, learns he is obliged to commit a crime or die in agony. He evades his unhappy responsibility by living a rustic life under the name of Robin Oakapple. His brother, Despard, believing him dead, has succeeded to the title. When the truth comes to light, Ruthven has to take the place of the suddenly reformed Despard. Ruthven is unhappy with his newly criminal life and solves the situation by refusing to perform the required daily deed. This means his death which, being suicide, is in turn a crime. "Despite its many minor felicities the animation is generally disappointing: the backgrounds (Ted Pettingell) in a style of pen-and-ink drawings with washes of colour, are attractive; but the more solid colour figures (John Cooper) are little more than conventional cartoon caricatures." (*Monthly Film Bulletin* July 1967.)

779 Flow Diagram (360)
Halas & Batchelor
P: John Halas, D:A: Harold Whitaker, S: Stan Hayward, Trevor Fletcher, M: Jack King
Eastmancolor

Instructional film. "Halas & Batchelor humorously introduce a mathematical process in this excellent example of the important new single-concept educational film." (*Cambridge Festival Programme* 1967.)

780   The Question (690)
Halas & Batchelor — MGM
P:D: John Halas, S: Stan Hayward, A: Tony Guy, Tony Whitehouse, DES: John Dick, ED:M: Jack King, V: David Henderson-Tate
Eastmancolor
Man tries to discover the meaning of a question mark by asking a priest, a politician, an artist, a businessman, a scientist, a psychiatrist, and a soldier. He gets the right answer from a girl.

781   The Revolution
Taylor Cartoons
P:D:A: Richard Taylor
Color
"The change of power and takeover by a revolutionary committee."

782   Fairy Tale (80)
Dick & Elizabeth Horn
D:A: Dick Horn, S: Stan Hayward
Color
"One man's brief flirtation with the promise of happiness." (*Cambridge Animation Festival* 1968.)

783   Functions and Relations (800)
Halas & Batchelor — Guild
P: John Halas, D: Harold Whitaker, S: Stan Hayward, Patrick Murphy, A: Tony Guy, C: Leo Rodgers, ED: Mike Crouch
Color
Instructional film. "Explains mathematical relations in terms of how each member of a family is related to each other, graphically illustrating the reflexive, symmetric, transitive, and equivalence relations." (*British National Film Catalogue* 1981.)

784   Tidy Why
TV Cartoons
P: George Dunning, D: Bill Sewell
Eastmancolor
Propaganda film for the National Coal Board promoting National Anti-Litter Week.

785   **The Furry Folk on Holiday**
      Hemsley – ROSPA
      P:D: Norman Hemsley
      Color
      Animated puppets featuring Tufty the Squirrel, made for the Royal
Society for the Prevention of Accidents. "Gives lessons about not swimming in an outgoing tide, not leaving broken glass on the beach, and
remembering curb drill when crossing the road." (*Film User* January 1968.)

786   **The Chair** (360)
      TV Cartoons
      P: George Dunning, D: Bill Sewell, A: Bill Sewell, Peter Bird
      Eastmancolor
      Humorous cartoon.

787   **Anima**
      Vester
      P:D:S:A: Paul Vester
      Color

788   **Repetition**
      Vester
      P:D: Paul Vester, S: Norman Mailer, A: Paul Vester, David Royle,
George Ward, Susan Branch, Susan Vester
      Color

789   **Henry Philpott** (180)
      Larkins Studio
      P:D: Beryl Stevens, A: Douglas Jensen, Peter Green, DES: Shirley
Rahman, V: Hattie Jacques, George Benson, Bernard Cribbins
      Eastmancolor
      Advertising cartoon for Barclays Bank.

790   **Same but Different**
      Phillips
      P:D:S:A: Derek Phillips, V: Trevor Begley
      Color
      Amateur cartoon. "The story of two people with opposite aims, il-
lustrating a poem told in a North Country accent." (*British National Film
Catalogue* 1978.)

791   **The Sailor and the Devil**
      Richard Williams – British Lion
      P: Richard Williams, D:A: Errol le Cain, C: Ted Gerald, M: Peter
Shade, V: Alex Bradford

Color

"Animated cartoon of a sailor, a high sea, a devilish island, and a song." (*British National Film Catalogue* 1970.)

792   The Rime of the Ancient Mariner
Argo Records – CETO
D: Bernard Queenman, S: Samuel Taylor Coleridge, A: John Ryan
ED: Richard Pettefer, V: Richard Burton, John Neville, Robert Hardy

Visual interpretation of the classic poem, sponsored by an American record company.

1968

793 Quodlibet
Biographic
P:D:S:A: Nancy Hanna, Vera Linnecar, ED: Keith Learner
Eastmancolor
"A little man is running. He goes through a variety of expressions –
laughing, frightened, tearful – but never stops running." (*British National
Film Catalogue* 1973.)

794 Dying for a Smoke
Halas & Batchelor – COI
P:D: John Halas, S: Joy Batchelor, Peter Sachs, A: Terry Harrison,
Alan Green, Mike Pocock, DES: Peter Sachs, M: Jack King, V: Warren
Mitchell
Eastmancolor
Propaganda film for the Ministry of Health. "The devil, old Nick
O'Tine, employs various tricks to persuade a young lad to take up smoking.
The rescue comes in the shape of a friendly lorry driver who points out the
disadvantages of smoking in terms of cash and improved physical fitness."
(*Film User* March 1968.)

795 Flurina
Halas & Batchelor – Condor Films
P: John Halas, Christian Feuter, D: John Halas, S: Selina Chonz,
SC: Joy Batchelor, A: Tony Whitehouse, DES: Alois Carigiet, ED: Jack King,
M: Paul Burkhart, V: Peter-Christian Feuter
Eastmancolor
Anglo-Swiss production. "The story deals with the relationship be-
tween Flurina and the small wild bird that she rescues from the claws of
an eagle in the Swiss Alps." (*British National Film Catalogue* 1968.)

796 What Exactly Is a Program?
ICE Films
A: Joan Garrick, C: Geoffrey Parsons, ED: David Martindale, V:
Ronald Baddiley

Eastmancolor
Instructional film for International Computers. "Explaining what a computer program consists of and how it is constructed. Machine coded instructions, programming languages, sub-routines, program libraries are explained in the 1900 series." (*British National Film Catalogue* 1968.)

797   Yellow Submarine (7830)
King Features–Subafilms–Apple–UA
P: Al Brodax, AP: Mary Ellen Stewart, SUP: John Coates, D: George Dunning, S: Lee Mintoff, SC: Lee Mintoff, Al Brodax, Jack Mendelsohn, Erich Segal, DES: Heinz Edelman, John Cramer, Gordon Harrison, AD: Jack Stokes, Robert Balser, A: Alan Ball, Hester Coblentz, Rich Cox, Anthony Cuthbert, Cam Ford, Ann Joliffe, Tom Halley, Jim Hiltz, Arthur Humberstone, Reg Lodge, Terry Moesker, Mike Pocock, Edrick Radage, Mike Stuart, Chris Caunter, C: John Williams, FX: Charles Jenkins, ED: Brian Bishop, M: John Lennon, Paul McCartney, MD: George Martin, SD: Donald Cohen, V: John Clive (John Lennon), Geoffrey Hughes (Paul McCartney), Paul Angelus (Ringo Starr), Lance Percival (George Harrison), Dick Emery (Lord Mayor; Boob)
Eastmancolor
Feature-length (87 minutes) cartoon set to the music of The Beatles. The people of Pepperland are enjoying a concert by Sergeant Pepper's Lonely Hearts Club Band when they are attacked by the Blue Meanies who want to rid the world of music. The invaders freeze people where they stand, but Old Fred the Conductor escapes to Liverpool in a yellow submarine. He rounds up the four members of The Beatles pop group who, with the aid of the super-intellectual Boob, rout the enemy and restore music and happiness to Pepperland. "Visually it is an anthology of contemporary art and graphic design, reflecting every fleeting fashion of the here and now from Aubrey Beardsley (the elongated Apple Bonkers) and Art Nouveau via Salvador Dali (distorted clock faces) to Rauschenberg and Op and Pop Art. Inevitably it has dated even in the transition from planning to completion." (*Monthly Film Bulletin* September 1968). The Beatles recorded their own singing and playing, but their speaking voices are impersonated by actors. Songs: "Yellow Submarine," "Sergeant Pepper," "Lucy in the Sky with Diamonds," "Eleanor Rigby," "It's All Too Much," "Altogether Now," "All You Need Is Love," "Hey Bulldog," "Nowhere Man," "Northern Swing," "When I'm Sixty-Four." Note: the international release version has a revised and partly remade final sequence.

798   Small Boats
Larkins Studio
P:D: Beryl Stevens, ED: Terry Brown, C: Robert Grey
Eastmancolor

Promotional film for the British National Export Council. "The background to the recent devaluation of sterling explained in simple terms, and how it will assist the British businessman competing in a foreign market." (*British National Film Catalogue* 1968.)

799   Dinosaur (90)
Nicholas Cartoons – COI
P:D:A: Nicholas Spargo, V: Peter Hawkins, John Harvey
Eastmancolor
Informational film for the Central Office of Information.

800   Refining
Larkins Studio
P: Beryl Stevens, D: Denis Gilpin, A: P. Green, C: Maurice Picot, Robert Grey, ED: Terry Brown, M: Tristram Cary, V: Roy Kinnear
Eastmancolor
Promotional film for B.P. "A tour of an oil refinery using animation, live action, and stills to comment on and simplify the technical jargon so often used." (*British National Film Catalogue* 1968.)

801   Credit
Phillips
P:D:S:A: Derek Phillips
Color
Amateur cartoon. "An inspector sees that a tree can keep its leaves tidy, so he sacks a road sweeper." (*British National Film Catalogue* 1978.)

802   Clean
Phillips
P:D:S:A: Derek Phillips
Color
Amateur cartoon. "About a man who attaches great importance to having a clean car." (*British National Film Catalogue* 1978.)

803   Perfect
Phillips
P:D:S:A: Derek Phillips
Color
Amateur cartoon. "A tramp gets knocked down by a car. In a coma he dreams of a perfect existence which he hates, so when he eventually comes round he is glad when the surgeons tell him he will not survive the accident." (*British National Film Catalogue* 1978.)

804   Round and Round
Phillips
P:D:S:A: Derek Phillips
Color
Amateur cartoon. "Black and White find their differences settled when they become Grey." (*British National Film Catalogue* 1978.)

805   Two Faces
Alison de Vere
P:D:S:A: Alison De Vere, ED: Gordon Grimward, M: Derrick Newman, V: William Abney
Color
"An image of two heads describes subjectively a meeting and a parting." (*Cambridge Animation Festival Programme.*)

806   The Pilgrim
Taylor Cartoons
P:D: Richard Taylor, A: Ginger Gibbons, Leonard Lewis, Eileen Matthews, M: Manfred Mann, Mike Higg, V: Nigel Stock, Derek Nimmo
Eastmancolor
Promotional film for Barclays Bank. "The case of our Pilgrim, his adventures in the mists and jungles of international dealings, and his eventual success, aided by the bank manager and the bank's overseas representatives, symbolised by the ever-present Barclay's Eagle." (*Film User* February 1969.)

807   The Princess and the Wonderful Weaver
Taylor Cartoons
P: Digby Turpin, D: Richard Taylor, A: Ginger Gibbons, Eileen Matthews, Leonard Lewis, M: Daphne Orcam, V: Avis Bunnage, George A. Cooper
Eastmancolor
Promotional film for National Wool Textile Export Corporation. "Light-hearted capsule history mainly in cartoon form, embodying a fairy-story about a princess (representing world demand) who is growing into a giant and must be clothed in wool in a matter of hours if she is to return to normal size." (*Film User* June 1968.)

808   Discovering Radar
TV Cartoons – British Lion
P: George Dunning, D: Jim Duffy, John Fletcher, S: Donald Holmes, Sarah Erulkar, A: Jim Duffy, ED: Brian Bishop, M: Bill Shepherd, V: John Carson
Eastmancolor
The history of radar, its discovery and progress.

809   Fairy Story
Wyatt—Cattaneo Productions
P: Ron Wyatt, D: Tony Cattaneo, S: Stan Hayward, A: Tony Cattaneo, Beth McFall, C: Leslie Green, ED: Steve Cox, M: Misha Donat, V: Kenneth Griffith
Eastmancolor
"A father sits reading his newspaper; his small son waits expectantly. Eventually father puts his paper down and begins to tell a fairy story. Suddenly a beautiful fairy appears." (*British National Film Catalogue* 1973.) Father swats it with his paper!

1969

810 The Trend Setter
Biographic Three
P:D:DES: Vera Linnecar, S: Stan Hayward, C: Gerry Walters, ED:
Mary Hughes
Eastmancolor
"Everything the Trendsetter does is immediately imitated by the
crowds who follow him wherever he goes. So he decides to start a trend
for suicide, but the result is not as happy as he expects." (*British National
Film Catalogue* 1973.)

811 The Arrow
British Film Institute
D:S:A: Mel Calman, M: Ron Matthewson
A little man blindly follows the direction of a pointing arrow. Print
preserved in the National Film Archive. Included in the feature film *Long
Shot* (1978).

812 Automatic Fare Collection and You
British Transport Films
P: John Shearman, D: Bob Privett, A: C. Whitby, C: Ron Craigen,
ED: R. Debenham
Instructional film for London Transport Board. "The correct and
incorrect ways of getting tickets and going through automatic gates."
(*British National Film Catalogue* 1971.)

813 Soft Orange
Donaldson – Idea Books
D: Antony Donaldson, Robert Graham, A: Antony Donaldson
Color
Animated wax. "Erotic images with an undertone of menace."
(*British National Film Catalogue* 1976.)

814   The Travellers and the Thieves
Eothen Films
P: Philip Sattin, S: C. Griffith, A: F. Langford, Ken Gray, ED: David Jenner
Color
"Free adaptation using animation of two West African folk stories incorporating a number of moral values." (*British National Film Catalogue* 1976.)

815   Two Off the Cuff (810)
Godfrey Films — Monarch
P:D: Bob Godfrey, S: Stan Hayward, A: Bob Godfrey, Bill Sewell, C: Bev Roberts, Ramon Modiano, ED: Tony Fish, Peter Hearn, V: Bob Godfrey, Deryck Guyler, Ronnie Barker
Eastmancolor
Two short cartoons: *Masks* and *Happenings*. In the first Harry's smiling face is a public image concealing his true gloomy self. In the second a man in a void wonders why nothing ever happens to him. "As with most of Godfrey's recent work, the style is far removed from the inconsequential, Goonish antics of his earlier films. The ideas are too obviously derivative of other cartoonists." (*Monthly Film Bulletin* April 1969.)

816   Linear Programming
Halas & Batchelor — EFC
P: John Halas, D:A: Harold Whitaker, S: Stan Hayward, Patrick Murphy, ED: Jack King
Color
Educational film illustrating the basic principles in plotting equations on graphs, using the problem of loading a cart with boxes as a demonstration.

817   Topology
Halas & Batchelor — EFC
P: John Halas, D:A: Harold Whitaker, S: Stan Hayward, Patrick Murphy, ED: Jack King
Color
Educational film combining two- and three-dimensional animation to demonstrate topological changes.

818   Bolly (450)
Halas & Batchelor
P: John Halas, D:S: Joy Batchelor, A: Tony Guy, M: Keith Potger, David Groom
Color
Adventures in space of Bolly and his friends among imaginary planets.

819 Metrication (800)
Halas & Batchelor – EFC – Guild
P: John Halas, D:A: Tony Whitehouse, V: Murray Kash
Color
Educational film in three parts: The meter and its subdivisions; long lengths and land divisions; volumes and weight.

820 To Our Children's Children's Children
Halas & Batchelor
P:D: John Halas, S: Derek Lamb, A: Tony Whitehouse, M: The Moody Blues
Color
Musical cartoon.

821 Who'll Pay My Mortgage?
Larkins Studio
P:D: Beryl Stevens, A: Douglas Jensen, DES: Edward McLachlan, V: George Benson, Bernard Cribbins
Eastmancolor
Advertising cartoon for Barclays Bank. "Tuneful explanation of the advantages of the painless way to pay your regular bills." (*Zagreb Animation Festival Programme.*)

822 Tell Mummy
Taylor Cartoons – COI
P:D:A: Richard Taylor
Color
Informational cartoon warning children not to talk to strangers.

823 Don't Talk to Strangers
Taylor Cartoons – COI
P:D:A: Richard Taylor
Color
Informational cartoon warning children not to talk to strangers.

824 Matrices
Halas & Batchelor – EFC – Guild
P: John Halas, Alan Burke, D:A: Harold Whitaker, S: Stan Hayward, Patrick Murphy, M: Jack King
Color
Educational film: "Illustrates the matrices that control the contraction, rotation and reflection of the shapes in relation to the X and Y axes on a graph." (*British National Film Catalogue* 1982.)

825   What Is a Computer
Halas & Batchelor — Argo
P: John Halas, XP: Ian Dalrymple, D:S: Stan Hayward, A: Bill
Sewell, Tony Whitehouse, ED: Jack King, V: Murray Kash
Color
Educational film: introduction to the principles of the computer.
Special computer animation by Tony Pritchett.

826   Cool and Calculating
Larkins Studio
P: Beryl Stevens, D: Terry Brown, S: Roy Alexander, A: Freddie
Shackell, C: Roy Beard, V: Richard Bebb
Eastmancolor
Informational film for Midlands Bank: a "filmagraph" combining still
pictures, animation and other optical effects." Traces the development of
methods of counting and calculating from the earliest times." (*Guild Films
Catalogue* 1972.)

827   The Curious History of Money
Larkins Studio
P:D: Beryl Stevens, A: Ann Joliffe, C: Robert Grey, ED: Terry
Brown, M: Tristram Cary, V: Jack Hulbert
Eastmancolor
Promotional film for Barclays Bank. "When the cavemen came out
of the caves and started to become tradesmen, the system of trading by
barter grew up. But it had its problems. How many spears equal one roast
leg of mammoth, for instance? So they invented money." (*Film User* June
1969.)

828   G.I.G.O.: Garbage in Garbage Out
Millbank Films
D:S: Richard Taylor, A: Richard Taylor, Ginger Gibbons, V: William
Rushton, Bernard Cribbins
Technicolor
Promotional film for Barclays Bank: live action and animation. "This
fine production shows us that the quality of what comes out of any com-
puter depends entirely upon the quality of what the operator feeds into it."
(*Film User* July 1970.)

829   The Air Show
Nicholas Cartoons
P:D:A: Nicholas Spargo, M: Jack Gregory
Eastmancolor
Promotional cartoon to mark the 50th anniversary of the British
branch of Atlas Copco. "Two cartoon figures introduce various big

contracts on which the sponsor's products have been used. Then they take it to a typical branch office before going to the big factory at Hemel Hempstead. We get two glimpses of the future." (*Film User* September 1969.)

830   Handyman
Phillips
P:D:S:A: Derek Phillips
Color
Amateur cartoon. "A nail is made from an enormous ingot, but when it is hammered into the wall, it bends." (*British National Film Catalogue* 1978.)

831   Oops!
Phillips
P:D:S:A: Derek Phillips
Color
Amateur cartoon. "Suggests that evolution relies on mistakes for its continuance, and so does inspiration." (*British National Film Catalogue* 1978.)

832   Mine All Mine
Phillips
P:D:S:A: Derek Phillips, M: Peter Ind
Color
Amateur cartoon. "The people in this film show their greed but are caught out by the person who wants to share." (*British National Film Catalogue* 1978.)

833   Hands, Knees and Boomps-a-Daisy
TV Cartoons
P:D: George Dunning, A: Tony Gearty, Ron Coulter, Denis Hunt, C: John Williams, ED: Brian Bishop, V: Stanley Unwin.
Eastmancolor
Instructional film for the National Coal Board. "The hazards of working in coal mines and the need to wear protective clothing." (*British National Film Catalogue* 1969.)

834   I Love You
Wyatt – Cattaneo Productions
P: Ron Wyatt, D: Tony Cattaneo, S: Stan Hayward, A: Tony Cattaneo, Franco Cristofani, Beth McFall, ED: Steve Cox, V: Graham Stark
Eastmancolor
"A man is nervously rehearsing the phrase 'I love you' in every possible intonation and expression. Then the telephone rings." (*British National Film Catalogue* 1973.)

835   Package Deal
Wyatt—Cattaneo Productions
XP: Derek Smythe, P: Ron Wyatt, D: Tony Cattaneo, S: Ron Wyatt,
Stan Hayward, A: Tony Cattaneo, Beth McFall, Franco Cristofani, Barry
Merritt, DES: Ron Wyatt, Tony Cattaneo, Beth McFall, ED: Steve Cox, M:
Misha Donat, V: Stanley Baxter
Eastmancolor
Advertising film for the United States Lines showing the advantages
of container shipping.

836   Cod Fishing
TV Cartoons
P: George Dunning, D: Bill Sewell
Eastmancolor

837   No Arks
British Film Institute Production Board
D:S:DES: Abu Abraham, A: Alan Kitching, Joanna Drake
Propaganda cartoon for the abolition of atomic bombs, made by
"Abu," an Indian cartoonist drawing for *The Guardian* and *The Observer*
newspapers.

1970

838 Airport
Phillips
P:D:S:A: Derek Phillips
Color
Amateur cartoon: "Film concerning a bomb scare at an airport."
(*London Film Festival Notes.*)

839 The Battle
Phillips
P:D:S:A: Derek Phillips
Color
Amateur cartoon: "The action takes place within the digestive
system of a soldier with a fried egg to be overcome by attrition." (*London
Film Festival Notes.*)

840 Now
Phillips
P:D:S:A: Derek Phillips
Color
Amateur cartoon: "The workaday world, relatively unseen." (*British
National Film Catalogue* 1978.)

841 Flags (90)
Nicholas Cartoons—COI
P:D:A: Nicholas Spargo, V: Wendy Craig, Peter Hawkins
Color
Informational film for the Central Office of Information. Couple on a
seaside beach come to grief when they ignore the danger warning flags.

842 Corporate Planning in British Railways (1800)
British Transport Films
P: James Richie, D: Richard Crosfield, A: Richard Taylor, C: Ronald
Craigen, ED: David Lochner, M: Eric Wetherall, V: Anthony Marsh, Gary
Watson

Color

Instructional film: live action and animation. "Explains the theory of corporate planning in relation to the sponsor's corporate plan." (*British National Film Catalogue* 1970.)

843 A Film
Amber Films
P:D:A: Peter Roberts
Color
"Story of a man who, unable to relate to his surroundings, adopts a series of disguises in a futile attempt to overcome his alienation." (*British National Film Catalogue* 1978.)

844 The Pied Piper of Hamelin
Argo Records
D: Bernard Queenman, S: Robert Browning, A: Allan Smith, M: David Munrow, V: Peter Ustinov
17-minute animated version of the classic poem for children.

845 Careful Charlie
British Transport Films
P: John Shearman, D: Bob Privett, ED: R. Debenham, V: Stephen Jack
Eastmancolor
Instructional film for the British Railways Board. Charlie, a railway worker, demonstrates the careless way of working.

846 Henry 9 Till 5 (548) (X)
Godfrey Films — British Lion
P:D: Bob Godfrey, S: Stan Hayward, A: Bob Godfrey, Denis Rich, Kathleen Houston, Bill Sewell, C: Bev Roberts, ED: Tony Fish, V: Bob Godfrey, Marilyn Rickard
Eastmancolor
Henpecked commuter spends all his working hours fantasizing about sex. Awarded an "X" (adults only) certificate. "The humour is broad and British, like animated Donald McGill; but not really sharp enough to be a comment on itself and trailing off into a predictable punchline." (*Monthly Film Bulletin* June 1973.) British Film Academy Award 1970.

847 Ways and Means
Godfrey Films — Halas & Batchelor
P: John Halas, D: Bob Godfrey, S: Lewis Carroll, A: Jeff Goldner, Bob Godfrey, Kathleen Houston, DES: Jeff Goldner
Eastmancolor
Animated adaptation of one of Lewis Carroll's nonsense poems.

848 Children and Cars (731)
Halas & Batchelor
P: John Halas, D: John Halas, David Williamson, S: John Halas,
Joy Batchelor, A: Harold Whitaker, M: Jack King, V: Edward Bishop
Eastmancolor
Promotional film for British Petroleum. Young children's pictorial
ideas of the motor car of today and tomorrow, animated from their own
original drawings.

849 The Five
Halas & Batchelor
P: John Halas, Joy Batchelor, D:S: Joy Batchelor, A: Harold Whitaker, M: The Aunties
Eastmancolor
Instructional film for British Life Assurance Trust. "Sets out to
create a positive attitude in the minds of young girls aged 8 to 12 years, and
to encourage them to look after their feet." (*British National Film Catalogue*
1970.)

850 Sputum
Halas & Batchelor
P: Joy Batchelor, D: Brian Borthwick, A: Brian Borthwick, Vic Bevis
Eastmancolor
Instructional film for Boehringer Ingelheim. "Presents a series of
logically related animated sequences, an up-to-date synoptic review of
bronchial secretion." (*British National Film Catalogue* 1970.)

851 The Wotdot (540)
Halas & Batchelor
P: John Halas, Joy Batchelor, D:S: Joy Batchelor, A: Vic Bevis,
Harold Whitaker, Jose Roxburgh, M: Jack King, V: Richard Carpenter
Color
Wotdot organizes the other dots to form a variety of shapes and
forms in different colors and sizes.

852 This Love Thing
Halas & Batchelor
P: John Halas, Joy Batchelor, D: Geoff Dunbar, S: Len Sugarman,
A: Tony Whitehouse, Denis Rich, C: Stephen Goldblatt, M: James Taylor,
Alan Parker, Paul Ryan, Barry Ryan
Color
Musical combination of live action and animation.

853   The Electron's Tale
Larkins Studio
P: Beryl Stevens, D: Peter Green, Bob Godfrey, S: Nicholas Spargo,
A: Jeff Goldner, Ian Moo-Young, Kathleen Houston, Ann Joliffe, C: Guy
Knight, Paul Wibley, Kevan Woolridge, ED: Scott Forrest, Tony Fish, M:
Tristram Cary, V: George Benson
Eastmancolor
Combined live action and animation, promotional film for the 50th
anniversary of Mullard. "The way in which electrons play such an impor-
tant part in our everyday lives." (*Film User* December 1970.)

854   The World of Automation
Larkins Studio – COI
P: William Leach, D: Denis Rich, A: Denis Rich, B. Moon, C:
Bob Hunter, Robert Grey, ED: Peter Heffran, M: John Mayer, Indo Jazz
Fusions, V: Lohna Phillipe
Color
Combined live action and animation; promotional film for the
Foreign Office. "The principles and advantage of automation, the basis of
modern industry and progress." (*British National Film Catalogue* 1977.)

855   Jobs for Early School Leavers
Taylor Cartoons – COI
P:D:S:A: Richard Taylor, V: Patrick Cargill
Eastmancolor
Instructional film made for the Central Office of Information.

856   The Patient Analyst
Taylor Cartoons
P:D:S: Richard Taylor, A: Richard Taylor, Ann Joliffe, V: Richard
Taylor
Eastmancolor
Promotional film for Vickers.

857   A Sense of Responsibility
TV Cartoons
P: George Dunning, D:A: Alan Ball, S: Jim Duffy, C: John Williams,
ED: Brian Bishop, V: Deryck Guyler, Wallas Eaton
Eastmancolor
Instructional film for National Coal Board. "Shows in a light-hearted
way how one incident sets off a chain reaction of disaster." (*British National
Film Catalogue* 1970.)

858   The Self-Rescue Breathing Apparatus
TV Cartoons
P: George Dunning
Eastmancolor
Instructional film for National Coal Board. "Drawing attention to the fatal consequences of not carrying a self-rescuer." (*British National Film Catalogue* 1971.)

859   After the Arrow
World Wide Pictures
P: Clifford Parris, D:S: Glyn Jones, Ric Wylam, A: Ric Wylam, Don Golding, Alan Gray, C: Kenneth Reeves, Charles Smith, ED: Arthur Stevens, M: Frank Spedding, V: Anthony Quayle
Eastmancolor
Promotional film for the Post Office. "Selected commemorative stamps trace the heritage of the British nation from the Norman Conquest to the Concorde." (*British National Film Catalogue* 1971.)

860   Problematics
World Wide Pictures
P: R. D'Ancona, D:A: R.A. Lord, C: Charles Smith
Amateur film advertising IBM. "A third year design student was asked to express his concept of the sponsors and this short animation film is the result." (*British National Film Catalogue* 1971.)

861   Magnetism
World Wide Pictures
P: Arthur Stevens, D:A: Eric Wylam, V: John Grahame
Educational film for Philips Electrical. In two parts: "The Lorentz Force and its Effect"; "The Origin of Magnetic Fields."

862   Moon Rock (720)
TV Cartoons
P:D: George Dunning, S: Edward de Bono, A: Diane Jackson, Roy Evans, Jeremy Hibbert, DES: Mike Crane, M: Ron Grainer, C: John Williams, ED: Brian Bishop, SD: Ron Geeson
Eastmancolor
Science-fiction cartoon based on the book *Lateral Thinking*.

1971

863　I'm Glad You Asked That Question
Biographic Films
P:D:A: Keith Learner, Nancy Hanna, Vera Linnecar, S: Stan Hayward, C: Gerry Walters, ED: Paul Huggett, M: Kenneth Jones, V: Deryck Guyler
Color
Promotional film for North Sea Gas; guided tour through the gas fields.

864　A Cat Is a Cat
Biographic Three
D:S: Vera Linnecar, M: Ludwig Beethoven
Color
"The cat as seen through a child's eye, through history ancient and modern." (*Zagreb Animation Festival Programme.*)

865　Sisyphus
Films of Scotland
D:A: Donald Holwill, S: Robert Garioch
Color
"Cartoon of the Greek legend which interprets the mood and style of Robert Garioch's poem." (*British National Film Catalogue 1977.*)

866　Kama Sutra Rides Again (802) (X)
Godfrey Films—Rank
P: Ron Inkpen, D: Bob Godfrey, S: Stan Hayward, Ralph Edney, John Lloyd, A: Ian Moo-Young, Jeff Goldner, Kathleen Houston, Bob Godfrey, Ann Joliffe, John Challis, Franco Cristofani, Peter Green, C: Paul Wibley, ED: Tony Fish, M: Johnny Hawkesworth, V: Bob Godfrey, L.J. Dickens
Eastmancolor
Apparently typical middle-class suburbanites, Stan and Ethel, devote their lives to discovering new ways to make love. Awarded "X" certificate (adults only). Nominated for the Academy Award. Animators included students from the West Surrey College of Art.

867 Milestones in Therapy
Halas & Batchelor
P: John Halas, D: Jack King, S: Bob Privett, A: Vic Bevis, Brian Borthwick, C: Ken Lee, Leo Rodgers, ED: Bernard Moss, V: Vernon Greeves
Eastmancolor
Instructional film for Abbott Laboratories. "The principles of Irofolc for coping with iron and folates deficiencies during pregnancy." (*British National Film Catalogue* 1971.)

868 The Condition of Man (90)
Halas & Batchelor: "Condition of Man" No. 1
P: John Halas, D: Geoff Dunbar, A: Alan Ball
Color
One-minute cartoon.

869 Quartet (90)
Halas & Batchelor: "Condition of Man" No. 2
P: Dick Arnall, D: Tony White, A: Tony White, John Perkins
Color
One-minute cartoon. "Comment on man's fight for the balance of power and humanity." (*Zagreb Animation Festival Programme.*)

870 Up (90)
Halas & Batchelor: "Condition of Man" No. 3
P: John Halas, D: Geoff Dunbar, A: Gillian Lacey, M: Terry Brown
Color
One-minute cartoon.

871 Let It Bleed (90)
Halas & Batchelor: "Condition of Man" No. 4
P: John Halas, D: Geoff Dunbar, A: Maggie Clarke, M: Terry Brown
Color
One-minute cartoon.

872 It Furthers One to Have Somewhere to Go (90)
Halas & Batchelor: "Condition of Man" No. 5
P: John Halas, D: Geoff Dunbar, A: Ginger Gibbons, M: Angela Morley
Color
"Our hero collects gun/cross/woman/clock/coffin and takes them home to mother." (*London Film Festival Notes.*)

873   **Xeroscopy** (90)
      Halas & Batchelor: "Condition of Man" No. 6
      P: John Halas, D: Geoff Dunbar
      Color
      One-minute cartoon.

874   **Cast**
      Intergalactic Films
      P:D:S: Peter Dockley, SD: Barry Guy
      Color
      Experimental cartoon. "Filmed on a set which was totally enclosed:
no windows, no doors. Inside is a table with bottles and glasses on it, and
six figures. A metamorphosis begins to take place which is both horrifying
and beautiful." (*Zagreb Animation Festival Programme.*)

875   **And Now for Something Completely Different**
      Kettledrum – Python – Columbia – Lownes – GSF
      XP: Victor Lownes, P: Patricia Casey, D: Ian Macnaughton, S:
Graham Chapman, John Cleese, Terry Gilliam, Eric Idle, Terry Jones,
Michael Palin, A: Terry Gilliam, C: Bob Godfrey, ED: Thom Noble
      Color
      Live-action feature film (88 minutes) with animation sequences.
Adapted from material used in the BBC Television series, *Monty Python's
Flying Circus.* "It's a relief to discover that this cinema version of a currently
successful comedy series was primarily intended for American distribu-
tion, since otherwise its rehash of well-used television sketches would
seem a rather pointless exercise." (*Monthly Film Bulletin* November 1971.)

876   **For Your Pleasure**
      Phillips
      P:D:S:A: Derek Phillips
      Color
      Amateur cartoon. "Constable's 'The Haywain' seems like a good
place for a picnic until the Town Planners move in." (*Phillips List.*)

877   **Joe and Petunia** (135)
      Nicholas Cartoons – COI
      P:D:A: Nicholas Spargo, V: Wendy Craig, Peter Hawkins
      Color
      Informational cartoon for the Central Office of Information. Further
misadventures of a married couple who ignore safety warnings.

878   **Love Affair**
      British Film Institute Production Board
      D:S: Roy Evans, M: Steve Jacobson
      Student's cartoon film.

879   Dreamcloud
NSH Animation
P:D:S: Hitch Hitchens, DES: Bill Sewell
Color
Advertising film for National Westminster Bank. "Couple share a dream house but it is beyond their means." (*Zagreb Animation Festival Programme.*)

880   A Short Tall Story
Halas & Batchelor — Concord
P: John Halas, Joy Batchelor, D: John Halas, S:DES: Tony White, A: John Perkins, Tony Guy, M: Jack King, V: Murray Kash
Color
"Animated fable dealing with the basic subject of human relationships between any two groups of people." (*British National Film Catalogue* 1980.)

881   Football Freaks
Halas & Batchelor
P: Richard Arnall, D:S: Paul Vesta, A: Paul Vesta, Madge Buckingham, Helen Whitty, Dorothy Lony
Eastmancolor
Series of gags, some of them involving a football, animated to snatches of music from old pop records by Paul Anka, the Crewcuts, Johnnie Ray, Johnny Bond, and Billy Williams.

882   The Square Deal
Larkins Studio
P: Beryl Stevens, D:S: Doug Jensen, A: Peter Green, Ralph Ayres, Roy Jackson, C: Guy Knight, ED: Michael Crane, M: Tristram Cary, V: Deryck Guyler
Eastmancolor
Promotional film for British Insurance Association. "Brief history of the development of British insurance, explaining the basis of sound insurance and that it is essentially an international industry." (*British National Film Catalogue* 1971.)

883   Who's Next
Phillips
P:D:S:A: Derek Phillips, M: Ron Littlefield
Color
Amateur cartoon: "A flower in a greenhouse longs for freedom, but when it gets it is devoured by the surrounding wildlife." (*British National Film Catalogue* 1978.)

884 The Saga of the Scrunge
Central London Polytechnic
D:A: Monica Mazure, S: Chris Burgon, V: Chris James
Color
Amateur cartoon: "A knight called Floop goes on his horse called Phleke to kill the fearful dragon Scrunge." (*British National Film Catalogue* 1973.)

1972

885 Windows
BFI Production Board
D:A: John Gibbons, M: Colin Stiff
Combined live action and animation. "A personal view of the surreal quality of windows." (*British National Film Catalogue.*)

886 I Had a Hippopotamus
DHP Productions – MGM – EMI
P:D: Dennis Hunt, S: Patrick Barrington, SC: Dennis Hunt, A: Dennis Hunt, Gordon Harrison, Diane Jackson, DES: Dennis Hunt, Gordon Harrison, ED: Brian Bishop, C: Ian Lett, John Williams, M: Boosey & Hawkes, Chappell
Color
A man's problems in trying to keep a pet hippopotamus.

887 Mothers and Fathers
Halas & Batchelor – Concord – EFC
P: John Halas, D: Vic Bevis, Ann Goodwin, John Halas, S: Dorothy Dallas, Jane Madders, M. Holmes, A: Brian Borthwick, Vic Bevis
Color
Educational film. "Sex education film for primary schools showing by means of animated drawings the mating of a hen and a cock, the laying of an egg, the growth of the embryo, and finally the hatching of the chick." (*British National Film Catalogue* 1976.)

888 Hot Water Bottles
Taylor Cartoons – COI
P:D:A: Richard Taylor
Color
Informational cartoon for the Home Office.

889   Panic Man
Taylor Cartoons – COI
P:D:A: Richard Taylor
Color
Informational cartoon for the Department of Trade.

890   Girls Growing Up
Halas & Batchelor – EFC
P: John Halas, D: Brian Borthwick, Vic Bevis, S:DES: Dorothy Dallas, A: Vic Bevis, Brian Borthwick
Color
Educational film. "Explains how the menstrual cycle helps the human egg start its development as an embryo." (*British National Film Catalogue 1977.*)

891   You Are Ridiculous
Melendez Productions
P: Steven Cuitlahuac Melendez, D: Alan Shean, DES:S: André Francois, A: Dean Spille, Jacques Vausseur, ED: John Farrow, M: Michel Roques, V: Dean Spille, Paul Nesbitt, Alan Shean
Color
Cartoon film designed by the famous French magazine cartoonist André Francois.

892   Pardon
Tupy
P:D:S: Peter Tupy
Color
"A little man plays a flute for a group of lions." (*Zagreb Animation Festival Programme.*)

893   The Gas Genie
Larkins Studio
P: Beryl Stevens, D:S: Sidney Mould, A: Kathleen Houston, V: Deryck Guyler
Eastmancolor
Instructional film for the Gas Council. "Demonstrates how to ensure complete safety using the cooker, the water heater, and other gas appliances." (*British National Film Catalogue 1972.*)

894   Sinderella (450) (X)
Oppidan Films – Border
P: David Grant, D: Ron Inkpen, A:S: not credited
Color

The first British pornographic cartoon, made by anonymous animators. Banned by the Bow Street Magistrates Court and the High Court of Appeal, but granted an "X" (adults only) Certificate after some 30 feet removed by the British Board of Film Censors. Sinderella arrives at the ball after being assaulted on the way by the Three Bears. She loses her bra in the Prince's bed. He eventually finds her, the only girl to fit the bra, and her jealous ugly sisters are compensated by being raped by the Three Bears. "The animation is crude and cheaply imitative of Terry Gilliam, while the drawings themselves have more than a passing resemblance to those of cartoonist Gahan Wilson. Embarrassingly puerile throughout." (*Monthly Film Bulletin* December 1973.)

895   The Gulf
Phillips
P:D:S:A: Derek Phillips
Color
Amateur cartoon: "About people who have difficulty in understanding each other." (*British National Film Catalogue* 1978.)

896   New Force
Phillips
P:D:S:A: Derek Phillips, V: David De Keyser
Color
Amateur film combining live action and animation. A spoof television commercial for "violence."

897   The Visitor
Phillips
P:D:S:A: Derek Phillips, M: Mat Ross
Color
Amateur cartoon. "A creature from outer space is enthralled by the Earth and its inhabitants until it is swamped by humans." (*British National Film Catalogue* 1978.)

898   Boom Bom Boom (400)
S.C. Films
P:D:S:A: Jack Stokes, C: Ian Lett, ED: Brian Bishop, M: Tony Archer
Color
Bearskinned bandsman bangs his drum.

899   The Film of Mr. Zyznik
Stewart Films
P: J.R.F. Stewart, D:S: John Tully, A: Jack Stokes, C: Leslie Dear, ED: Gordon Hales, Ron Tanner, V: Peter Hawkins, Frank Duncan

Eastmancolor

Promotional film for the Gas Council: combined live action and animation. "The uses of natural gas in industry presented by means of a cartoon character commissioned to make a film on the subject." (*British National Film Catalogue* 1972.)

900 Cluster Analysis

Teamwork Films – Compufilm

D: John Daborn, A: John Daborn, Derek Phillips, Stuart Wynn Jones, ED: Stein Falcenberg, V: John Witty

Eastmancolor

Instructional film. "Computer programme designed for the grouping of large quantities of items in terms of many variables." (*Central Film Library Catalogue* 1977.)

1973

901 Think Twice
Ferson
P: Peter Ferson, D: Digby Turpin, A: Bill Sewell, C: J.M. Burgoyne-Johnson, ED: John Scott, V: Frank Muir
Color
Promotional film for Arthur Guinness. "How the sponsor looks after bottled Guinness at every stage of production in the brewery."(*British National Film Catalogue* 1974.)

902 Grape Expectations
Halas & Batchelor
P: Alan Burke, D: John Challis, S: Jeremy Baird, A: Len Lewis, John Challis, Peter Green, ED: Terry Brown, V: Robert Stephens
Eastmancolor
Advertising film for H. Sichel & Sons. "Henry finds out where wines come from and what makes them special, just in time for a dinner party with his girl friend." (*British National Film Catalogue* 1973.)

903 Neville and the Problem Pump
Halas & Batchelor
P: Alan Burke, D: John Challis, Alan Burke, S: George Tapner, A: Peter Green, Len Lewis, ED: Terry Brown, V: Bernard Cribbins
Eastmancolor
Instructional film for Crane Packing Company. "Two cartoon characters explain the right way of fitting gland packings in pumps." (*British National Film Catalogue* 1973.)

904 Children Making Cartoon Films
Halas & Batchelor – EFC
P:S: John Halas, Joy Batchelor, D: Paul Halas, C: Clive Tickner, ED: Martin Amstell, M: Andreas Ranki, V: John Craven
Color
Combined live action and animation. Based on the 1972 award-winning animated films in a competition organized jointly by the British

241

Broadcasting Corporation, the Association International du Film d'Animation, and the International Council of Graphic Design Associates.

905   Carry on Milkmaids
Halas & Batchelor – EFC
P: John Halas, Joy Batchelor, D: Joy Batchelor, Garrie Fotheringham,
S: Joy Batchelor, A: John Quinn, Lorraine Calora, Ian Emes, Brian Larkin,
DES: Suzanne Villanyi, C: Hugh Gordon, ED: Mike Crouch, V: Evelyn
Elliott, Derek Partridge
Color
Combined live action and animation; promotional film for the Scot-
tish Milk Marketing Board. "How drinking milk can bring a new vitality into
the lives of a typical family." (*British National Film Catalogue* 1975.)

906   Making Music Together
Halas & Batchelor
P: Alan Burke, D: Lee Mishkin, A: Pete Arthy, John Challis, Jeff
Goldner, Eden Anthony, Ian Moo-Young, Peter Green, Oscar Grillo, Len
Lewis, Annie O'Dell, Sandra Hill, DES: Jim Duffy, Geoff Dunbar
Color
Promotional film for the Schering Corporation.

907   This Is B.P.
Larkins Studio
P:S: Beryl Stevens, D: Sidney Mould, A: Kathleen Houston, Eileen
Matthews, Peter Green, C: Guy Knight, Charles Lagus, Kevan Woolridge,
ED: Mike Gascoyne, M: Tristram Cary
Eastmancolor
Combined live action and animation. Promotional film for British
Petroleum. "Reviews the history and integrated operations of the BP group
of over 600 companies in more than 80 countries." (*British National Film
Catalogue* 1973.)

908   The Case of the Metal Sheathed Elements
Larkins Studio
P: Beryl Stevens, D: Sidney Mould, C: Kevan Woolridge, ED: Hugh
O'Donnell, V: Norman Bird, Frank Duncan
Eastmancolor
Instructional film for the Electricity Council. "Sherlock Holmes and
Dr. Watson explain the construction and use of metal sheathed elements."
(*British National Film Catalogue* 1974.)

909   Disgusted, Binchester
Nicholas Cartoons – COI

P:D: Nicholas Spargo, A: Keith Roberts, Pip Shuckburgh, Mary Spargo, C: Jane Keeley, Ian Sheath, ED: Michael Crane, V: Derek Nimmo, Peter Hawkins, Noel Johnson
Color
Propaganda film for the Race Relations Board. "The story of a typical character who, throughout the ages, has never stopped protesting about social change." (*Zagreb Animation Festival Programme.*)

910   The Ostrich
London Film School
D:S: John Verbeck, M: Paul Meixner
Color
Student's cartoon: "Story of a bashful one-legged ostrich who is exploited by a cruel showman." (*Zagreb Animation Festival Programme.*)

911   Green Men Yellow Woman
London Film School
D:S:A: Thalma Goldman
Color
Student's cartoon. "Yellow woman prepares herself to meet Clark Gable, but instead five little green men appear who pretend to be him." (*London Film Festival Notes.*)

912   Jellyfish
Roberts
D:S:A: Peter Roberts
Color
Experimental cartoon. "This work employs a variety of experimental techniques to create a mood of threat and anxiety around a series of people and objects linked together only by their presence on a beach." (*Cambridge Animation Festival 1980.*)

913   Custard
Hayes & Austin
D:S:A: Derek Hayes, Philip Austin
Color
"The story of Percy who works in the maintenance department of Crumbs Custard Factory. He likes custard so much that he has his own private custard making machine at home. One evening Percy fails to notice that his vat has sprung a leak and is spurting custard on a courting couple outside his flat. A mob breaks into his room and smashes up his vat. Driven to revenge Percy decides to flood the city with custard." (*Cambridge Animation Festival 1980.*)

914   **Generation Gap**
British Film Institute Production Board
P: Bob Godfrey, D:A: Peter Hickling, M: John Hawkesworth, ED:
Tony Fish, C: Paul Wibley
Color
Experimental cartoon.

915   **Dandruff**
TV Cartoons
P:D:S:A: Jim Duffy, C: John Williams
Color
"A man has a very bad case of dandruff. Will someone produce a
solution to his problem?" (*Annecy Animation Festival Programme.*)

916   **Benny**
Melendez Productions
P: Steven Cuitlahuac Melendez, D:S:DES: Jim Duffy, A: Jacques
Vausseur, Dick Horn, ED: John Farrow, M: Gordon Haskell
Color
"A surreal kind of tribute to the Silly Symphony cartoons of 1930,
but the environment has somewhat changed!" (*Annecy Animation Festival
Programme.*)

917   **Snow White and the Seven Perverts** (984) (X)
Oppidan Films – Small
P: David Grant, D: Ron Inkpen, S:A: not credited
Color
Pornographic cartoon, granted an "X" (adults only) certificate; made
by anonymous animators. The Wicked Queen, jealous of Snow White's
bust dimensions, attempts to kill her. Sheltered by the Seven Dwarfs, all of
whom are exhibitionists, Snow White is restored to life when the Prince
makes love to her corpse. "Grant's studied vulgarisation of the tale is largely
confined to crude phallic and mammary embellishments; his graphic style
resembles Terry Gilliam's (especially in a sequence where the raincoated
perverts scamper over photographs of Piccadilly Circus) but his cut-price
animation is mostly achieved through jointed cutouts irresistibly reminiscent of John Ryan's *Captain Pugwash* TV series." (*Monthly Film Bulletin*
December 1973.) Reissued 1978 with the new title *Some Day My Prince Will
Come.*

918   **The Sculpture**
Phillips
P:D:S:A: Derek Phillips, M: Mat Ross
Color

Amateur cartoon: "The artist kills himself over his work and the critic contributes by saying he does not like it." (*British National Film Catalogue* 1978.)

919 Weird
Phillips
P:D:S:A: Derek Phillips
Color
Amateur cartoon: "They meet and each one thinks the other somehow peculiar." (*British National Film Catalogue* 1978.)

920 Horses of Death
TV Cartoons
P: John Coates, D: George Dunning, Jim Duffy, S:A: Jim Duffy, ED: Brian Bishop, C: John Williams
Eastmancolor
Instructional film for the National Coal Board. "Coal miner pushes control button on large coal face shearing machine, and is given a terrifying demonstration of the potential danger of the horsepower within." (*British National Film Catalogue* 1973.)

921 Plant a Tree
TV Cartoons
P: George Dunning, A: Mike Crane, V: Clive Swift
Eastmancolor
Promotional film for the Department of Environment. "Intended to stimulate interest in trees and to encourage tree planting." (*British National Film Catalogue* 1973.)

922 Fooling About
Nicholas Cartoons—COI
P:D:A: Nicholas Spargo, C: Jane Keeley, V: Peter Hawkins
Color
Promotional cartoon for safety at work.

923 How Not to Lose Your Head While Shot Firing
TV Cartoons
P: John Coates, D: George Dunning, Jim Duffy, S:A: Jim Duffy, C: John Williams, ED: Brian Bishop, V: Paul Whitsun-Jones
Eastmancolor
Instructional film for the National Coal Board. "Coal mine lecturer gives demonstration on how not to prepare for a coal face shot fire, and loses his head in the process." (*British National Film Catalogue* 1973.)

924 The Maggot
TV Cartoons – Righteous Apple – Concord
P: John Coates, D: George Dunning, S: Topper Carew, A: Jeremy Hibbert, Roy Evans, DES: Mike Crane, C: John Williams, ED: Brian Bishop, M: Topper Carew, V: Harry Poe, Ebony Impromptu
Color
Propaganda cartoon. "When the drug pusher prowls about the school, it behoves kids to turn away from him and therefore reduce him to unemployment." (*London Film Festival Notes.*)

925 Damon the Mower
TV Cartoons
P:D: George Dunning, A: George Dunning, Roy Evans, Jeremy Hibbert, S: Andrew Marvell, C: John Williams, ED: Brian Bishop
Color
Interpretation of a 17th century poem.

926 Jumping Joan
Bristol University
P: John Loveless, D:S:A: Janet Johns
Color
Student's cartoon: "Series of nursery rhymes and traditional street songs which are linked together by Jumping Joan." (*Zagreb Animation Festival Programme.*)

927 Many Moons (468)
Royal College of Art (Contemporary)
D:S:A: Rachel Igel, Eric Money, S: (Story) James Thurber, M: Johann Sebastian Bach, N: Robert Morley, V: Emma Spiller, Howard Heywood, David Grant, Eric Money
Student's cartoon for children. Sick Princess asks for the moon to make her well, so the court jester makes her one of cardboard. "Fairly simple animation and background design complement a straightforward narrative approach." (*Monthly Film Bulletin* April 1976.)

928 Who Needs Finance?
World Wide Pictures – EMI
P: Peter Bradford, S: Philip Harland, S: Nick Goldstream, A: Peter Neal, C: Bill Marshall, ED: Ronald Glenister
Color
Live action with animation sequences. "Explains the building of a balance sheet illustrated by a series of business transactions recorded on an animated balance sheet." (*British National Film Catalogue* 1974.)

1974

929 Dialogue
BFI Production Board – Avon
D:S:A: Chris Majka
Experimental cartoon. "Animated fable about people who come upon a mysterious and disturbing edifice in the wilderness." (*British National Film Catalogue* 1979.)

930 Lautrec (540)
Dragon – Curzon – Concord
P:D:S: Geoff Dunbar, A: Geoff Dunbar, Oscar Grillo, Jill Brooks, Ginger Gibbons, Len Lewis, ED: Terry Brown, M: Offenbach, Laurie Scott-Baker, C: Gerry Knowlden, V: Yvette Guilbert
Color
Art film sponsored by the Arts Council; based on the paintings and drawings of Toulouse-Lautrec. "Geoff Dunbar's suitably exhilarating and tantalisingly brief film conjures up the painter's work and environment with an animated kaleidoscope of his pet subjects, based on the original drawings and paintings. We see the night club's Can Can dancers, swirling shapes of black, red and yellow; Lautrec's favourite singer, Yvette Guilbert; circus clowns, acrobats and equestrians; the remarkably accurate yet unfussy sketches of mice, snails, ducks and suchlike." (*Monthly Film Bulletin* February 1976.)

931 As Girls Grow Up
Eothen Films
P: Philip Sattin, David Jenner, D:ED: Vivian Collins, A: Tom Bailey, Ted Pettingell, V: Dorothy Gordon
Color
Educational film for the Thomson Organisation. "Animated cartoon set in a classroom. Using appropriate audio-visual aids the teacher outlines the basics necessary to an understanding of the changes that take place during puberty." (*British National Film Catalogue* 1975.)

932 How Babies Are Born
Eothen Films
P: Philip Sattin, David Jenner, D:ED: Vivian Collins, A: Tom Bailey, Ted Pettingell, V: Andrew Lodge
Color
Educational film for primary school children, made for the Thomson Organisation. "Animated cartoon which uses a story format to introduce fundamental concepts of human reproduction." (*British National Film Catalogue* 1975.)

933 Kitchen Think
Halas & Batchelor—Stewart Films
P: Ann Kotch, John Stewart, D: Lee Mishkin, A: Kathleen Houston, M: Johnny Hawkesworth, V: Frank Muir
Color
Promotional film for the Gas Council. "Light-hearted look at the ways in which man has developed the art of cooking. Traces the progress of kitchens from a fire in a prehistoric cave to the streamlined split-level kitchen of today." (*British National Film Catalogue* 1974.)

934 Contact
Halas & Batchelor—EFC
P:D: John Halas, Joy Batchelor, S: Joy Batchelor, Jean-Pierre Braillard, A: Ian Emes, John Quinn, George Borzyskowski, Brian Larkin, Graham Ralph, Franco Cristofani, DES: Janos Kass, C: Hugh Gordon, ED: Mike Crouch, M: Andreas Ranki, V: Peter Barkworth
Eastmancolor
Promotional film for the 75th Anniversary of the Compagnie Générale d'Electricité. "Animated history of the development of electricity and its wide applications, including the growth of telecommunications and its possible future developments." (*British National Film Catalogue* 1974.)

935 Five Problems in Communications
TV Cartoons
D:S: Jim Duffy
Color
"The subject of communications is humorously treated in five basic situations." (*Zagreb Animation Festival Programme.*)

936 Monty Python and the Holy Grail (8073)
Python Pictures—Michael White—EMI
XP: John Goldstone, P: Mark Forstater, D: Terry Gilliam, Terry Jones, S: Graham Chapman, John Cleese, Terry Gilliam, Eric Idle, Terry Jones, Michael Palin, A: Terry Gilliam, ED: John Hackney, M: Neil Innes

Technicolor

Live-action feature (90 minutes) with animation sequences. King Arthur and his knights seek the Holy Grail. "Terry Gilliam's occasional animated inserts draw on medieval painting and manuscript illuminations (though the neatest one is in modern style – a sun and two clouds all with legs, noisily bouncing up and down). (*Monthly Film Bulletin* April 1975.)

937   The Glorious Musketeers
AKA: **D'Artagnan L'Intrepide**
Pendennis – Michelangelo Cinematografica
P: Steven Pallos, Patrick Wachsberger, D: John Halas, Jeffrey Veri, S: Alexandre Dumas, SC: Howard Clewes, Paolo di Girolamo, A: Brian Larkin, Ian Emes, Bob Balser, A. Marks, Colin Ruddock, Stuart Welch, Ronald Murdoch, Edrick Radage, Franco Cristofani, C: Ian Lett, Alan Foster, ED: Mike Crouch, M: Michel Polnareff, Martin Shear, V: John Fortune (D'Artagnan), Howard Clewes (Athos), Peter Bull (Porthos), Maurice Denham (Aramis), Roy Kinnear (Louis XIII), Adrienne Corri (Milady), Peter Hawkins (Rochefort), Madeleine Smith (Constance), Joyce Windsor (Queen)
Technicolor
Anglo-Italian coproduction; feature (70 minutes) adaptation of *The Three Musketeers*. "Thanks to a percussive animated cartoon, here is a D'Artagnan new and transfigured with smashing adventures which unroll at triple gallop over the music and rhythms of Michel Polnareff." (*Film Francais* 8 November 1974.)

938   The Christmas Feast
Halas & Batchelor – EFC – Corona Cinematografica
P:S: John Halas, Joy Batchelor, D: John Halas, A: Ian Emes, Brian Larkin, DES: Susan Villanyi, M: Mario Migliardi
Color
Anglo-Italian coproduction.

939   The Ass and the Stick
Halas & Batchelor – EFC – Corona Cinematografica
P:S: John Halas, Joy Batchelor, D: Joy Batchelor, A: Ian Emes, Brian Larkin, DES: Tom Bailey, M: Mario Migliardi
Color
Anglo-Italian coproduction.

940   Butterfly Ball
Halas & Batchelor – Aurelia Enterprises
P: Jack King, D: Lee Mishkin, DES:S: Alan Aldridge, A: Harold Whitaker, Nicholas Spargo, John Perkins, Lee Mishkin, M: Roger Glover, ED: Roy Piper

Eastmancolor
Adaptation of the children's book illustrated by Alan Aldridge. A frog leads a merry crowd of forest animals to the butterfly's ball.

941　A Better Mousetrap
Larkins Studio
P: Beryl Stevens, D: Sidney Mould, S: Beryl Stevens, Peter Cliffe, C: Kevan Woolridge, Wolfgang Suschitzky, ED: Hugh O'Donnell, M: Tristram Cary, V: John Le Mesurier
Eastmancolor
Promotional film for IBM. "Industrial fairy tale showing how a terminal process system increases the efficiency by integrating the effort and activities of the various departments and locations within a business." (*British National Film Catalogue* 1974.)

942　Emsleigh Dockyard Computer System
Larkins Studio
P: Beryl Stevens, D: Sidney Mould, A: David Tuffnell, ED: Michael Crane, C: Maurice Picot, V: Gordon Davies
Color
Instructional film for the Ministry of Defence. "Uses a combination of live action and graphics to show how the projected Emsleigh Dockyard Computer System is designed to meet the provisioning demands of the Royal Navy." (*British National Film Catalogue* 1975.)

943　The Losers Club
Phillips
P:D:S:A: Derek Phillips
Color
Amateur cartoon: "Everyone's a loser in the rat race of modern life." (*London Film Festival Notes.*)

944　The Day That Battersea Power Station Flew Away (108)
Rockley
P:A:C: Ted Rockley, D: Dave Pescod, Ted Rockley, S: Dave Pescod, V: Alf Paulding
Eastmancolor
The trouble that follows when a power station flies to the moon. "Using cutouts of photographs and drawings the film is attractively designed and children will no doubt find it great fun." (*Monthly Film Bulletin* August 1978.)

945　The Inventor (198)
Rockley
P:D:S:A:C: Ted Rockley

Eastmancolor

A caveman's inventions continually fail until he invents a rifle: he is promptly shot. "A typical Rockley product making excellent use of pleasing drawings set against the director's habitual plain backgrounds, this time entirely black and aptly suggesting the dawn of time." (*Monthly Film Bulletin* August 1978.)

946   Join the Army (36)
      Rockley
      P:D:S:A:C: Ted Rockley
      Eastmancolor
A soldier is shot to pieces beside a recruiting poster. "Simply because of its brevity, which is shockingly effective, Rockley's film succeeds in being a timely reminder of the folly of war." (*Monthly Film Bulletin* August 1978.)

947   Tree Top Tales (series)
      Seabourne Enterprises
      XP: John Seabourne, P: Ken Holt, D: Mary Turner, S: Peter Seabourne, C: John Reed, ED: Harry MacDonald, M: Peter Murray
      Color
      1: Hoppy's Hiccups, 2: Dazzling Diamonds, 3: Learning Fast, 4: The Black White Kitchen, 5: How Does Your Garden Grow, 6: Time to Wake Up
Series of animated puppet films for children, featuring a group of forest creatures including an owl, a frog, and a squirrel.

948   Alice in Label Land
      Taylor Cartoons — COI
      P:D: Richard Taylor, A: Richard Taylor, Denis Rich, Roger McIntosh, ED: Janet Spiller, V: Carleton Hobbs, William Rushton, Elizabeth Proud
      Color
Instructional film for the Ministry of Agriculture, inspired by Lewis Carroll's story *Alice in Wonderland*. "Characters from the story explain in simple terms certain sections of the Labelling of Food regulations 1970, which came into force on 1 January 1973." (*British National Film Catalogue* 1975.)

949   French Windows
      Timeless Films — Fair Enterprises
      P:D:A: Ian Emes, M: Pink Floyd
      Color
Musical cartoon. "An anonymous figure waits by the windows, which open and draw the viewer into a world of expanding perspectives." (*British National Film Catalogue* 1977.)

950 How to Lie with Statistics
Videological Productions
P: Anthony Jay, Peter Robinson, S: Darrell Huff, Irving Geis, SC: Robert Reid, A: Tony Hart, ED: Graham Aza, V: John Cleese
Color
Instructional cartoon based on a book. "Concentrates on the suppression of zero and the change of scale in graphs." (*British National Film Catalogue* 1975.) For sequel see 1041.

951 This Is the Life
Welsh Arts Council
P:D:S:A: Clive Walley, V: Alan McPherson
Color
"The events take place in the near future on a typical tourist beach. The lifeguards who are in charge find themselves forced to confront an unusually powerful public nuisance." (*British National Film Catalogue* 1978.)

952 Puttin' on the Ritz
Starkiewicz
D:S:A: Antoinette Starkiewicz, M: George Gershwin
Color
"Cartoon in which the characters create themselves out of an ever-changing dancing line." (*London Film Festival Notes.*)

953 Herb the Verb
West Surrey College of Art
D:S:A:M: Chris Jelley
Color
"Educational film for children in light-hearted style." (*London Film Festival Notes.*)

954 Ondra
Keen
D:S:A: Lesley Keen, M: Neil Morrison
Color
"Children's cartoon about a little boy who visits the Man in the Moon." (*London Film Festival Notes.*)

955 The Castaway
Central School of Art
P:D:S:A: Clive Pallant, M: Ligetti
Color
"Mysogyny in two measures: how to turn to account a situation, or how to use the female as an object." (*London Film Festival Notes.*)

956   The Miracle of Flight
Gilliam
P:D:S:A: Terry Gilliam, ED: John Hackney
Color
"Some of man's abortive attempts, whether he was an illustrious scientist or a humble worker, to fulfil his longing for flying." (*London Film Festival Notes.*) Made for the television show *The Marty Feldman Comedy Machine,* but released theatrically.

957   Trans-Siberian Express
Richard Williams
P: Carl Gover, D: Rowland Wilson
Color
"A long and hazardous journey across the Russian countryside to deliver passengers of the Trans-Siberian Express to the court of Count Pushkin." (*London Film Festival Notes.*) Advertisement for Count Pushkin Vodka.

958   Classical Cartoon
Mather Animations
P:D: Bill Mather
Instructional cartoon: "A teaching aid to the sonata form relying on the recreation of paintings." (*Annecy Animation Festival Programme.*)

959   Who Needs the Computer
World Wide Pictures – EMI
P: Peter Bradford, D: Philip Harland, S: Philip Harland, Kit Grindley, A: Bill Sewell, ED: Tony Fish, V: David Jason, Lee Peters, Josephine Tewson
Color
Educational cartoon. "Intended to illustrate some of the misconceptions about the use of computers and to define the role of computers in business and society." (*British National Film Catalogue* 1974.)

1975

960 Support Your Local Poet
Churches Television & Radio Centre
P: Bill Stevenson, D: Norman Stone, S: Steve Turner, A: Norman
Stone, C: Chris Pettit, ED: Roger Shufflebottom, M: David Cooke, V:
Graham Stark, David Barry, Deryck Guyler, Derek Nimmo
Color
Combined live action and animation. "About truth and hypocrisy,
love and communication, life and death, as seen through the eyes of a
young Christian poet." (*British National Film Catalogue* 1975.)

961 Is This a Record
Ferson
P: Peter Ferson, D: Digby Turpin, S: *The Guinness Book of Records,*
SC: Barry Took, A: Bob Godfrey, Bill Sewell, Richard Taylor, Corona
Marker, C: Larry Pizer, FX: Nobby Clark, M: Stanley Myers, V: Frank Muir,
John Cleese, Terry Jones
Color
Combination of animation, live action, and stills. Advertising film
for Arthur Guinness. A light-hearted look through *The Guinness Book of
Records.*

962 Amateur Night (674)
Goldman – British Lion
P:D:S:A: Thalma Goldman, M: Paul Lewis
Eastmancolor
Three ill-assorted females perform a strip-tease dance.

963 Great: Isambard Kingdom Brunel (2539)
Grantstern – Godfrey – British Lion
P:D: Bob Godfrey, SUP: Hester Coblentz, S: Bob Godfrey, Richard
Taylor, Joe McGrath, Robin Smyth, Paul Weisser, AD: Jeff Goldner, Ann
Joliffe, A: John Challis, Mark Shepherd, Bob Godfrey, Graeme Jackson, Ian
Moo-Young, Denis Rich, Kevin Attew, Hester Coblentz, Chris Jelley,

Video Animation, C: Julian Holdaway, Kent Houston, DES: Oscar Grillo, Mark Shepherd, ED: Tony Fish, Peter Hearn, M: Jonathan P. Hodge, V: Richard Briers, Harry Fowler, Barbara Moore, Angus Lennie, Peter Hawkins, Dick Graham, Imogen Claire, Cyril Shaps
 Musical biography of Isambard Kingdom Brunel (1806–1859), the Victorian engineer who built the Clifton Suspension Bridge, the Great Western Railway, and the *Great Eastern,* a steam ship too large to launch — plus some items he did not invent, such as sliced bread, the living bra, and the self-exploding hat. "Godfrey mixes his ingredients with such skill that the results are delightfully fresh. The jokes, as expected, are often out-rageously low (Queen Victoria makes her entrance rising out of a lavatory bowl, pulling the chain to celebrate the beginning of her glorious reign), but they all work, and the exuberant clowning is accompanied by a ge-nuine affection for the hero and his creations." (*Monthly Film Bulletin* June 1976.) First British cartoon film to win an Academy Award: 1976. British Film Academy Award 1975.

964 Handle with Care
 Stewart Hardy Films – COI
 P: Stewart Hardy, D: Guy Ferguson, A: Robin Thomas, C: Leslie Dear, John Sharples, Maurice Picot, ED: Jim Elderton, V: Vernon Greeves
 Color
 Combined live action and animation; instructional film for Ministry of Defence. "The rules to be observed in the first aid handling of casualties in various situations." (*British National Film Catalogue* 1976.)

965 How Not to Succeed in Business: Parkinson's Law
 Halas & Batchelor – EFC
 P:D: John Halas, S: Norman Parkinson, A: Harold Whitaker, DES: Mel Calman, M: Jack King, V: London Shakespeare Company
 Color
 "Short humorous cartoon featuring the Parkinson Institute, named after Sir Norman Parkinson, inventor of *Parkinson's Law.* The Institute's principal conducts the audience through the various departments, each of which deals with the problems of business technology." (*British National Film Catalogue* 1976.)

966 Discovering Electricity
 Larkins Studio
 P: Beryl Stevens, D: John Spencer, S: John Spencer, Sidney Mould, A: Martin Wansborough, DES: David Tufnell, C: Martin Hailey, Bill Glass, ED: Brian Schwegman, V: Trevor Churchman
 Color
 Educational film for the Electricity Council. Live action and anima-tion sequences: Dr. Trevor Churchman lectures to children at the Royal

Institution. "Traces the story of electricity from the amber of the Ancient Greeks to the fundamental researches of Faraday." (*British National Film Catalogue* 1975.)

967 What Is Electricity?
Larkins Studio
P: Beryl Stevens, D: John Spencer, A: Martin Wansborough, C: Martin Hailey, Bill Glass, ED: Brian Schwegman, V: Trevor Churchman
Color
Educational film for the Electricity Council. Live action and animation sequences: Dr. Trevor Churchman lectures to children at the Royal Institution.

968 Around the World in Eighty Ways
Larkins Studio
P: Beryl Stevens
Color
Advertising film for Barclays Bank Travellers Cheques.

969 Operation Teastrainer
Larkins Studio
P: Beryl Stevens, D: Sidney Mould, ED: Terry Brown, V: Timothy Bateson
Color
Propaganda film for the Ministry of Defence: live action with animation sequences. "300 years of keeping the Royal Navy afloat have meant changes to the system, but not to the traditions of the Royal Navy Supply and Transport Service." (*British National Film Catalogue* 1975.)

970 Dick Deadeye or Duty Done (7251)
Bill Melendez Productions—CIC
XP: Leo Rost, P: Steven Melendez, AP: Graeme Spurway, D: Bill Melendez, SUP: Mike Hayes, S: William S. Gilbert, Arthur Sullivan, SC: Robin Miller, Leo Rost, Gene Thompson, Victor Spinetti, Casey Kelly, DES: Ronald Searle, AD: Dick Horn, Jacques Vausseur, A: Bill Melendez, Mike Hibbert, Peter Green, Ron Coulter, Doug Jensen, Annie O'Dell, Franco Milia, Don Mackinnon, Rafaella Lombardi, Terry Harrison, George Jackson, Kathleen Houston, Janet Nunn, Jeff Loynes, Ann Elvin, April Spencer, Olive Scott, Tancy Baran, ED: Steven Melendez, Babette Monteil, M: William S. Gilbert, Arthur Sullivan, Robin Miller, MD: Jimmy Horowitz, V: Victor Spinetti, Peter Reeves, George A. Cooper, Miriam Karlin, John Newton, Linda Lewis, Julia McKenzie, Francis Ghent, Barry Cryer, Beth Porter, John Baldry, Casey Kelly, Liza Strike, Ian Samwell
Produced in England by the American animation company responsible for the *Charlie Brown* television series, to celebrate the Gilbert

and Sullivan Centenary. Dick Deadeye is commissioned by Queen Victoria to recover the Ultimate Secret which has been stolen by the Sorceror. The secret scroll is given to the King of the Penzance Pirates in exchange for gold. Dick crews the HMS *Pinafore* with prisoners from the Tower of London and pursues the pirates. Poo, the evil twin of Nanki, steals the scroll and escapes to the Isle of Utopia, populated entirely by beautiful girls who are ruled by Princess Zara. The undecipherable scroll, when reflected in water, reveals the message: "It's love that makes the world go round." Nanki and Poo conjoin as one and everybody embraces one another." A splendid showcase for the bizarre imaginings of Ronald Searle, the movie's designer, but a poor one for Gilbert and Sullivan. Songs are sung only in snatches, and for the most part with newly satirical lyrics which have none of Gilbert's wit and verve, and the storyline is unintelligently manufactured from the plots and characters of the best-known operas, and finally dribbles into inanity." (*Monthly Film Bulletin* September 1975.)

971 The Ballad of Lucy Jordan
Moo Movies
P: Tony Cash, D:S:A:C: Ian Moo-Young, ED: Janet Spiller, M: Dr. Clock and the Medicine Show
Color
"The last day of an unhappy housewife." (*British National Film Catalogue* 1977.)

972 Way Out (126)
New Fields
P:D:C:A: Ted Rockley, S: Stan Hayward, M: Derek Phillips
Ektachrome
A man tries various ways to commit suicide and finally succeeds accidentally." A delightful and engaging example of all three artists working on top form." (*Monthly Film Bulletin* August 1978.)

973 Super Natural Gas
Nicholas Cartoons
P:D: Nicholas Spargo, C: Ian Sheath, ED: Michael Crane, V: Kenneth Williams, Noel Johnson, Peter Hawkins
Color
Instructional film for British Gas. "Uses humorous treatment to explain what natural gas is, and how it is brought ashore at high pressure." (*British National Film Catalogue* 1975.)

974 "A" Concert
Phillips
P:D:S:A: Derek Phillips
Color
An orchestra tunes up: amateur cartoon.

975 Mickey's Nasty Turn
Abattoir Fillums
P:D:S:A: Jeff Goldner
Color
Single gag of Mickey Mouse turning his head to reveal flat ears.

976 Newsflash
Kevin Attew
D:A: Anna Brockett
"Science fiction story of the homeless in deserted London." (*Annecy Animation Festival Programme.*)

977 Switched On
Phillips
P:D:A: Derek Phillips, S: Stan Hayward, V: Ann Murray
Color
Amateur cartoon: "Switched on to sexual desires." (*British National Film Catalogue* 1975.)

978 Bigger Is Better
Phillips–Concord
P:D:S: Derek Phillips, A: Derek Phillips, John Daborn
Color
Amateur cartoon: "In which enormous combines are taken a stage further to produce a monster society." (*British National Film Catalogue* 1977.)

979 A Tale of Two Cities (288)
Rockley
P:D:S:A:C: Ted Rockley
Eastmancolor
Two cities go to war and destroy each other, and a third city is revealed. "Although it is a little short on jokes, the drawings are attractive and unusual enough to hold the interest throughout." (*Monthly Film Bulletin* August 1978.)

980 Safety Senses Series
TV Cartoons
P: George Dunning, D: Jim Duffy, M: Ron Goodwin
Eastmancolor
Instructional cartoons for the National Coal Board; a series of six one-minute films. "Illustrating the importance in safety of the faculties of sight, hearing, taste, smell and feel, with a final summation on the Sixth Sense." (*British National Film Catalogue* 1976.)

981 Café Bar
Wyatt – Cattaneo Productions
P: Ron Wyatt, Tony Cattaneo, D:S:A: Alison De Vere, C: Ted Gerald
ED: Sean Lenihan, M: Reg Tilsey
Eastmancolor
The extraordinary visions that are created in the minds of a man and a woman as they chat over a cup of coffee in a café.

982 A to A
Yorkshire Arts Association
D: John Gibbons, M: David Kershaw
Color
"Animated film which explores a woman's mental landscape." (*British National Film Catalogue* 1976.)

983 Who Needs Nurseries? We Do!
Leeds Animation Workshop
Color
Propaganda cartoon. "Four year old Tracy runs away from her mum in a supermarket. She comes across a meeting of other children with family problems, presided over by three chairbabies. A child expert, age about three months, presents the facts and figures about nursery places, and the children discuss the problems they have arising from the lack of places. In the end the children decide to take action." (*Cambridge Animation Festival* 1979.)

984 All Sorts of Heroes
Megginson & Hughes
P:D:A:S: Rick Megginson, Steve Hughes, ED: Roy Newton, M: Steve Hopkinson
Color
"At night amidst the dark, derelict skyscrapers of a city, a bunch of delinquent frogs infest the street and attack an innocent passer-by. He defends himself with the contents of his wonderful bag. It yields up all kinds of devices which the stranger puts to creative use." (*Cambridge Animation Festival* 1979.)

985 Icarus (90)
Taylor Cartoons
P:D:A: Richard Taylor
Color
One-minute cartoon about a man who tries to fly.

986   The Twelve Tasks of Asterix
       AKA: **Les 12 Travaux D'Asterix**
       Halas & Batchelor – Dargaud – Goscinny – Idefix – EMI
       P: Rene Goscinny, Albert Uderzo, Georges Dargaud, D:S: Rene
Goscinny, Albert Uderzo, A: Harold Whitaker, Brian Larkin, Graham
Ralph, John Perkins, Dave Unwin, Borg Ring, Christopher Evans, John
Halas, Tessa Jones, C: Denis Gruel
       Color
       Episode for a French feature cartoon (82 minutes): the final task.
Asterix the Gaul defeats the beasts and gladiators in the Roman arena.
"Bearable for its occasional witty scenes and isolated laughs, it is ultimately
depressing because of the massive labour which has clearly gone into its
making." (*Monthly Film Bulletin* March 1978.)

1976

987 Search for Source
Andrews
D: Catherine Andrews, M: Rubicon, Tangerine Dream
Color
"Abstract lights, lines, forms in a pummelling rhythm." (*London Film Festival Notes.*)

988 I'm Sorry You've Been Kept Waiting
Biographic
P:D:A: Keith Learner, Nancy Hanna, Vera Linnecar
Color
Promotional film for IBM.

989 High Fidelity (369)
British Film Institute – Contemporary
D:S:A: Annette Starkiewicz, M: Richard Hartley, C: Graham Orrin, ED: Tork Stewart, V: Neil Campbell
Color
Experimental cartoon. "A woman, naked except for a pair of ruby red tights, sings and dances with a black-suited partner." (*British National Film Catalogue* 1977.)

990 The Mathematician (120)
British Film Institute
P:D:S: Stan Hayward, DES: Ted Rockley, V: Robert Gladwell, Computer Programmer: Peter Chandler, Computer Operator: Nick Yates
Color
Experimental computerized cartoon. Harry, a mathematician, deduces that a certain mathematical combination could destroy the world. When nobody believes his theory, he puts the ingredients into a small black box. It makes him very rich and very dead: the world blows up. "Unfortunately, judging from this anticlimactic and poorly designed film, the prospects for the future of this method of animation seem far from encouraging." (*Monthly Film Bulletin* February 1978.)

991 The Miracle
British Film Institute
D:S:A: Jack Daniel
Color
"Animated cartoon with surrealistic approach." (*British National Film Catalogue* 1978.)

992 Responsibility: A Film About Contraception
Eothen Films
P: David Jenner, D: Vivian Collins, A: Tom Bailey, Ted Pettingell, Arthur Humberstone, Geoff Chennell, C: John Hardman, V: Susan Barnes, Ray Gosling
Color
Educational film for LR Industries: live action with animated sequences. "A schoolgirl finds that she is pregnant and, using animation, the film explains some of her possible courses of action – a shotgun wedding, abortion, adoption, etc." (*British National Film Catalogue* 1977.)

993 Moving On
Sheila Graber Animated Films
P:D:S:A: Sheila Graber
Color
"Tracing the history of transport on land, sea and in the air." (*British National Film Catalogue* 1979.)

994 Four Views of Landscape
Sheila Graber Animated Films
P:D:S:A: Sheila Graber
Color
Art film. "Contrasts in the style of four artists in their approach to landscape painting: Constable, Turner, Monet and Van Gogh." (*British National Film Catalogue* 1979.)

995 Michelangelo
Sheila Graber Animated Films
P:D:S:A: Sheila Graber
Color
Art film. "Shows the artist's major works in chronological order and attempts to put over his dynamic energy." (*British National Film Catalogue* 1979.)

996 The Twelve Days of Christmas
Sheila Graber Animated Films
P:D:S:A: Sheila Graber

Color
Animated version of the old Christmas song, sung by a school madrigal group.

997 The Lady of Shallot
Sheila Graber Animated Films
P:D:A: Sheila Graber, S: Alfred Tennyson
Color
Animated version of the classic poem.

998 I Am the Very Model of a Modern Major General
Sheila Graber Animated Films
P:D:A: Sheila Graber, S: William S. Gilbert, Arthur Sullivan
Color
Animated version of the comic-opera song.

999 When I Went to the Bar
Sheila Graber Animated Films
P:D:A: Sheila Graber, S: William S. Gilbert, Arthur Sullivan
Color
Animated version of the comic-opera song.

1000 The Boy and the Cat
Sheila Graber Animated Films
P:D:S:A: Sheila Graber, M: Brenda Orwin
Color
"Set to a specially composed piano score telling the adventures of a boy and his cat in the snows of Christmas." (*British National Film Catalogue* 1981.)

1001 The Boy and the Song
Sheila Graber Animated Films
P:D:S:A: Sheila Graber
"A boy and a cat who soldier on against great adversity arising from the words of four well-known songs." (*British National Film Catalogue* 1981.)

1002 Deadlock (450)
Halas & Batchelor – EFC
P: John Halas, D:S: Janos Wiktorowsky, A: Mike Hibbert, C: Leo Rodgers, M: Francis Chagrin
Color
"One man tries to sink a shaft into the earth trying to reach the other side, only to discover that another man is doing the same on the other side." (*British National Film Catalogue* 1979.)

1003 Chromatographic Separation
Halas & Batchelor — Guild Sound & Vision
P: John Halas, A: Brian Borthwick, S: John Hargreaves, C: Leo Rodgers, ED: Jack King
Combined live action and animation. "The analysis of chromatic separation." (*British National Film Catalogue* 1981.)

1004 Reel People
Chris James
P:D:S:A: Chris James
Animated caricatures of Jeremy Thorpe MP, Edward Heath MP, Harold Wilson MP, Margaret Thatcher MP, Spike Milligan, Dwight D. Eisenhower, John F. Kennedy, Lyndon Johnson, Richard Nixon, Spiro Agnew, Gerald Ford.

1005 A Helluva Bet in the Wet
London International Film School
D:S: Frank Bren, A: Frank Bren, Nick Beeks-Sanders, M: Chris Tingley
Color
Students' film. "Caterpillars involve themselves in an unusual horse race." (*British National Film Catalogue* 1976.)

1006 Arrival of the Iron Egg
North West Artists Association — Open Eye
D: Brodnax Moore, S: Boris Howarth, Di Davies, Steve Gumbley, A: Di Davies, Steve Gumbley, Hannah Fox, ED: Annette Kuhn, Brodnax Moore, C: Brodnax Moore, John Chapman, Lou Chadfield
Students' film: live action and animation. "Depicts the arrival and discovery of an iron egg from outer space." (*British National Film Catalogue* 1980.)

1007 Creation
North Yorkshire Education Committee
D: Tom Chadwick, C: Tom Chadwick, Peter Bell, M: Peter Bell, Malcolm Marker, Joan Meeke
Color
Animated cartoon made by 11–14 year old children of a Whitby secondary school. "Chronological view of the story of creation." (*British National Film Catalogue* 1979.)

1008 Animal Alphabet Parade (series)
Seabourne Enterprises
P: John Seabourne, D: John Williams, A: Stewart Hardy, M: Peter Murray

Color

Series of 27 animated films for children. The first film uses animals to represent each letter of the alphabet; the remaining 26 feature one letter of the alphabet each.

1009 La Forza Del Destino
London International Film School
D:A: Hans Glanzmann
Color

"Tragic destiny of a man seduced by a woman: if you intend to jump over a chasm, measure the run up." (*Annecy Animation Festival Programme.*)

1010 Strip Cartoon
Sharp
P:D:S:V: Chris Sharp, M: John Sinclair

"A girl strips off her clothes inside a public bar. She imagines herself to be a star stripper, and in a flight of fancy is transported to the night sky, where she walks through the stars." (*British National Film Catalogue* 1978.)

1011 Metamorphosis
Sharp
P:D:S:A: Chris Sharp

Experimental cartoon, scratched directly onto the film. "About women and sex, natural and magical changes of form which depict sensuality and image association." (*British National Film Catalogue* 1978.)

1012 I Told You So
Timeless Films
P:D:S:A: Ian Emes, M: Tom Lehrer
Color

"Male and female symbols are shown ageing together through marriage." (*British National Film Catalogue* 1977.)

1013 Freefall
Timeless Films
P:D:S:A: Ian Emes, M: Pink Floyd
Color

"Trip through geometry, time and space at breakneck speed, ending inevitably with a collision." (*British National Film Catalogue* 1977.) Made as a back-projected image behind the pop group Pink Floyd performing live, but re-edited for exhibition.

1014 The Case of the Sulphuric Acid Plant
    Video Arts
    P: Peter Robinson, D: Robert Reid, A: Tony Hart, C: Peter Middle-
ton, ED: Peter Clarke, M: Roland Harker, V: John Cleese
    Color
    Combined live action and animation; instructional film for ICI.
"Showing both the chemistry and the industrial process of making sulphuric acid." (*British National Film Catalogue* 1976.)

1977

1015 Loop
British Film Institute Production Board
D: Anna Fodorova, ED: Anna Fodorova, Vera Neubauer, C: Philip Mulloy, M: Simon Desorgher, V: Mike Gold
Color
Experimental cartoon. "Meditates on the nature of animation and the power of the animator." (*British National Film Catalogue* 1978.)

1016 Schizophrenia
Jack Warner – London College of Printing
D:SC: Stephen Lowe, S: R.D. Laing, M: Fats Domino
Color
"Survey of the most important ideas within the book, *The Divided Self.*" (*Zagreb Animation Festival Programme.*)

1017 Man and the Motor Car
Concord Films
D: Peter Hickling, S: David Evans, A: Peter Hickling, Don Coleman, Brian Simpson, Andre Fontenoy, C: Tom Connor, Don Coleman, Peter Hickling, M: Russ Law, V: Liz Denmark
Color
"Deals humorously with man's relationship with the motor car and the effects it has had on the world." (*British National Film Catalogue* 1977.)

1018 The Mysterious Moon
Concord Films
D: Peter Hickling, S: David Evans, A: Peter Hickling, Don Coleman, Brian Simpson, Andre Fontenoy, C: Tom Connor, Don Coleman, Peter Hickling, M: Alan Parker, V: Liz Denmark
Color
"Portrays some of the facts already known about the moon, showing how much is still unknown." (*British National Film Catalogue* 1977.)

1019 Phil the Fluter's Ball
Sheila Graber Animated Films
P:D:S:A: Sheila Graber
Color
Animated illustration of the old Irish comic song.

1020 The Cat and the Tune (270)
Sheila Graber Animated Films
P:D:S:A: Sheila Graber
Color
"A cat leads an animal band through musical adventures to an orchestrated version of 'Eye Level.'" (*British National Film Catalogue* 1981.)

1021 Cathedral
London International Film School
D:S:A:ED: Ian Cook
Student's cartoon: "In a cathedral you find all sorts of pilgrims, but today with group travel and charters..." (*Annecy Animation Festival Programme.*)

1022 Make-Up
Fryer Productions
P:D: Joanna Fryer
Color
"While putting on her makeup a woman fantasises about the types of men who will take her out, only to be disappointed." (*Annecy Animation Festival Programme.*)

1023 Be a Good Neighbour
Sheila Graber Animated Films
P:D:S:A: Sheila Graber, V: Geoffrey O'Connell
Color
Informational film for the Northumbrian Police Force. "Many of the simple precautions that can be adopted by householders to protect their homes and property during their absence." (*British National Film Catalogue* 1979.)

1024 Making It Move
Halas & Batchelor— EFC
P:D: John Halas, S: John Halas, Roger Mainwood, A: Roger Mainwood, M: Kraftwerk, C: Dee Simpson
Color
Live action with animation sequences. "Film showing how to line up a production for animation, which goes through the various steps from conception to final show print." (*British National Film Catalogue* 1978.) Shows Roger Mainwood working on *Autobahn*.

1025 Skyrider (720)
Halas & Batchelor
P:D: John Halas, S: John Halas, Derek Lamb, A: Tony Guy, Harold Whitaker, M: Jack King
Color
"Set against a lavish interplanetary background with an innocent small citizen who builds his own rocket in his backyard and penetrates with it into outer space. This parody ends with him being awarded a knighthood by the Queen." (*Art & Animation* 1980.)

1026 Measure of Man (900)
Halas & Batchelor – EFC – Guild
P: John Halas, D: Tony Guy, John Halas, S: Stan Hayward, Patrick Murphy, A: Tony Guy, M: Jack King
Color
The first half of the film deals with a humorous recollection of the history of measuring, the second half deals with metrication and the conversion of Imperial units to SI units." (*British National Film Catalogue* 1982.)

1027 Noah's Arc
Halas & Batchelor – EFC
P: John Halas, D: Elphin Lloyd-Jones, DES: Dino Katopoulis, Paul Shardlow, A: Harold Whitaker, Brian Larkin, Graham Ralph, Kathleen Houston, M: Wilfred Joseph, V: Orson Welles
Educational film for the Genesis Project.

1028 Duo
Stuart Wynn Jones
P:D:A:S: Stuart Wynn Jones, M: Gordon Jacob, William Waterhouse, Thea King
Color
Experimental cartoon. "Visual interpretation of a musical composition exploring the cinematic medium in the way that abstract posters explore the medium of paint and canvas." (*British National Film Catalogue* 1978.)

1029 Topiary
MGR Productions – Guild
Color
"A hedge is cut into the shape of a bird, which comes to life." (*British National Film Catalogue* 1979.)

1030 Hotel
MGR Productions – Guild
Color

"Story of a boy and his dog who go away on holiday but are refused admittance to a hotel. A good deed by the boy gains them entrance." (*British National Film Catalogue* 1979.)

1031 Max Beeza and the City in the Sky (1800)
    National Film School—Animation City
    D: Derek Hayes, Philip Austin, A: Derek Hayes, Philip Austin, Ginny d'Santos, M: Nick Symes
    Color
    Students' cartoon. "Science fantasy cartoon about a future Britain where everyone lives in a tower city under threat by a mysterious airship. Max Beeza is a preacher, magician, and con-man who discovers who the real enemy is." (*British National Film Catalogue* 1978.) A stunning 20-minute musical cartoon by two students of the National Film School, the film was contracted for commercial distribution by Twentieth Century–Fox, but the arrangement was aborted by the Musicians Union.

1032 When I'm Rich (472)
    New Fields—Contemporary
    P: Derek Phillips, D: Stan Hayward, Ted Rockley, Derek Phillips, S: Stan Hayward, A: Ted Rockley, V: Nigel Stock
    Color
    A disgruntled man tells the audience that when he is rich he will have new clothes, a new car, and throw a lavish party. He will also knock down his wall and throttle his annoying neighbor. Then he hears through the wall a voice telling his neighbor he has won a football pool. Immediately a hammering begins on the other side of the wall. "Touching that familiar Stan Hayward preoccupation, the sexual fantasies of the shabby, middle-aged British male, this collaborative snippet offers a tonic celebration of curmudgeonly behaviour." (*Monthly Film Bulletin* February 1978.)

1033 Dear Margery Boobs (480) (X)
    Oppidan Films—New Realm
    P: David Grant, D: Bob Godfrey, S: Stan Hayward, A: Jeff Goldner, Ann Joliffe, Ted Rockley, C: Julian Holdaway, ED: Tony Fish, M: Jonathan P. Hodge, V: Imogen Claire, Bob Godfrey
    Eastmancolor
    Middle-aged "Worried, Streatham," writes a series of letters to a newspaper columnist describing his escalating sexual aberrations. She falls in love with him! "From anxiety about his anatomical inadequacy, through experiments with an unwisely electrified inflatable doll and a bicycle machine that tans his bottom, to his final circus extravaganza, 'Worried' provides animator Godfrey with another excuse for creating second-generation Heath Robinson machines." (*Monthly Film Bulletin* September 1977.) Certified "X" for adults only.

1034 Man the Inventor: The History of the Heat Engine
Perkins Engines Group
S: Michael Smee, Joe Hind, A: David Oliver, Frank Brown, C:ED: M. Jones, M: Merrick Farrar
Color
Instructional film. "History of heat engine development from Hero of Alexander to Rudolph Diesel." (*British National Film Catalogue* 1977.)

1035 The Two Stroke
Random Films
P: Stephanie Tennant, D: Peter Mills, S: John Tolly, A: Frances Rodker, C: Gordon Lang, ED: Cyril Roth, V: Roy Skelton, Patrick Jordan, Nigel Rathbone
Color
Instructional film for Shell. "Using animated drawings the film explains the difference between the operation of two and four stroke engines." (*British National Film Catalogue* 1978.)

1036 How the Motor Car Works: The Carburettor
Shell Film Unit
D: George Seager, A: John Halas, Joy Batchelor, C: Alan Fabian, Bob Taylor, Rian Mitchinson, ED: Roy Piper, Chris Joyce
Color
Instructional film for Shell. "Demonstrates by the use of direct experiment combined with animated diagrams the need for mixing air and gasolene in the correct proportions to make an efficient fuel." (*British National Film Catalogue* 1978.)

1037 Too Much Monkey Business
National Film School
D: Andrew Walker
Color
Student's cartoon. "A primeval monkey's dream of civilization and his reaction towards it." (*Zagreb Animation Festival Programme.*)

1038 The Cage (120)
Royal College of Art – BFI
D:S:A:C: Roger Mainwood
Eastmancolor
Student's cartoon. A lioness is agitated by a persistently buzzing fly. "Particularly to devotees of the cat family, this is an unusual and diverting entertainment that holds the attention despite its flimsy storyboard." (*Monthly Film Bulletin* February 1978.)

1039 Teamwork
TV Cartoons
P: George Dunning, S: Jim Duffy, A: Malcolm Draper, M: Ron Goodwin
Color
Instructional film for the National Coal Board. "Emphasises the importance of team effort in productivity and safety." (*British National Film Catalogue* 1977.)

1040 Heart's Right
Timeless Films
P:D:S:A: Ian Emes, M: Roger Daltry
Color
"Pop star Roger Daltry as a cartoon comic strip hero returning home to the East End aboard a squadron of airborne records, only to find that the city is inhabited by strange creatures of the media." (*British National Film Catalogue* 1977.)

1041 How to Lie with Statistics: The Average Chap
Video Arts
P: Peter Robinson, S: Darrell Huff, Irving Geis, SC: Robert Reid, A: Tony Hart, M: Sidney Sager, V: John Cleese
Color
Instructional film based on a book. "Concentrates on the use and misuse of averages." (*British National Film Catalogue* 1977.) See also 950.

1042 Swimming Pool (270)
West Surrey College of Art
D:S:A: Jo Beedel
Student's cartoon.

1043 Night Call
Julian Roberts
D:S:A: Thalma Goldman
Color
"Man rushes to save a friend from suicide but discovers it to be an April Fool joke." (*Zagreb Animation Festival Programme.*)

1044 Witchflight
Timeless Films
P:D:A: Ian Emes
Color
"Visually stunning film by a British animator whose work has often been with major British pop musicians." (*London Film Festival Notes.*)

1045 Imperial Guard Cavalry
Richard Williams
P: Richard Williams, D: Russell Hall
Color
Advertisement film for Count Pushkin Vodka.

1046 That'll Be the Dei
Central School of Art and Design
D:A: Ian Henderson
Color
Student's cartoon. "Animated ideas around a medieval illuminated manuscript." (*London Film Festival Notes.*)

1047 Kalamazoo
Leeds Polytechnic
D:S:A: Rob Hopkin
Color
Student's cartoon. "Witty illustration of a pop song." (*London Film Festival Notes.*)

1048 Bob
Walker
D:S:A: Andy Walker
Color
"Science fiction film about sending a giant canary into outer space." (*London Film Festival Notes.*)

1049 Lane Discipline
Film Troupe
D: Ken Brown, S: Diana Humphrey
Color
"Computer animation used to demonstrate lane discipline on today's busy roads." (*London Film Festival Notes.*)

1050 Nostalgie de la Boue
Rimmer
P:D:A: Peter Rimmer
Color
"Account of Liverpool children's street games in a highly individual graphic style evoking memories of L.S. Lowry." (*London Film Festival Notes.*)

1978

1051 The Vital Spark
Animated Productions
V: Philip Stone
Promotional film for Smiths Industries. "The early history of the sponsor and their long connection with the design and manufacture of spark plugs." (*British National Film Catalogue* 1978.)

1052 The Water Babies (8280)
Adriadne — Miniatur Filmowych — Productions Associates — Pethurst
XP: Ben Arbeid, P: Peter Shaw, D: Lionel Jeffries, S: Charles Kingsley, SC: Michael Robson, Lionel Jeffries, Denis Norden, DES: Edward McLachlan, AD: Jack Stokes, Tony Cuthbert, Miroslaw Kijowicz, A: Jan Baudouin, Leszek Galysz, Adrezej Kozlowski, Elzbieta Morawska, Jaroslaw Jakubiec, Alexsander Piatkowski, Cecylia Terlikieqicz, Joanna Zacharzewska, ED: Hanna Michaelwicz, Adam Sendyk, Brian Bishop, FX: Roy Turk, M: Phil Coulter, V: Jon Pertwee, Olive Gregg, Lance Percival, David Jason, Cass Allan, Liz Proud, Una Stubbs
Color
Anglo-Polish production; live-action feature (92 minutes) with animation sequences. Adapted from the novel by Charles Kingsley set in the London of 1850. Tom, a 12-year-old orphan boy, escapes from a cruel chimney sweep by becoming able to live under water. Helped by Jock the Lobster and Terence the Seahorse, he escapes from a shark and an electric eel, thanks to Claude the Swordfish, and reaches the Eternal Playground of the Water Babies. He ventures to the polar regions to seek help from Kraken, Lord of the Oceans, and after leading the Babies against a wicked Shark, he returns home. "The animation sequences are surprisingly successful, despite a certain monotony and lack of inventiveness in the backgrounds (B. Kuznicki, M. Kijowicz). The human figures as so often are distressingly arch, the Water Babies themselves being the height of Disney cuteness, but the other denizens of the deep are characterized with prolific wit." (*Monthly Film Bulletin* April 1979.)

274

1053 About Face
Arts Council
D:S:A: Chris James, ED: Chris James, Bill Hopkins, C: Julian Holdaway, M: Claude Jouvin
Animated caricatures of Mick Jagger, Henry VIII, Oscar Wilde, Lord Alfred Douglas, Queen Elizabeth II, Prince Philip, Prince Charles, Pablo Picasso, Salvador Dali, Adolf Hitler, Idi Amin, the Marx Brothers, David Bowie.

1054 Hokusai
Arts Council – Concord
D: Tony White, A: Tony White, Tass Heron, Richard Burdett, DES: Katsushika Hokusai, C: Peter Wood, ED: Rod Hawick, M: Howard Blake, Susi Sakashita, V: Michael Bates, Erik Chitty
Color
Animated tribute to the Japanese painter Katsushika Hokusai (1766–1849) featuring sixty of his 30,000 sketches. British Film Academy Award 1978.

1055 Engineering Matters or the Continuing Story of Ogg
Sygnet Guild Communications
P:S: Julian Dinsell, D: Tim Thomas, A: Sidney Mould, C: Martin Rissen, ED: John Beaton, V: Gary Watson
Color
Promotional film for ICI. "Uses animation and historical content to set the scene for the working life of today's professional engineer." (*British National Film Catalogue* 1978.)

1056 Screen Test Series
Godfrey Films – CTVC
D: Bob Godfrey, S: Norman Stone, A: Ted Rockley, C: Julian Holloway, ED: Tony Fish, Peter Hearn
Color
1: The Hand, 2: The Trap, 3: The Line, 4: The Shadow, 5: The Key
Propaganda cartoons for CTVC. "Series of humorous cartoons intended to provide an insight into the meaning of salvation from a Christian viewpoint." (*British National Film Catalogue* 1979.)

1057 The Owl and the Pussy Cat
Lyn O'Neill
P:D:A: Lyn O'Neill
Color
Animated adaptation of Edward Lear's poem for children.

1058 Marking Time
Sheila Graber Animated Films
P:D:S:A: Sheila Graber
Color
"History of how time has been marked from moon calendar to clocks and relativity." (*British National Film Catalogue* 1979.)

1059 Mondrian
Sheila Graber Animated Films
P:D:S:A: Sheila Graber
Color
Art film. "Set to piano boogie-woogie, traces the gradual development of the artist's style from early naturalism to late neo-plasticism." (*British National Film Catalogue* 1979.)

1060 William Blake
Sheila Graber Animated Films
P:D:S:A: Sheila Graber, M: Carl Orff
Color
Art film. "Animates the major works by William Blake to show some of his powerful philosophy as sensed in his painting and poetry." (*British National Film Catalogue* 1979.)

1061 Ubu (1800)
Grand Slamm-Concord
P:D:SC: Geoff Dunbar, S: Alfred Jarry, A: Geoff Dunbar, Annabel Jankel, Len Lewis, Ginger Gibbons, ED: Terry Brown, C: Richard Wolff, M: Laurie Scott-Baker, V: William Mitchell
Eastmancolor
Adaptation of Alfred Jarry's 1896 play, *Ubu Roi,* as translated by Julia Rowntree; produced for the Arts Council. The monstrous Pa Ubu is persuaded by his wife, Ma Ubu, to murder King Wenceslas. He does so, making Captain Drubbish his scapegoat, and revels in the prospect of unlimited power. Prince Bugrelas raises an army and defeats him in battle, but Pa and Ma sail away to further adventures. "The play's unique verbal force is retained through the use of dialogue in comic strip bubbles of various colours (Pa's vilest oaths suitably appear in vile green)." (*Monthly Film Bulletin* (December 1978.)

1062 Mercurious
Stuart Wynn Jones
P:D:S:A: Stuart Wynn Jones, M: Mat Camison
Color
"Abstract designs to music giving the impression of a firework display." (*London Film Festival Notes.*)

1063 Marx for Beginners
Cucumber Studios – Readers & Writers Publishing Cooperative
P: Bob Godfrey, Ed Berman, D: Clive Morton, Kevin Attew, A: Annabel Jankel, Marcus Parker-Rhodes, Graeme Jackson, Gale Wright, ED: Tony Fish, Clennel Rawson, C: Julian Holdaway, M: John Hawkesmith, V: Dirty Linen
Color
"Potted history of philosophy up to and including Karl Marx." (*London Film Festival Notes.*)

1064 Out of Silence
Central School of Art
D:S:A: Inni Karine Melbye
Color
"A 45-second television interlude between children's programmes." (*London Film Festival Notes.*) Student's cartoon.

1065 Doctor Nightmare
Royal College of Art
D:S:A: Morgan Sendall
Color
Student's cartoon. "Visit to the psychiatrist with a surprising twist." (*London Film Festival Notes.*)

1066 Discovery Train
Williams Animation
XP: Richard Williams, P: Carl Gover, D: Russell Hall, DES: Bruce Doward, ED: Rod Horrick, M: Terry Bush
Color
Promotional cartoon. "A train which gives the opportunity to Canadians of discovering the history of their country." (*Annecy Animation Festival Programme.*)

1067 The Adventures of Flutterguy
British Film Institute Production Board
D:S:A: Donald Holwill
Color
Flutterguy, secretly a super-hero, works in a human being factory. Receiving a call from headquarters, he is sent on a mission by Fatman.

1068 Safe in the Sea (75)
Bob Godfrey Movie Team
P: Bob Godfrey
Color
"A film to warn of the dangers of swimming in the open sea." (*Zagreb Animation Festival Programme.*)

1069 The Garden of Eden

Kuperberg
P:D:S:A: Marcia Kuperberg
Color

Experimental animation: the cartoon is drawn and colored on screen. "An outdoor scene with a child holding a balloon. The artist and the child disagree over the colouring of the balloon." (*British National Film Catalogue* 1979.)

1070 Oriental Nightfish

MPI Communications – Timeless Films
P: Paul McCartney, Linda McCartney, D:S: Ian Emes, A: Ian Emes, Margaret Grieve, Robert Grigg, M: Linda McCartney, Wings, V: Linda McCartney
Color

Musical cartoon: creature descends from outer space and metamorphoses a girl. "The Oriental Nightfish is everything we know and all that we cannot comprehend." (*Zagreb Animation Festival Programme.*)

1071 Watership Down (8290)

Nepenthe Productions – CIC
P: Martin Rosen, Philip Alton, D:SC: Martin Rosen, S: Richard Adams, SUP: Philip Duncan, AD: Tony Guy, A: Arthur Humberstone, George Jackson, Tony Guy, Philip Duncan, Edrick Radage, Bill Littlejohn, Ruth Kissane, John Perkins, Ralph Ayres, Brian Foster, Chris Evans, Marie Szmichowska, Alan Simpson, Colin White, Doug Jensen, Bill Geach, Kathleen Houston, Barrie Nelson, ED: Terry Rawlings, C: Tony Haines, M: Angela Morley, Malcolm Williamson, MD: Marcus Dods, V: John Hurt (Hazel), Richard Briers (Fiver), Michael Graham-Cox (Bigwig), John Bennett (Captain Holly), Ralph Richardson (Chief), Simon Cadell (Blackberry), Terence Rigby (Silver), Roy Kinnear (Pipkin), Richard O'Callaghan (Dandelion), Denholm Elliott (Cowslip), Lyn Farleigh (Cat), Mary Maddow (Clover), Zero Mostel (Kehaar), Harry Andrews (General Woundwort), Hannah Gordon (Hyzenthlay), Nigel Hawthorn (Captain Campion), Clifton Jones (Blackavar), Derek Griffiths (Vervain), Michael Hordern (Frith), Joss Ackland (Black Rabbit), Michelle Price (Lucy)
Technicolor

Feature-length (92 minutes) adaptation of the fantasy novel by Richard Adams; production work commenced by John Hubley. When young Fiver, a rabbit, has a prophetic vision of the warren's destruction, Hazel leads a group of companions to seek a safer home. After many adventures they reach the safety of a high down, but realize they have no does in their colony. They try capturing some from a neighboring warren ruled by the tyrannical Wondwort, and are helped in their fight by Kehaar, a seagull. Hazel releases a fierce farm dog who routs the rival rabbits, and the new colony prospers. "Rosen has claimed that his film is not a children's picture, yet with most of its running time filled with standard harum-scarum battles and adventures, lightly veneered with a sort of pseudo-mysticism, it's hard to imagine that there is much here for the adult admirers of Adams' long, literary novel." (*Monthly Film Bulletin* October 1978.)

1072 Jack and the Beanstalk
Sheffield Polytechnic
D: Nick Park
Student's film: version of the old fairy story.

1073 The Beard
Summerfield – Kendon – Electronic Picture Palace – Timeless Films – Boyd's Company
XP: Nicholas de Rothschild, Don Boyd, P: Chris Brown, D: Ian Emes, S:DES: Peter Till, A: Ian Emes, Margaret Grieve, Robert Grigg, C: Roy Watford, M: Adrian Wagner, V: William Rushton
Color
The horrible consequences of a man's beard suddenly growing to monstrous proportions.

1074 The Devil May Care
TV Cartoons
P: George Dunning, D: Jim Duffy
Eastmancolor
Instructional film for National Coal Board. "Intended to reduce the frequency of carbon-copy accidents." (*British National Film Catalogue* 1978.)

1075 The Interview
West Surrey College of Art & Design
D:A: Michael Dudok de Wit
Color
Student's cartoon. "What is it that makes the public flee from the sight of a tape recorder?" (*London Film Festival Notes.*)

1076 T'Batley Faust
Yorkshire Artists Association
D:A: Tony Hall
Color
"Version of the Faust legend set in Yorkshire and involving a mean-spirited industrial tycoon who sells his soul to the Devil in exchange for his lost youth." (*British National Film Catalogue* 1980.)

1979

1077 The Adventures of Captain Mark and Krystal Klear
Alexander Productions
D: Brian Early, A: Stewart Hardy, C: Adrian Jeakins, ED: Eddie Powell, V: James Smilie, Sue Sheridan
Color
Promotional film for Reed Paper. "Two characters from a future world which has developed the ultimate communicating technique. Illustrates the uses of chemical carbonless paper." (*British National Film Catalogue* 1979.)

1078 The Code It Story
Roger Cherrill Associates
P: Arthur Sterns, D: Eric Wylam, A: Photomation, S: Eric Wylam, Gerald Borer, ED: Howard Birkett, V: Deryck Guyler
Color
Promotional film for the Post Office. "Light-hearted look at the history of communicating by letter illustrates the efficiency of the postcode system." (*British National Film Catalogue* 1979.)

1079 Father Christmas Forgets
Honeycomb – Eastern Arts Association
P:D:S: Simon Bor, Sara Bor, A:ED: Simon Bor, M: Edward Bor, V: Margaret Bor
Color
Santa Claus forgets a small girl's present, so takes her to his castle to choose her own.

1080 Black and White Magic
TV Cartoons
P: John Coates, D: Jeremy Hibbert, A: Jeremy Hibbert, Hilary Andus, Joanna Fryer, Richard Fawdry, DES: Ion Cramer, Mike Crane, C: Peter Turner, ED: Mick Manning

1081 Yellow Submarine Sandwich
Harold Friedman Consortium
D: George Parker, A: Tony White
Color
Lampoon of the 1968 Beatles cartoon feature *Yellow Submarine*. Made originally as an item for the BBC2 television show, *The Rutles*.

1082 Dream Doll (1150)
Godfrey Films – Halas & Batchelor – Zagreb Studio
P: Bob Godfrey, John Halas, D: Bob Godfrey, Zlatko Grgic, S: Stephen Penn, A: Ted Rockley, Alastair McIlwain, Kathleen Houston, Zlatko Grgic, Turido Paus, ED: Tony Fish, Peter Hearn, C: Julian Holdaway, Frank Malogorsky, Ian Lett, M: John Hyde
Eastmancolor
Anglo-Yugoslavian coproduction. A lonely little man falls in love with an inflatable rubber woman. "This cartoon spoof of *The Red Balloon* is distinguished by its lightness of tone. Godfrey's distinctly personal film is a very rare example of a British sex comedy, however slight, that is actually amusing." (*Monthly Film Bulletin* December 1980.) Adults only certificate.

1083 Instant Sex
Godfrey Films
P: Bob Godfrey, D: Graeme Jackson, S: Stephen Penn, A: Graeme Jackson, Chris Rayment, ED: Tony Fish, Peter Hearn, C: Julian Holdaway, Robert Murray, M: Peter Shade, V: Imogen Claire, Pat Morris, Bob Godfrey
Eastmancolor
An old man buys a tin of Instant Sex from a supermarket and uses it with ludicrous results. Adults only certificate.

1084 Nocturna Artificiala (Those Who Desire Without End) (780)
British Film Institute Production Board
P: Keith Griffiths, D:S:A:C:ED: Stephen Quaij, Timothy Quaij, M: Stefan Cichonski, MD: Martin Weaver
Eastmancolor
Puppet animation: "The precincts of an alien behind the closed eyelids of that deep sleep usually reserved for epileptics." (*Zagreb Animation Festival Programme.*)

1085 Christmas Round the World
Sheila Graber Animated Films
P:D:S:A: Sheila Graber, M: Brenda Orwin
Color
"Set to an arrangement of 'Jingle Bells' the film traces the action-packed journey of Santa Claus round the world on Christmas Eve." (*British National Film Catalogue* 1979.)

1086 The Listeners
Greater London Arts Association
D:A: Keith Greig, M: Bob Taylor, Meira Shore, V: Terry Beakman,
S: Walter de la Mare
"Animated film illustrating the poem." (*British National Film Catalogue* 1980.)

1087 Autobahn
Halas & Batchelor — EFC
P:D: John Halas, S: John Halas, Roger Mainwood, A:DES: Roger Mainwood, M: Kraftwerk, C: Peter Petrino, ED: Tork Stewart
Eastmancolor
Visual interpretation of music by the pop group Kraftwerk, featuring a green figure wearing goggles swimming through space occupied by floating lips and eyes. The making of this film is featured in *Making It Move* (No. 1024).

1088 Crackers
Luther-Smith
P:D:S:A:ED: Vanessa Luther-Smith, C: Graham Orrin, M: The Henderson Twins
"Humorous visual interpretation from an original 78 rpm recording of Shirley Temple's 'Animal Crackers in My Soup,' 'On the Good Ship Lollipop,' and 'When I Grow Up.'" (*British National Film Catalogue* 1981.)

1089 Boolean Procedure
Muscle Films — Greater London Arts
P:D: Michael Coulson, Nicola Bruce, M: George Thorn, Dave Henderson, C: Tony Cook, V: Terry McGinty
Color
Live action (Nigel Hawley) and animation. "Expresses the idea that each individual has a variety of avenues and procedures open to them, especially concerning work and leisure." (*British National Film Catalogue* 1979.)

1090 Mack the Knife
National Film School
D:A: Margaret Allen, C: Terry Handley, Carine Vogel, M: Kurt Weill, Bobby Darin
Students' film: live action and animation, interpreting the Bobby Darin recording of "Mack the Knife" from *The Beggar's Opera*. "An anonymous dancer attempts to upstage Mack the Knife, and wins." (*British National Film Catalogue* 1980.)

1091 Spare a Thought
Oxfam – Christian Aid – Concord
P: Doron Abraham, S: Peter Stalker, A: Ray Bruce, V: Adrian Juste
Color
Propaganda film for Oxfam. "Three part cartoon which aims to bring home to young people the legacy of Britain's colonial past and the price paid by the world's poor for what people in Britain consider to be everyday essentials." (*British National Film Catalogue* 1979.)

1092 Ersatz
Premier
D: Christopher Taylor
Color
Animated puppets. "Pastiche featuring small puppets playing Humphrey Bogart and juggling with popular Forties movies." (*British National Film Catalogue* 1980.)

1093 Together for Children: Principle 10
AKA: **Ten for Survival**
UNICEF – Halas & Batchelor – EFC
P: John Halas, Max Massimino Garnier, D: John Halas, S: Joy Batchelor, A: Roger Mainwood, Brian Larkin, Graham Ralph, DES: Roger Mainwood, C: Peter Petronio, M: Luis Bacalov, V: Judi Dench
Color
Animated feature in ten parts in which ten countries (Mexico, East Germany, Canada, Finland, USSR, Hungary, Italy, Sweden, Poland and Great Britain) combined to illustrate the ten principles of the United Nations Charter for Children. Initiated by the Italian UNICEF Committee, a ballot drawn out of a hat decided which nation should produce each principle. The Halas & Batchelor studio, selected to represent British animation, drew the final principle, No. 10. "Principle 10: The child shall be protected from practices which may foster racial, religious and any other forms of discrimination." A small fairy brings black and white neighbors together at a colorful carnival.

1094 What Is a Computer
Video Arts
P:S: Robert Reid, A: April Johnson, DES: Tony Hart, M: Michel Le Grand, V: Maya Brandt, Mick Shipley, Frank Sinatra
Color
Instructional film for International Computers. "Illustrating the basic elements of the computer and its functions." (*British National Film Catalogue* 1979.)

1095 The Great Rock'n'Roll Swindle (9325)
Virgin Films — Boyd's Company — Matrixbest
XP: Jeremy Thomas, Don Boyd, P: Joyce Herlihy, D: Julien Temple
(live action), S: Julien Temple, A: Phil Austin, Bill Mather, Derek Hayes, Gil
Potter, Andy Walker, M: Steve Jones, the Sex Pistols
Color
Live-action feature with animation sequences: the rise and split-up
of the punk rock group the Sex Pistols. "Many gaps in the narrative, such
as the Pistols reported ransacking of record company offices, the mis-
demeanours at airports, and attacks in the street on members of the group
during the Jubilee, are covered by animation sequences. The end credits
appear over a cartoon of the Pistols on a sinking ship to the tune of Steve
Jones' ribald sailor song, 'There was Friggin' in the Riggin.'" (*Monthly Film
Bulletin* July 1980.)

1096 Saxkrazy
West Surrey College of Art
D: Mike Smith
Color
Student's cartoon. "The sax crazy hero gets carried away literally
with his passion for the saxophone." (*British National Film Catalogue*
1980.)

1097 Mr. Pascal
Wyatt Cattaneo — Essential Cinema
P: Tony Cattaneo, D:S:A: Alison De Vere, C: Ted Gerald, ED: Sean
Lenihan, M: Derek Hodgson, John Smith
"A shoemaker who sees the very human face of his saviour." (*British
National Film Catalogue* 1980.)

1098 Funny Valentine
COW Films
D: Maya Brandt
Color
"A cautionary tale of romance and married life using plasticene
figures." (*British National Film Catalogue* 1981.)

1099 Stanley
Goldman
P:D:A: Thalma Goldman, ED: Terry Brown
Color
"A one-night encounter between two individuals. Their union is as
short-lived as it is cold." (*London Film Festival Notes.*)

1100 Read the Road
Film Troupe – COI
P: Christine Crawshaw, D: Ken Brown
Color
Informational film for the Central Office of Information.

1101 The Bunyip
Caricature Films
P:D:A: Frank Koller
Color
An adventure of "Mr. Eppynt and Klara the Cow"; cartoon for children, made in Wales.

1102 Coastguard Telephone
Taylor Cartoons – COI
P:D:A: Richard Taylor
Color
Informational film for the Central Office of Information.

1103 Fishing Accident
Taylor Cartoons – COI
P:D:A: Richard Taylor
Color
Informational film for the Central Office of Information.

1104 Four Moving Pictures
Andrews
P:D:A: Alan Andrews
Color
"A Fischingeresque silent abstract." (*London Film Festival Notes.*)

1105 Animation for Live Action
British Film Institute Production Board
P: Philip Mulloy, D:S: Vera Neubauer, A: Vera Neubauer, Anna Fodorova, Ravi Swani, Nick Xypnitos, M: Alan Lawrence
Eastmancolor
Live action with animation: experimental film. Female filmmaker tries to solve her problems through an animated surrogate. "The stylistic jostle is relatively easy to enjoy, with the two media of the title constantly invading each other's territory." (*Monthly Film Bulletin* November 1979.)

1106 The Chinese Word for Horse
Jacques
P: Peter Jacques, D: Kate Canning, S: John Lewis, A: Anna Brockett, Peter Tupy, Kate Canning, DES: Peter Rigby, M: Dixie Dean, V: Jim Cranmer

Color
"In Chinese the ideogram for horse looks in fact like a horse. And the word for forest looks like a stylized tree." (*London Film Festival Notes.*)

1107 Accidents Will Happen
Cucumber Studios
D: Clive Morton, Annabel Jankel, DES: Patricia Hackman, Wendi Ellis
Color
Pop cartoon: "Zany film made from Elvis Costello's latest hit." (*Cambridge Animation Festival* 1979.)

1108 The Face in Art
Sheila Graber Animated Films
P:D:S:A: Sheila Graber
Color
How the human face has been depicted by artists over the centuries.

1109 Monty Python's Life of Brian (8425)
Handmade Films—CIC
XP: George Harrison, Denis O'Brien, Tarak Ben Ammar, P: John Goldstone, D: Terry Jones, S: Graham Chapman, John Cleese, Terry Gilliam, Eric Idle, Terry Jones, Michael Palin, A:DES: Terry Gilliam, ED: Julian Doyle, M: Geoffrey Burgon
Eastmancolor
Live-action feature (93 minutes) with animation sequences. Sole survivor of a clash between the Judean People's Front and the Campaign for Free Galilee poses as a prophet and is mistaken for the Messiah. "The film might also be taken seriously as an attempt to demystify Christ and religious fanaticism, while it successfully sends up the kind of reverent, choir-laden, star-studded gospel dramatizations habitually perpetrated by the cinema industry on behalf of God and Mammon." (*Monthly Film Bulletin* November 1979.)

1110 Story Time (808)
Monty Python Pictures—CIC
D:S:A: Terry Gilliam
Color
Series of unpleasant incidents occur to the characters in traditional Christmas cards.

1980

1111 Do I Detect a Change in Your Attitude (560)
Biographic Films
P:D: Vera Linnecar, A: Nancy Hanna, Vera Linnecar, Elizabeth Horn, ED: Keith Learner
Color
"A continuing battle between two enemies who change their attitudes to meet their changing circumstances. They change once too often. The changing attitudes are represented by sudden changes of background and styling." (*Cambridge Animation Festival* 1981.)

1112 Seaside Woman (400)
Boreweald – Dragon – MPL Communications – ITC
XP: Paul McCartney, P: Kevin Molloy, D:DES: Oscar Grillo, A: Barry Baker, Motti Cohen, Joanne Gooding, Ray Newman, Steve Woods, C: Richard Wolff, ED: Terry Brown, M: Linda McCartney, Wings
Color
Musical cartoon: a little black girl has fun on a sunny day in the Caribbean. Cannes Film Festival Award: best short film 1980.

1113 Evolution
Sheila Graber Animated Films – Marble Arch
P:D:S:A: Sheila Graber
Color
Educational cartoon. "Traces the history of evolution from vibrating atoms, through amoebas, fish, reptiles, and finally man, leaving the viewer with a question as to whether or not it was all worth while." (*British National Film Catalogue* 1980.)

1114 Sunbeam
Speedy Cartoons – Gandon Productions
P: Christian Gandon, D: Paul Vester, A: Paul Vester, John Challis, Alistaire McIlwaine, Franco Milia, C: Ian Lett, ED: Terry Brown, Sue Michie, V: Vicky Silva, M: Hugh Charles, Sonny Miller

287

Color
Musical cartoon in Thirties style; Anglo-French coproduction for the Arts Council. Set to the song, "What Is on Top of a Sunbeam?"

1115 John Barleycorn
Leicester Polytechnic
D:A:DES: Nik Lever, M:V: Mik Parsons
Color
Student's cartoon. Visual interpretation of the traditional folksong about the growing and harvesting of wheat.

1116 Once Upon a Time
Royal College of Art
D:S:A: Jonathan Richardson
Color
Student's cartoon: "a sci-fi parable." (*London Film Festival Notes.*)

1117 Escher
Emes Films
P:D:A: Ian Emes, C: Roy Watford, M: Mike Oldfield
Color
Art cartoon: "Escher's *trompe-l'oeil* designs brought to life." (*London Film Festival Notes.*)

1118 Space Invaders
St. Martins School of Art
D:A: Matt Forrest, Andy Morahan
Color
Student's cartoon: "Who will win the young man's attention, the girl or the space invaders?" (*Cambridge Animation Festival* 1981.)

1119 Air Beds
Taylor Cartoons – COI
P:D: Richard Taylor, A: Joanne Gooding
Color
Informational film for the Central Office of Information.

1120 Frozen Ponds Can Be Dangerous
Taylor Cartoons – COI
P: Richard Taylor, D: Roger McIntosh, Richard Taylor
Color
Informational film for the Central Office of Information.

1121 Bring It All Home
Animation City – Liberty United Records – Rock Biz Pix
D: Phil Austin, Derek Hayes, A: Phil Austin, Derek Hayes, Keith Grahame, M: Gerry Rafferty
Color
"Interpretation of Gerry Rafferty's recent hit." (*London Film Festival Notes.*)

1122 Punch and Judy
Atelier Koninck – Arts Council
P:D: Keith Griffiths, DES:A: Timothy Quaij, Stephen Quaij, S: Stephen Pruskin, M: Harrison Birtwhistle
Color
Animated puppets perform a one-act operetta founded on the traditional Punch and Judy show, to music played by the London Sinfonietta.

1123 Pandora
Gwent College
D:S:A:ED: Pete Turner, M: Philip Slass
Color
Student's cartoon: "A woman with piercing eyes and moving gracefully is the depository of a secret." (*Annecy Animation Festival Programme.*)

1124 Kremmen the Movie
Alan Carr Film Productions (Columbia – EMI – Warner)
P: Alan Carr, D: John Sunderland, S: Kenny Everett, A: Roy Cameron, V: Kenny Everett
Color
Sexy science-fiction adventures of an unlikely spaceman. Adapted from episodes first heard in Kenny Everett's radio disc-jockey programmes, then adapted to his Thames Television series. 25-minute cartoon certified "A" (adult).

1125 The Chord Sharp (903)
Moo Movies – Handmade Films
P: Joachim Krek, Ian Moo-Young, D:S: Joachim Krek, Ian Moo-Young, Volker Kriegel, Alastair McIlwain, A: Alistair Campbell, Gustl Haas, Elizabeth Horn, Rudiger Laske, Joan McLean, Paul O'Hagan, Hubertus Petroll, Alma Sachs, Wolfgang Ziemssen, C: Julian Holloway, ED: Terry Brown
Color
Series of gags about a guitarist who persistently plays the wrong chord. Shown February 1982.

1981

1126 Bio Woman (900)
Godfrey Films – 20th Century–Fox
P: John Halas, Bob Godfrey, D: Bob Godfrey, S: Stephen Penn,
SC: Jeff Goldner, Ann Joliffe, A: Mike Smith, Ted Rockley, Peter Green,
Paul Stone, Clennell Rawson, Bridget Colgan, Peter Neame, M: Peter
Shade, C: Julian Holdaway, Robert Murray, ED: Tony Fish, Peter Hearn
Color
Promotional cartoon for Rank Aldis Training Films. "A henpecked
husband and his encounters with a nubile bubble woman who comes out
of a washing machine." (*British National Film Catalogue* 1982.)

1127 In Flagranti
Greater London Arts Association
P: Neil Thomson, D:A: Ravi Narayanswami, ED: Don Carter, S:DES:
Max Klinger, M: Martin Watson, Buzz Chanter
Color
Art cartoon. "Animated film in Gothic style which deals with a series
of mysterious events that lead up to a conclusion portrayed in an etching
by the German artist, Max Klinger." (*British National Film Catalogue* 1982.)

1128 Face to Face
Sheila Graber Animated Films
P:D:S:A: Sheila Graber
Color
"Using a smudge-and-click pastel animation technique, traces the
history of a life from cradle to grave." (*British National Film Catalogue* 1982.)

1129 Dilemma
Halas & Batchelor – EFC – Computer Creations – Gala
P:D: John Halas, A: Eric Brown, Shaun Reynolds, Kathy Levy,
DES: Janos Kass, M: Michael Arnell, David Hewson
Computer animation; Anglo-American coproduction. "A fully digi-
tized computer-animated film which shows the progress of civilization

through the ages, but poses the question whether man will use his inventive abilities for destruction, or as the key to progressive creation." (*British National Film Catalogue* 1982.)

1130 First Steps
Halas & Batchelor – EFC
P: John Halas, D:A: Roger Mainwood, S: Roger Mainwood, Rosemary Fost, Beryl Kingston, C: Peter Petronio, ED: Sean Lenihan, V: Judi Dench
Color
Educational cartoon. "Deals with various aspects of ante-natal care, attitudes to children, caring for new babies, and the importance of education for parenthood." (*British National Film Catalogue* 1982.)

1131 After Beardsley
James – Arts Council
P:D:A:S: Chris James, C: Julian Holdaway, Richard Wolff, M: Ronald Fowler, DES: Aubrey Beardsley, Patricia McCourt
Color
Art cartoon. "Cartoon in the style of Beardsley in which the spirit of Aubrey Beardsley journeys to modern times." (*British National Film Catalogue* 1982.)

1132 Keep Off the Grass
Lincolnshire & Humberside Arts
D:A: Porl Smith
Color
Amateur cartoon. "Handpainted film dealing with the unforeseen dangers of walking on the grass." (*British National Film Catalogue* 1981.)

1133 The Wife
London Filmmakers Cooperative
D:A: Brenda Horsman, M: Steve Penatti
Color
Cut-out animation. "A woman's search for self-discovery after her husband leaves her for a younger woman, which brings her into contact with women anxious to implement their liberating theories. The woman returns to her husband." (*British National Film Catalogue* 1982.)

1134 You're the Cream in My Coffee
Honeycomb Animation – Middlesex Polytechnic
D:A: Sara Bor, M: DeSylva, Brown and Henderson
Color
Student's cartoon: "Thirties style high-kicking illustration of the popular song." (*Cambridge Animation Festival* 1981.)

1135 The Decision
British Film Institute
D:A:S: Vera Neubauer, C: David Anderson, Gerry Knowlden, M: Gary Carpenter, V: Nick Burton
Color
Live action with animation sequences. "Contrasts the fantasy and romantic ideals of the traditional fairy tale with the life of an ordinary woman confined in her home." (*Cambridge Animation Festival* 1981.)

1136 Act V
Miller Productions
P:D: John J. Miller, S: William Shakespeare, A: John J. Miller, R.A. Smith, ED: Terry Brown, C: Peter Turner, M: Mark London, V: John Junkin, Peter Marinker, Peter Dennis
Color
Animated version of the Gravedigger Scene from Act V of Shakespeare's play *Hamlet.*

1137 The Vision
Prater—Church Army
D:ED: Sue Tee, S: John Bunyan, SC: Irene Cockroft, A: Raymond Moore
Color
Religious cartoon series for the Church Army, in four parts of 19 to 24 minutes each. "Reinterprets *Pilgrim's Progress* in space age terminology." (*British National Film Catalogue* 1983.)

1138 Bal Masque
Royal College of Art
D: Lys Flowerday, A: Lys Flowerday, Stephen Quaij, ED: Larry Sider, C: Atelier Konick, M: Bela Bartok
Color
Animated puppets. "Showing a glimpse of a masked ball as viewed (or invented) by a solitary mannequin figure who stands alone in a room of a ruined domain." (*British National Film Catalogue* 1982.)

1139 Expressionism
Sheila Graber Animated Films—Interama
P:D:S:A: Sheila Graber
Color
Art film combining plasticene models, cels, and direct painting. "Traces the use of the expressive image from African masks to the twentieth century expressionist movement." (*British National Film Catalogue* 1981.)

1140 Heavy Metal
Columbia—EMI—Warner
XP: Leonard Mogel, P: Ivan Reitman, AP: Michael Gross, Peter Lebensold, Lawrence Nesis, SC: Dan Goldberg, Len Blum, M: Elmer Bernstein, Royal Philharmonic Orchestra
Metrocolor
American produced feature (90 minutes) with the following four sequences animated in England (1141-1144):

1141 Soft Landing
TV Cartoons
P: John Coates, D: Jimmy Murikami, S: Dan O'Bannon, DES: Thomas Warkentin, A: Joanna Fryer, Hilary Audus, C: Peter Turner, ED: Mick Manning, M: Jerry Riggs, Marc Jordan

1142 Den
TV Cartoons
P: John Coates, Jeremy Hibbert, D: Jack Stokes, S: Richard Corben C: Peter Jones, Graham Orrin, Peter Turner, Richard Wolff, A: Hilary Audus, Bob Balser, Rich Cox, Michael Dudok de Wit, Jeremy Hibbert, Dick Horn, Reg Lodge, Alastair McIlwain, Edrick Radage, John Perkins, Mike Williams, ED: Ian Llande

1143 Grimaldi
Halas & Batchelor
P: John Halas, D: Harold Whitaker, A: Harold Whitaker, Roger Mainwood, John Perkins, Euen Frizzell, C: Peter Petronio

1144 So Beautiful and So Dangerous
Halas & Batchelor
P:D: John Halas, S: Angus McKie, A: Brian Larkin, Harold Whitaker, Roger Mainwood, John Cousen, Borge Ring, DES: Angus McKie, Neal Adams, C: Peter Petronio
Episodic science-fiction fantasy centering on a green jewel, "the sum of all evil." "The result, to put it mildly, is something of a hodge-podge." (*Monthly Film Bulletin* December 1981.)

1145 The Big Hit
RSTC Rosc
D:A: Charlotte Jennings
Color
"A high ball from the batsman during a cricket match makes an unexpected launch into the galaxy, bound for the sun." (*Cambridge Animation Festival* 1981.)

1146 Opus
University of York
D:A: David Kershaw
Color
Student's cartoon: "Explores audio-visual inter-relationships of the electronic music soundtrack." (*Cambridge Animation Festival* 1981.)

1147 Fifty Ways to Look More Lovely
Davies
P:D:A: Strinda Davies
Color
"Prescriptive ideas for female loveliness." (*Cambridge Animation Festival* 1981.)

1148 Henry King
Fletcher
P:D:A: Tara Fletcher, S: Hillaire Belloc
Color
"From the poem." (*Cambridge Animation Festival* 1981.)

1149 Last Respects
Mole Hill
P: Julian Roberts, D:A: Matthew Hill
Color
Amateur film: animated plasticene. "A murder in the criminal underworld. The funeral of Big Boss is attended by all and sundry." (*Cambridge Animation Festival* 1981.)

1150 How the Kiwi Lost Its Wings
Houston
P:D:A: Kathleen Houston
Color
"Based on an original story from a Maori legend about Tane, the god of the forest, and the birds who dwell there." (*Cambridge Animation Festival* 1981.)

1151 Movieola
Cerebelle Productions
P:D:S:A: Nick Kavanagh, ED: Fran McLane, SD: Ken Freeman
Color
"Story of a working day in an editing room, but the film has a life of its own: sometimes it cooperates with the editors, sometimes it is rather more whimsical." (*Cambridge Animation Festival* 1981.)

1152 Carousel
>TV Cartoons
>P: John Coates, D: Jimmy Murakami, A: Alan Ball, Jim Duffy, Diane Jackson, C: Peter Turner, ED: Mick Manning, M: Jonathan Hodge
>Color
>"No musicals, no jogging, no smoking, kissing prohibited, no cameras, elephants not allowed." (*Cambridge Animation Festival* 1981.)

1153 Risky Business
>Leeds Animation Workshop—British Safety Council
>M: Chris Reason, Steve Trafford, Liz Mansfield, V: Liz Mansfield
>Color
>Instructional cartoon. "A look at health and safety hazards at work." (*Cambridge Animation Festival* 1981.)

1154 Second Sight
>West Surrey College of Art
>D:A: Michael Smetham
>Color
>Student's cartoon. "Animated film about blind ambition." (*British National Film Catalogue* 1982.)

1155 Alarm Call
>West Surrey College of Art
>D:A: Daniel Greaves
>Color
>Student's cartoon: "A man's home is his castle, but what if the house itself and its contents turn carnivorous?" (*Cambridge Animation Festival* 1981.)

1156 The Pudding Factor
>Hull College of Higher Education
>D:A: Keith Roberts
>Color
>Student's cartoon: "Visit to Silacosia, a nightmare vision of the future." (*Cambridge Animation Festival* 1981.)

1157 Proserpine
>Goldsmiths College
>D:A: James Heyworth
>Color
>Student's cartoon: "A wistful tale of a girl and a flower." (*Cambridge Animation Festival* 1981.)

1158 A Tale of Gothic Horror
Goldsmiths College
D:A: James Heyworth
Color
Student's cartoon: "A British Rail horror story." (*Cambridge Animation Festival* 1981.)

1159 The History of the Alphabet Part One
London College of Printing
D:A: Brian Golding, Barry O'Keefe
Color
Student's cartoon: "From cave painting to photographs, a chronological development of writing." (*Cambridge Animation Festival* 1981.)

1160 Manzigo
London College of Printing
D: "D.J."
Color
Student's cartoon: "Prehistoric man visits the twentieth century." (*Cambridge Animation Festival* 1981.)

1161 Dog Day Afternoon
London College of Printing
D: Renan Tolon
Color
Student's cartoon: "A little dog goes swimming in the sea – at least he thinks he does." (*Cambridge Animation Festival* 1981.)

1162 Sleeping Beauty
London College of Printing
D: Renan Tolon
Color
Student's cartoon: "What can a man do when his wife's snoring keeps him awake?" (*Cambridge Animation Festival* 1981.)

1163 Creation
London College of Printing
D: Foundation Studies Dept.
Color
Student's cartoon: "Evolution of life depicted in a variety of styles." (*Cambridge Animation Festival* 1981.)

1164 Life Drawn
Liverpool Polytechnic
D: Chris Yarwood
Color
Student's cartoon.

1165 The Egg and the Griffin
Gwent College
D:A: Richard Fawdry
Color
Student's cartoon: "Mythical metamorphoses." (*Cambridge Anima-tion Festival* 1981.)

1166 Spring Sonata
Exeter College of Art
D:A: Martin Cheek, S: Bernice Robins
Color
Student's cartoon. "The adventures of a foetus who is a virtuoso violinist, based on a novel." (*Cambridge Animation Festival* 1981.)

1167 To Mom with Love
Goldsmiths College
D:A: Steve Watts, Garry Martin, Paddy Morris
Color
Student's cartoon: "Mom receives a series of surprise presents that are not quite what they seem." (*Cambridge Animation Festival* 1981.)

1168 Dogs
Liverpool Polytechnic
D:A: Jonathan Hodgson
Color
Student's cartoon: "The many facets of a dog's life." (*Cambridge Animation Festival* 1981.)

1169 Opus 1 2 3
Liverpool Polytechnic
D:A: Chris Bowman
Color
Student's cartoon: "Studies based on the dance." (*Cambridge Anima-tion Festival* 1981.)

1170 Weekend Epic
St. Martin's School of Art
D:A: Augur Schiff
Color
Student's cartoon: "Are the obstacles real or imaginary? Whichever they are, it is important that they remain our own." (*Cambridge Animation Festival* 1981.)

1171 Just Walking
St. Martin's School of Art
D:A: Ravi Narayanswami
Color
Student's cartoon: "In the not very distant future, walking for pleasure will be seen as a suspicious activity. All good folk should be tucked up with their video screens." (*Cambridge Animation Festival* 1981.)

1172 Panopticon: The Firm's Eye View
Croydon College of Art
D: Tim Summers
Color
Student's film. "In a world of police states, who is watching whom?" (*Cambridge Animation Festival* 1981.)

1173 The Idol Breakers
Croydon College of Art
D: Shahryar Bahrani
Color
Student's cartoon: "In the desert an Islamic city is ruined as images of destruction march inexorably on. The peacock throne crumbles and soldiers slaughter the protesting civilians." (*Cambridge Animation Festival* 1981.)

1174 Louis the Conqueror
Gwent College
D: Stephen Shore
Color
Student's cartoon: "Louis Bleriot attempts to cross the English Channel, but his flight takes him on a rather strange route." (*Cambridge Animation Festival* 1981.)

1175 Macbeth
Gwent College
D: Joan Ashworth, S: William Shakespeare
Color
Student's film: "Puppets and silhouettes are used to illustrate scenes from the tragedy, focussing primarily on the witches." (*Cambridge Animation Festival* 1981.)

1176 In the Mood, in the Nude
Hull College of Higher Education
D:A: Anne Whiteford
Color
Student's cartoon: "An examination of a blue movie." (*Cambridge Animation Festival* 1981.)

1177 Comic Story
West Surrey College of Art
D:A: Russell Brooke
Color
Student's cartoon. A small boy goes into a strange bookshop run
by a strange character.

1178 Organic Canonic Icon
Stuart Wynn Jones – SE Arts
P:D:S:A: Stuart Wynn Jones, M: Johann Pachelbel
Color
Experimental cartoon. "Organic implies the idea of growth, the
development of a complicated structure from a simple beginning.
Canonic – a musical composition in which different voices or instruments
take up the same theme successively. Icon means simply an image, not
necessarily a religious one." (*London Film Festival Notes* 1981.)

1179 Pretend You'll Survive
Leeds Animation Workshop
M: Steve Trafford, Chris Reason
Color
"One woman's nightmare experience of living through the holo-
caust with the help of the Government pamphlet." (*Cambridge Animation
Festival* 1981.)

1180 The Way of the Fool
Whiteman – West Midlands Arts
P:D:A: Robin Whiteman
Color. "Two alternative journeys through the Tarot, the 22 picture
cards said to contain universal symbols of an eternal wisdom." (*Cambridge
Animation Festival* 1981.)

1181 Ein Brudermord: A Fratricide
Koninck Studios – Greater London Arts
P: Keith Griffiths, D:A: Timothy Quaij, Stephen Quaij, S: Franz
Kafka, ED: Larry Sider, V: Lutz Becker
Color
Animated puppets. "Kafka's harsh, cold, pathetic narrative rendered
as a 'melodrama for marionettes,' in which the assassin and the assassinated
are viewed entymologically as two insects." (*London Film Festival Notes*
1981.)

1182 Flora Dance
National Film School
D:A: Alex Brychta

Color

Student's cartoon. "A brass band plays the Floral Dance but their instruments are flowers and plants."

1183 Still Life

Wolff Productions

P:D:S: Richard Wolff, ED: Terry Brown, M: Brian Eno, V: Gary Bond

Color

"Uses artwork, animation and photographic effects to give a vivid picture of the life and aesthetics of the Scottish painter Lawrence Angus McConi." (*London Film Festival Notes* 1981.)

1982

1184 Danse Macabre
Sheila Graber Animated Films – Interama
P:D:S:A: Sheila Graber, M: Camille Saint-Saens
Color
"Ghosts, skeletons, witches, and the devil himself act out the story behind the tune." (*British National Film Catalogue* 1983.)

1185 The Nightingale
Sands Films
P: Richard Goodwin, D:A: Christine Edzard, C: Christopher Challis, S: Hans Christian Andersen, V: Richard Goolden, John Daltry
Color
Live action with animation sequences. Picturization of the familiar fairy story.

1186 Arcade Attack (2327)
Fifth Channel – Animation City
P: Mike Wallington, D: Phil Austin, Derek Hayes, A: Mario Szmichowska, Anna Brockett, C: Terry Handley, M: Dirk Higgins, Dave Westbrook
Color
Live action and animation sequences. "Pinballers meet videodrones in swinging high-tech London. The clash of generations is inevitable."

1187 Cochlea Heroes
Nucleus Films
P: John Allinson, D: Peter Tupy
Color
Promotional cartoon for Velosef. "Spoof on World War II films to persuade doctors to buy an antibiotic." (*Cambridge Animation Festival* 1983.)

1188 Genius of Love
Cucumber Studios
P:D:A: Clive Morton, Annabel Jankel
Fujicolor
Musical cartoon paying homage to black musicians: George Clinton, Bootsy Collins, Smokey Robinson, Bob Marley, Sly Dunbar.

1189 Give Me Some Action
Royal College of Art
D:A: Gill Bradley
Color
Student's cartoon: cut-out animation synchronized to a disco tune.

1190 The Plague Dogs (9261)
Nepenthe – UIP
P:D:SC: Martin Rosen, S: Richard Adams, AD: Tony Guy, Colin White, A: George Jackson, Arthur Humberstone, Colin White, Phil Robinson, Tony Guy, Alan Simpson, Bill Hajee, Marie Szmichowska, Retta Scott, Mary Carol Millican, Karen Peterson, Terry Hudson, Brad Bird, DES: Gordon Harrison, M: Patrick Gleeson, Antonio Vivaldi, Kronos Quartet, V: John Hurt (Snitter), Christopher Benjamin (Rowf), James Bolam (The Tod), Nigel Hawthorne (Dr. Robert Boycott), Warren Mitchell (Tyson/Wag), Bernard Hepton (Stephen Powell), Brian Stirner (Assistant), Penelope Lee (Lynn Driver), Geoffrey Matthews (Farmer), Barbara Leigh-Hunt (Wife), John Bennett (Don), Bill Maynard (Editor), Judy Geeson (Pekingese), Philip Locke (Civil Servant), Anthony Valentine (Civil Servant), William Lucas (Civil Servant), Dandy Nichols (Phyllis), Rosemary Leach (Vera), Percy Edwards (Animal Vocalization)
Technicolor
Feature-length cartoon (103 minutes) made in Britain by an American production company. A fox helps two dogs who escape from a research laboratory. "The production team responsible for *Watership Down* have again reduced Richard Adams' imaginatively detailed renderings of animal life to the wholesale, if updated, anthropomorphism of a Disney cartoon." (*Monthly Film Bulletin* October 1982.)

1191 Smile Please
Brandt – COW
P:D:S:A: Maya Brandt
Color
Mixed media film. "The concept of female liberty as defined by a male dominated society." (*Regional Film Directory* 1984.)

1192 Sredni Vashtar
Hull College of Higher Education
D:A: Liz Spencer, S: "Saki" (H.H. Munro)
Color
Student's cartoon. "A child whose only companion is a hen and who worships a ferret as a god." (*Cambridge Animation Festival* 1983.)

1193 Them
Motion Picture Company
D:A: Bill Mather
Color
"Alien spacecraft delivers a slide-show on evolution which owes more to Marx (Groucho) than to Darwin." (*London Film Festival Notes.*)

1194 The Three Knights
West Surrey College of Art
D:A: Mark Baker, S: Mark Baker, Bob Godfrey, Stan Hayward, M: Rimsky-Korsakov, Shostakovitch
Color
Student's cartoon: clumsy knights' adventures with a witch, a giant, and a three-headed dragon.

1195 The Snowman
Snowman Enterprises – Channel 4
XP: Iain Harvey, P: John Coates, D: Diane Jackson, Jimmy Murakami, S: Raymond Briggs, SC: Diane Jackson, Hilary Audus, Joanna Fryer, DES: Jill Brooks, A: Roger Mainwood, Alan Ball, Edrick Radage, Arthur Button, Tony Guy, Steve Weston, Robin White, ED: John Cary, C: Peter Turner, M: Howard Blake, V: Aled Jones
Rank Color
Adapted from the book by Raymond Briggs. Boy's snowman comes to life and flies him to snowman's land. Made for television, shown theatrically.

1196 Pink Floyd: The Wall (8556)
Tin Blue – Goldcrest – MGM – United International
XP: Stephen O'Rourke, P: Alan Marshall, D: Alan Parker, S: Roger Waters, SUP: Lance Paul, AD:DES: Gerald Scarfe, A: Roland Carter, Mike Stuart, Greg Miller, Chris Caunter, Bill Hajee, Les Matjas, Alistair McIlwain, Judy Howieson, Carol Slade, ED: Gerry Hambling, M: Roger Waters, David Gilmour, Nick Mason, Richard Wright, MD: Michael Kamen
Metrocolor – Scope
Live action feature (95 minutes) with animation sequences. Burnt-out rock star recalls his life. "Gerald Scarfe's contributions are interesting only in that they show his much-vaunted savagery as something available for rent, toned down anyway, and slotting quite happily into a deeply reac-

tionary overall scheme. The animated sequences are also in effect redundant, since they serve no specific function apart from the live action. Where the two are combined, however (Bob Geldoff as Pink menaced by a cartoon monster), the result is at least unintentionally funny." (*Monthly Film Bulletin* August 1982.)

1197　Imbrium Beach (500)
　　Panama Studio
　　D: Marcus Parker-Rhodes, ED: Sean Lenihan
　　Color
　　"Surreal picnic for the little creatures who live, presumably, on the moon." (*Cambridge Animation Festival* 1983.)

1198　Lost Causes
　　Selkirk
　　P:D:ED: Stewart Selkirk, A: Stewart Selkirk, Susan Nelson, Andy Zermanski, Peter Johnston
　　Color
　　Bird's-eye view of the last night on earth, linking a gravedigger at work with a corrupt boxing match.

1199　Players (720)
　　Halas & Batchelor – EFC – Kratky
　　P:D: John Halas, S:DES: Peter Sis, A: Chris Fenna, Roger Mainwood, ED: Sean Lenihan, C: Peter Petronio, M: Jiri Stivin
　　Color
　　"Using two well-known tennis players, the film is a satire on aggression as the players metamorphose into increasingly aggressive armies/ weapons until their victory is won at the expense of the spectators." (*Cambridge Animation Festival* 1983.)

1200　The Secret Army
　　Brooks
　　P:D:A: Jon Brooks, M: Dirk Higgins
　　Color
　　"Militarism in miniature: a toyshop is the setting for this anti-war film." (*Cambridge Animation Festival* 1983.)

1201　Hawk Roosting
　　Selkirk – Northern Arts
　　P:D:A: Stewart Selkirk, S: Ted Hughes
　　Color
　　"The animalistic strength, aggression and violence of the poem is translated into film imagery and the higher human implications are treated symbolically." (*Regional Film Directory* 1984.)

1983

1202 Just So Stories (series)
Marble Arch – Interama – Strengholt
P: Nicole Jouve, D:A:C: Sheila Graber, S: Rudyard Kipling, M: Brenda Orwin, V: Ronald Pickup, Michael Hordern
Color
Adaptation of the stories for children by Rudyard Kipling.

1203 Iron Lady
Goldsmith's College/Other Cinema
D:A: John Le Pelley
Student's film: animated puppets. "Cast iron Conservative policies send the forces to the Falklands, issued by the robot figure of a metallicized Maggie." (*Cambridge Animation Festival* 1983.)

1204 Bits
Pearce Studios
Color
Computer animation.

1205 Stolen Pride
Royal College of Art
D:A:S: Gary McCarver
Color
Student's cartoon. "A monster leaves his mansion and steals a peacock's feathers." (*London Film Festival Notes* 1983.)

1206 First Sight (900)
Wolff Productions
P:D:S:A:C: Richard Wolff, M: John Whitehall, ED: Charlotte Evans, V: Phyllis King, Matthew Guinness, Sally Grace
Color
Live action with animation. "Journey through the personal daydream interpreted through the flow of a river." (*Cambridge Animation Festival* 1983.)

1207 Thin Blue Lines
Liverpool Polytechnic
D: Susan Young
Color
Student's cartoon. "Animated observations on the 1981 Toxteth riots." (*London Film Festival Notes* 1983.)

1208 Gypsy
West Surrey College of Art
D: Paul Rosevear
Color
Student's cartoon. "An evocation of gypsy life and music." (*London Film Festival Notes* 1983.)

1209 Dada
London College of Printing
D: Brigitte Hartley
Color
Student's cartoon. "An evocation of the world of Dada and contemporary events." (*London Film Festival Notes* 1983.)

1210 Taking a Line for a Walk
Persistent Vision
D:SC: Lesley Keen, A: Lesley Keen, Donald Holwill, C: Donald Holwill, DES: Paul Klee, M: Lyell Cresswell
Color
Made for the Scottish Arts Council. "An exploration and expansion of the ideas of Paul Klee on colour and movement, using some of his works as a starting point." (*London Film Festival Notes* 1983.)

1211 New Frontier
Cucumber Studios
D:A: Clive Morton, Annabel Jankel
Color
Promotional cartoon for the rock song by Donald Fagen. "Fallout shelter romance to Fifties style graphics." (*Cambridge Animation Festival* 1983.)

1212 Night Club
Royal College of Art—Merseyside Arts
D:M: Jonathan Hodgson, A: Jonathan Hodgson, Janet Miller
Color
Student's cartoon. "An observation of young people in a social situation, restraining or giving vent to frustration, boredom and loneliness." (*London Film Festival Notes* 1983.)

1213　The Princess and the Musician

Sailsbury Arts Centre

P:D:A: Ariane Dixon, Tim Darlow, S: Fiona French, V: Alaric Cotter

Color

"Cut-out animation based on a Persian tale and Eastern graphics."
(*London Film Festival Notes* 1983.)

1214　Give Us a Smile

Leeds Animation Workshop – BFI – COW – Yorkshire Arts

M: Lindsay Cooper, V: Maggie Nichols

Color

"Through its inventive use of animation, distorted perspective, words and sounds made concrete and physically assaulting the heroines, it achieves a kind of expressionism appropriate to the theme of women belittled by media images." (*Monthly Film Bulletin* October 1984.)

1215　Noblesse Oblige

Mole Hill

P:C: Julian Roberts, D:S:A: Matthew Hill, M: Arne Richards

Color

Animated plasticene: "The white man's burden: another Gothic fantasy." (*Cambridge Animation Festival* 1983.)

1216　The View

Brooks

P:D:A: Jon Brooks, C: Terry Handley, M: Dirk Higgins

Color

"An old man lives alone in an English inner city and observes the people living around him. Events then take over which break his isolation." (*Cambridge Animation Festival* 1983.)

1217　History of Grease

Moo Movies

P:D: Ian Moo-Young

Color

"Sponsored film on the discovery of lubrication." (*Cambridge Animation Festival* 1983.)

1218　Swimsong

Taylor Cartoons – COI

P:D: Richard Taylor

Color

Promotional film to encourage children to learn how to swim.

1219 Cabaret
Bath Academy of Art
D: Art Parker
Color
Student's film: "The birds step out." (*Cambridge Animation Festival* 1983.)

1220 The Fridge D'or
Bath Academy of Art
D: Alastair Taylor
Color
Student's cartoon: "A premonition of breakfast." (*Cambridge Animation Festival* 1983.)

1221 Gigue
Bath Academy of Art
D: Alastair Taylor
Color
Student's cartoon: "A lively dance." (*Cambridge Animation Festival* 1983.)

1222 Fruit Machine
Croydon College
D: Victor Kulisz
Color
Student's cartoon: "Playing a different kind of fruit machine." (*Cambridge Animation Festival* 1983.)

1223 Struggle After Death
Croydon College
D: Janet Simmonds
Color
Student's cartoon: "The mythic battle continues." (*Cambridge Animation Festival* 1983.)

1224 Who Exploits Whom
Goldsmith's College—Pictures of Women
D: Charlotte Worthington
Color
Student's cartoon: "The hypocrisy and double standards of prostitution where those who condemn exploit." (*Cambridge Animation Festival* 1983.)

1225 Clown
  Leicester Polytechnic
  D: Nicola Gibson
  Color
  Student's cartoon: "Explorations of the expressive possibilities of a clown." (*Cambridge Animation Festival* 1983.)

1226 Holiday on Death Row
  Leicester Polytechnic
  D: Jane Beecham, S:V: Roger McGough
  Color
  Student's cartoon: Death throes of a marriage." (*Cambridge Animation Festival* 1983.)

1227 Roger the Dog
  Leicester Polytechnic
  D: Carol Ziegler, S: Ted Hughes
  Color
  Student's cartoon: "The hedonistic life of Roger the Dog." (*Cambridge Animation Festival* 1983.)

1228 Jaws
  Leicester Polytechnic
  D: Harry Dorrington
  Color
  Student's cartoon. "The battle of art materials against the anglepoise." (*Cambridge Animation Festival* 1983.)

1229 Space Visitor
  Leicester Polytechnic
  D: King Mon Chan
  Color
  Student's cartoon: "A little visitor from space." (*Cambridge Animation Festival* 1983.)

1230 Drawing with Light
  Liverpool Polytechnic
  D: Arthur White
  Color
  Student's film: "Experiments with a light pen." (*Cambridge Animation Festival* 1983.)

1231 Gallery
  Liverpool Polytechnic
  D: Mark Fuller

Color

Student's film: "Visit to an art gallery where interest in the painting and sculptures is diminished by the presence of 'real' people." (*Cambridge Animation Festival* 1983.)

1232 Dream Land Express (1021)
National Film School
D:A:C: David Anderson, ED: Tom Priestley
Color
Student's cartoon. "Small boy is aroused from sleep by a train whistle and begins a journey into a strange world where the train itself will be his guide and companion." (*Cambridge Animation Festival* 1983.) British Film Academy Award 1983.

1233 The Golden Grape
National Film School
D: Nick Willing
Color
Student's film: "In the atomic ballroom, the little fellow in search of the Golden Grape comes face to face with the extraordinary firecracker madness." (*Cambridge Animation Festival* 1983.)

1234 1884
National Film School
D: Dennis de Groot, Tim Ollive
Color
Student's film: "Showing yesterday's future which might have been but never was." (*Cambridge Animation Festival* 1983.)

1235/6 Arty Film
Royal College of Art
D: Jonathan Hodgson
Color
Student's film: "A parody of those of this ilk, the result of going to too many festivals." (*Cambridge Animation Festival* 1983.)

1237 Trafalgar Square
Royal College of Art
D: Susan Young
Color
Student's film: "Impressionistic view of the London landmark." (*Cambridge Animation Festival* 1983.)

1238 Basics
St. Martin's School of Art
D: Rashad Salim, M: Tara Jaff
Color
Student's film: "Muslim chant to the elements using the symbolism of the hand and the eye." (*Cambridge Animation Festival* 1983.)

1239 The Poet of Half Past Three
St. Martin's School of Art
D: Joanna Woodward
Color
Student's film: "Daring confrontation of the linear and the literate." (*Cambridge Animation Festival* 1983.)

1240 In the City
Trent Polytechnic
D: Carlo Briscoe
Color
Student's film: "Experimental ride around London." (*Cambridge Animation Festival* 1983.)

1241 The Journey
West Surrey College of Art
D: Malcolm Hartley, A: Steve Whitfield, Vince Couldman
Color
Student's film: "A journey used as a visual metaphor for seeing and recounting." (*Cambridge Animation Festival* 1983.)

1242 Peacock Feathers
Royal College of Art
D: Stephen Pride, Christopher Delaney
Color
Student's film: "A peacock retrieves his feathers stolen by a somewhat vain dragon." (*Cambridge Animation Festival* 1983.)

1243 Clip
Muscle Films – GLAA
D: Nicola Bruce, Mike Coulson, A: Andy Modlecki
Color
"Instantness, five minutes' worth. The length of time it takes to walk up the road, talk on the phone, have a dance, press a button. Woomph – all gone." (*Sounds* 1984.)

1244 Jazz Man
Royal College of Art
D: Clive Heaven, A: Clive Heaven, Andrew Smith
Color
Student's cartoon, painted directly onto film. "Impression of an evening in a jazz club." (*London Film Festival Notes* 1984.)

1984

1245 Tempting Fate
Royal College of Art
D:A: Susan Young, M: Carl Washington
Color
Student's cartoon, cutout animation. Allegory set in the Garden of Eden featuring a black Adam, a white Eve, a banana and a snake.

1246 Beasley Street
Kingston Polytechnic
D:A: Mo Shodi, Neil Donoghue, Martin Baffen, M: John Cooper Clarke
Color
Student's cartoon. "Second year graphic design students introduced to animation for the first time." (*London Film Festival Notes* 1984.)

1247 Blues for Mingus
Kingston Polytechnic
D:A: Lucilla Scrimgeour, M: Stanley Clarke
Color
Student's cartoon. Tribute to the jazz musician Charlie Mingus.

1248 Christmas for Sale
Liverpool Polytechnic
D:A: Iain McCall, M: Ravel
Student's cartoon: white outlines on black background in the early style of Émile Cohl. "A moody evocation of the Christmas preparations." (*London Film Festival Notes* 1984.)

1249 Oh for a Prince
West Surrey College of Art
D:A: Stephen Roberts
Color
Student's cartoon. "Warning that frogs don't always turn into princes when kissed." (*London Film Festival Notes* 1984.)

1250 Low Odds
West Surrey College of Art
D:A: Simon Margetts, Julian Caldow, Caroline Grebble
Color
Student's cartoon.

1251 Second Class Mail
National Film School
D:S: Alison Snowden, A: Alison Snowden, David Fine, Suzanne Clive, Mark Baker, Barry Baker
Color
Student's cartoon. Old lady goes shopping by post for an inflatable rubber man, who explodes in her embrace.

1252 Adoption
Taylor Cartoons – COI
P:D: Richard Taylor, S: Richard Taylor, Diana Humphrey, A: Richard Taylor, Roger McIntosh, V: Tim Woodvine
Color
Information film for the Central Office of Information on the topic of adopting underprivileged children.

1253 Pleasure of Love
Cucumber Studios
P:D:A: Clive Morton, Annabel Jankel, DES: Jimmy Rizzi, C: J. Swinnerton, M: Tom Tom Club
Color
Promotional cartoon for Tom Tom Club, a pop group.

1254 Inside Job
Red Spot Films
P:D:S:A:ED: Maya Brandt, C: Jude Groves, M: Martin Veysey, Dick Truscott, Peter Brandt, V: Maya Brandt, Martin Veysey
Color
"A zany subjective view of gynaecological examinations." (Cambridge Animation Festival 1985.)

1255 Heaven of Animals
Animate Films
P:D:S:A: Nick Gordon Smith, M: Nick Gordon Smith, M. Greaves
Color
"Allegorical journey, passing to and fro, reducing boredom, egged on by the evangelist Brother Prince." (Cambridge Animation Festival 1985.)

1256 The World of Children
Spectre Productions
P: Simon Hartog, D: Vera Neubauer, C: Bill Foulk, M: Gary Carpenter
Color
Live action with animation sequences. "How does the environment affect the child? Is it possible to learn to talk without adopting the prejudices built into the language?" (*Cambridge Animation Festival* 1985.)

1257 The Burglar
Fletcher
P:D:S:A: Tara Fletcher, ED: Mark Fletcher, C: Russell Ryman, M: Boosey & Hawkes, V: Jonathan Cecil, Anna Starkey
Color
Animated puppets. "Adaptation of a *Punch* story from the 1920s about an impoverished flautist who turns to crime." (*Cambridge Animation Festival* 1985.)

1258 Silence
Polstead Productions
P: John Cannon, D:S:A: Miroslaw Kijowicz, C: Peter Tupy, M: B. Mazurek
"Watching a succession of people passing his home, a farmer remains indifferent until he faces the inevitable himself." (*Cambridge Animation Festival* 1985.)

1259 Polygamous Polonius Revisited
Bob Godfrey Films
P: Mike Hodges, D:A: Bob Godfrey, M: Temperance Seven
Color
New version of Bob Godfrey's famous cartoon of 1960 updated to reflect contemporary tendencies.

1260 Ghost Town
Kingston Polytechnic
D:S:A: Damian Gascoigne
Color
Student's cartoon. "The problems of urban decay and the dissaffection of youth by the oppression of unemployment." (*Cambridge Animation Festival* 1985.)

1261 The Aeronauts
Newman Productions
P: Robert Newman, D: Alan Hodge, S: Edwin John, SC: Robert Newman, Alan Hodge, A: Robert Newman, Alan Hodge, Peter Kidd, Clinton Priest, Nigel Rutter, Kay Widdowson, V: John Kendall

Color

Animated cartoon affectionately burlesquing the Anson Dyer/ Stanley Holloway "Old Sam" cartoons of the Thirties, complete with rhyming monologue told in a Lancashire accent. Young Arty wins a football sweepstake and buys an aeroplane, flying to New York with his Uncle Bill and encountering Public Enemy Number One in Central Park. Made with the assistance of Cosgrove Hall Productions.

1262 Rupert and the Frog Song

MPL Communications – Grand Slamm

XP: Paul McCartney, Linda McCartney, P:D: Geoff Dunbar, A: Geoff Dunbar, Dave Unwin, Steve Weston, John Perkins, Dan Greaves, Greg Hill, Mike Smith, Alan Green, Mario Cavelli, Eric Goldberg, S: Paul McCartney, Linda McCartney, Geoff Dunbar, SC: Geoff Dunbar, Denis Rich, ED: Tony Fish, Peter Hearn, M: Paul McCartney, George Martin, Ray Merrin, V: Paul McCartney, Windsor Davies, June Whitfield, Barry Rose, the King Singers, the St. Paul's Choir

Color

Based on the characters in the "Rupert Bear" comic strip created by Mary Tourtel and continued by Alfred Bestall in the *Daily Express*. Rupert Bear sets out from his parents' cottage in Nutwood and has an underground adventure with singing frogs, two evil black cats and a white owl. Introduces the original song by Paul McCartney, "We'll All Stand Together." Originally intended to be a feature-length cartoon film, but released as a short.

1985

1263 Circus
COW
P:D:A: Ann Barefoot, M: Rosemary Schonfield, Jana Runneals, V:
Interchange Workshop
Color
"The rush and excitement of a circus performance." (*Cambridge Animation Festival* 1985.)

1264 I'm Not a Feminist But
Rimmisen Animation
P: Dick Arnall, D: Marjut Rimmisen, S: (book) Christine Roche, DES:
Christine Roche, A: Jeff Goldner, ED: Charlotte Evans, M: Dick Hestall-
Smith, V: Lena Rowe, Tracey King, Helen Durst, Julie Hocking, Rose
Wayner
Color
Feminist film adapted from a book of cartoons.

1265 Monster Man
Middlesex Polytechnic
D:S:A: Jeff Newitt, M: The Revillos
Color
Student's film: animated puppets perform to a pop record.

1266 The Attention Seeker
Humberside College
D:S:A: Nigel Winfield
Color
Student's cartoon. "A young man tries in vain to gain the attention
of passers-by with seemingly extravagant behaviour. Finally he joins the
crowd." (*Cambridge Animation Festival* 1985.)

1267 The Black Bicycle
National Film School
D:S:A: Mark Baker, V: Nick Park

Student's cartoon: "A cycling enthusiast decides that the climb up a steep hill will be more than rewarded by the pleasure of freewheeling down the other side." (*Cambridge Animation Festival* 1985.)

1268 Berlin
West Surrey College of Art
D:A: Tim Webb, Ron McRae, Terry Donner, S: George Grosz
Student's cartoon. "The satirical drawings of George Grosz documenting the slide from the Weimar Republic into Nazism." (*Cambridge Animation Festival* 1985.)

1269 The Wreck of the Julie Plante
Flying Horse Films
P:ED: Taylor Grant, D:DES:A: Stephen Weston, S: (poem) William Hay Drummond, C: Peter Turner, M: Howard Blake, V: Barry Dransfield
Color
"Based on a poem about a small steamboat and its crew caught in a terrible storm on Lac St. Pierre." (*Cambridge Animation Festival* 1985.)

1270 The Journalist's Tale
National Union of Journalists
D:S:DES: Steve Bell, P: Dave Rushton, A: Malcolm Hartley, Rick Villeneuve, Jeff Goldner, Susan Horner, Julia Gibbs, John Corse, C: Roy Watford, ED: Tony Fish, Peter Hearn, V: The Joeys, Bill Wallis, Jenny le Court, Steve Bell, Bob Godfrey
Color
Propaganda cartoon. "Steve Bell examines the role of the National Union of Journalists as it defends itself against the march of Fleet Street." (*Cambridge Animation Festival* 1985.)

1271 Me and My Shadow
Kingston Polytechnic
D:A: Naomi Davies, S: (poem) Robert Louis Stevenson (*My Shadow*), V: Mareka Carter
Color
Student's cartoon. Visual interpretation of the poem and the popular song "Me and My Shadow."

1272 Back in the Playground
London College of Printing
D:A: Andrew Wayne Barrass, S:V: Adrian Mitchell
Color
Student's cartoon. "The poet's memories of a childhood playground." (*Cambridge Animation Festival* 1985.)

1273 Bar Code
West Surrey College of Art
D:A: Quentin Mills
Student's cartoon in monochrome.

1274 Carnival
Royal College of Art
D:A: Susan Young, M: Carl Washington
Color
Student's cartoon. "A response to the visual experience of carnival exploring the formal qualities of colour, line and sound." (*Cambridge Animation Festival* 1985.)

1275 Electric Palace
West Surrey College of Art
D:A: Simon Margetts
Student's cartoon in monochrome. "Homage to the pleasures and fascination of the cinema." (*Cambridge Animation Festival* 1985.)

1276 Menagerie
Royal College of Art
D:A: Jonathan Hodgson
Student's cartoon in monochrome. "A day at the zoo from the animals' point of view (*Cambridge Animation Festival* 1985.)

1277 Money Money
London College of Printing
D:A: Andrew Wayne Barrass, M:V: Liza Minelli, Joel Grey
Color
Student's cartoon. "Images from the twenties and thirties are used to interpret the song performed by Lisa [*sic*] Minelli and Joel Grey." (*Cambridge Animation Festival* 1985.)

1278 This Unnameable Little Broom
Atelier Koninck – Channel 4 – BFI
P:ED: Keith Griffiths, D:S:A:C: Stephen Quaij, Timothy Quaij, M: R. Walter
Color
Animated puppets. Tricycle-man's adventures among insects, inspired by "Epic of Gilgamesh." Made for television, but shown theatrically.

1279 Siamese Cat Song
St. Martin's School of Art
D:S:A: Cathryn Marshall
Color
Student's cartoon.

1280 Flight
Royal College of Art
D:A: Christine Tongue, M: Jonathan Hodgson
Student's cartoon in monochrome. "Experimental first film exploring movement, atmosphere and social comment." (*Cambridge Animation Festival* 1985.)

1281 The Day That the Circus Left Town
Humberside College
D:A: Belinda Moores, C: Alan Jeffrey, M:V: Eartha Kitt
Color
Student's cartoon. "An illustration of the song performed by Eartha Kitt." (*Cambridge Animation Festival* 1985.)

1282 Ms Moon
Ruby Studios
P:D:A: Anna Brockett, C: Julian Holdaway, M: Steve Collis, Neil McDonald
Color
"The intrepid and seductive Ms Moon comes down to Earth to play against the husky he-men." (*Cambridge Animation Festival* 1985.)

1283 Train of Thought
Royal College of Art
D:A: Jonathan Hodgson
Student's cartoon.

1284 Gas Naturally
World Wide Pictures
D:S: Clive Mitchell, DES:A: Nicholas Spargo, ED: Peter Batty
Color
Sponsored cartoon promoting British Petroleum: 22 minutes. "Homo Sapiens – Sap for short – tells the story of the discovery and use of oil, and the later realisation that the natural gas which escaped with it when it was found could itself be adapted as an energy source." (*Films* April 1985.)

Index